What's a
HOSTESS
to Do?

What's a HOSTESS to Do?

SUSAN SPUNGEN

ARTISAN
NEW YORK

Published by Artisan
A division of Workman Publishing Company, Inc.
225 Varick Street
New York, NY 10014-4381
artisanbooks.com

Published simultaneously in Canada by Thomas Allen & Son, Limited

What's a . . . to Do? is a trademark of Workman Publishing Company, Inc.

Library of Congress Cataloging-in-Publication Data
Spungen, Susan.
  What's a hostess to do? / Susan Spungen.
      pages   cm
  Includes index.
  ISBN 978-1-57965-368-2
1. Entertaining. 2. Parties. I. Title.
  TX731.S684 2012
  793.2—dc23   2012029219

Design by Kara Strubel

Printed in the United States of America
First printing, March 2013

10 9 8 7 6 5 4 3 2 1

CONTENTS

Acknowledgments vi

Introduction 1

THE GIFTED HOSTESS 2

SETTING THE SCENE 28

THE COCKTAIL HOUR 50

THE BUFFET 94

THE DINNER PARTY 126

HOLIDAYS AND OTHER SPECIAL DAYS 178

OUTDOOR PARTIES 230

THE PARTY'S OVER 264

Resources 274

Index 277

ACKNOWLEDGMENTS

A huge thanks goes to everyone at Artisan who spent their time and attention on this project during its long gestation period. Thank you, Ann Bramson, for your faith in me and your unending patience, and most of all your friendship. A big giant thanks goes to Judy Pray, without whom I would not be at the end of this project. Words cannot express my gratitude. To Trent Duffy, Nancy Murray, Sibylle Kazeroid, Lia Ronnen, Michelle Ishay-Cohen, and Kara Strubel—thank you.

For their very important contributions, many thanks go to Kathryn Kellinger, Nina Lalli, and Andrew Pollock. For her always-cheerful hands-on help, thanks to Maria Washburn. Thanks for all of the cooking and shopping and schlepping. Thanks also go to Emma Feigenbaum and Rachel Michael for their help with the shoots. Thanks to Evan Sung for taking pictures when I couldn't. Thanks to Mason Adams for his technical help. To my agent, Kim Witherspoon at Inkwell Management, thank you.

To my husband, Steve, who gave me good advice from the beginning of this project, I thank you for your patience and your help.

"Noncooks think it's silly to invest two hours' work in two minutes' enjoyment; but if cooking is evanescent, well, so is the ballet."

—JULIA CHILD

INTRODUCTION:
FINDING YOUR INNER CLIPBOARD-WIELDING PARTY PLANNER

This book is an all-purpose handbook for the host or hostess. Whether you are hosting Thanksgiving for the first time or throwing your hundredth dinner party, there will be plenty of help here to make you a confident novice or a better veteran host. Whether you are looking for tips on icing a birthday cake, hiring a caterer, handling seating arrangements, or doing your own flowers, you will find it here, along with an arsenal of recipes for every occasion.

The first order of business is deciding what kind of party you want to have. A sit-down dinner for eight? a casual brunch? a big blowout for all of your friends and family? a holiday open house? swanky cocktails and hors d'oeuvres? Figure out how much time and money you want to spend and, of course, what would be most appropriate to the celebration at hand. Then get out the clipboard and start making lists (see page 6).

And by the way, while the title of this book, and the feminine pronouns used throughout, would seem to imply that any person throwing a party is female, the advice here is truly meant for everyone. Real men may not eat quiche, but they can certainly serve it up. So, guys, please strap on your aprons and get to work! This book is for you, too.

THE
GIFTED
HOSTESS

A gifted hostess makes it look easy. She knows the shortcuts that make entertaining less laborious and more enjoyable for everyone. Some of us were raised by this sort of woman, but if these skills skipped a generation, this book will help you look as though you learned it all at your mother's knee.

1 A Hostess's Four Golden Rules

1. Coddle your guests. Make them feel comfortable and welcome. Be hyper thoughtful: make a guest's favorite dessert; provide comfy, inexpensive Chinese slippers to wear indoors on a wintry evening; or use the tableware that was a gift from the guests. Let people know you're thinking about them.

2. Plan ahead. A realistic plan is the key to success. Choose a menu with dishes that can be prepared ahead of time, leaving only the simplest tasks—like heating a dish, cooking pasta or rice, or dressing a salad—for the last minute. Your goal should be to have as little sweat on your brow (and mess in the kitchen) as possible when the doorbell rings.

3. Less can be more. A few beautiful, well-conceived, and well-prepared dishes will go over big. If you have to make a million different things, something—or everything—will suffer. If you drive yourself to the edge of sanity in preparing the food and cleaning the house, you'll feel like collapsing by the time your guests arrive. Keep it simple and you'll be ready when it's time to have fun.

4. When the party starts, be in it. If you are running around frantically, with your guests asking, "Are you *sure* there's nothing I can do?," who can relax? You want to enjoy the party *with* your guests. They came to see you, and a good hostess is present and engaged.

2 How to Plan a Menu

The goal is to get the maximum impact for the least amount of work, or at least figure out how to streamline the work, spreading it over several days, so you aren't going crazy at the last minute. Trial and error is the best way to learn what not to do, but you will find some examples of good and bad menus at the start of each main section, so you can see how good menu planning applies to cocktail parties (see pages 52–55), buffets (see pages 96–97), brunches and lunches (see pages 180–182), and dinner parties (see pages 128–130), as well as how to avoid common pitfalls.

3 Ten Important Questions

1. Who are the guests?

2. What time of day is the party?

3. Is it going to be a formal or casual affair?

4. How many people will there be?

5. Is it all adults or will there be children, too?

6. Is it a carnivorous crowd or are there any vegetarians?

7. Does anyone have special dietary needs?

8. Is it buffet-style or a sit-down meal?

9. Is my menu well balanced, with rich and light flavors, colors, textures, carbs, protein, and veggies?

10. Am I forgetting anything?

4 TIP: Do What You Love

When planning a menu, let your passion guide you. Try not to overthink it. Make something you really love and, preferably, have made before. If you love the food, your guests will too.

Three Lists You Can't Live Without

Spending a few minutes making lists will save you immeasurable time, not to mention stress, later on. Put little boxes next to each item so you can have the satisfaction of checking them off as you accomplish each task. In the end, even if you don't refer back to the lists frequently, the act of making them will help you organize your thoughts and stay focused.

1. The Guest List.
Strive for a "mixer": instead of inviting a group of people who all know one another well, mix it up a bit and invite friends and acquaintances who may not know one another well, or at all. It's always nice if a guest knows someone, and he or she will know you, the hostess. Unless the party is an intimate affair, be a bit of a matchmaker, and try to bring together people who you think have things in common and who will enjoy meeting one another. You'll be surprised at how seemingly disparate friends will find common ground.

2. The Shopping List.
Try to get everything you'll need for cooking, except for perishable foods like salad greens, all at once, so you can spend your time in the kitchen, not running out for forgotten ingredients. Divide your master shopping list by sections of the store—dairy, meat, fish, grocery, produce—or by different stores if you need to make more than one stop for groceries. Add additional list sections for liquor and wine, other party supplies, and flowers.

3. The Prep List.
Break your planning down into a list of tasks, day by day, and put them in order as best you can. (See "How to Break It Down," entry 163.) What can you make ahead of time? Plan to get those jobs done early, so you can cross them off the list. Seeing it all on paper will give you a more realistic view of what you can accomplish, too, and whether you're being overly ambitious.

At the end of each day, revise the list as you cross some things off and get more detailed about the tasks still remaining. For the "day of" list, order the jobs chronologically with the first things first and ending with the tasks you need to do just before your guests arrive.

6 *In Praise of* Good Ol' Pencil and Paper

You might think you've got it all figured out with your smartphone, but keep your lists tangible, on actual paper—and a clipboard is not a bad idea. It fits well in the front part of a shopping cart, and it keeps all your lists, notes, and receipts together.

SPREADING THE WORD

7 Invitations

Invitations should convey the who, what, when, and where of your event and evoke the tone of the party. From engraved to e-mailed, the invitation should embody the formality—or dress code—of the occasion. Throwing a ladies' lunch? Go for something classic and comfortable like stationery engraved with your initials. Hosting a potluck for coworkers? An e-mailed invitation means it's an easygoing affair. Try using a casual, colorful electronic invitation for a big birthday bash. That way friends and relatives can keep track of who is coming, helping to build anticipation for the event.

8 Save the Date

Sending out a printed "save the date" notice is usually reserved for weddings. It should be sent out six months ahead of time, especially if there is travel involved. If you are planning a less formal party at a busy time of year, such as around the holidays or July Fourth, you can send a save-the-date by e-mail a month before you send the actual invitation.

9   How to Time an Invitation

Whether you're mailing invitations or inviting guests by phone, timing is key. Send an invitation too late and your friends may already be booked; send it too early and it might be misplaced or forgotten. The following advice should serve as a guideline for various occasions. Use your best judgment for your specific event.

EVENT	INVITATION LEAD TIME
Anniversary party	3 to 6 weeks before the event
Bar or Bat Mitzvah	8 weeks
Birthday party	3 weeks
Bon voyage party	Last minute to 3 weeks
Casual party	Same day to 2 weeks
Charity ball	6 weeks to 3 months
Christmas party	1 month
Cocktail party	1 to 4 weeks
Formal dinner	3 to 6 weeks
Graduation party	3 weeks
Housewarming party	1 to 3 weeks
Informal dinner	1 to 3 weeks
Lunch or tea	Last minute to 2 weeks
Thanksgiving dinner	6 to 8 weeks
Wedding	2 weeks to 2 months

10   When Is Mailing an Invitation a Must?

Weddings, anniversaries, milestone birthdays, christenings, and the like announce themselves elegantly and traditionally with a written invitation. Your invitation can be simple and handwritten, or creative and crafty; or you can splurge on gorgeous printed stationery. The look is up to you and should fit the occasion, but the act of mailing a tangible invitation is a statement in itself: it says the event is significant and tells the guest that his or her presence is meaningful.

11   The DIY Invite

Homemade snail-mail party invitations are easy to create and can look very professional. There is a plethora of Web sites that make it easy to make your own professional-looking invitations at home using your computer and printer. Just type "homemade invitations" into your favorite search engine, and you will find a variety of companies that want to help you; see Resources (page 274).

12   E-mail Invitations

An e-mail invitation can be just that—a regular e-mail containing the pertinent details; or if you want to catch people's attention, and at the same time give them some idea of the mood of the party, use an e-vite from an online service, or create a unique invitation that you can attach to your e-mail in PDF format. A quick browse on the Internet will lead you to Web sites that will help you do this quickly and easily; see Resources (page 274).

13 Phone Invites

If you're having a small dinner party (say, six to eight people), a phone call is a warm and wonderful way of inviting guests. As your friend may be feeding the kids or be otherwise distracted, follow up with an e-mail to be sure each guest has the correct date and address on his or her calendar.

14 How to Elicit the Elusive RSVP

One of the anxieties any hostess has is wondering who's going to show up. Here are a couple of tips on handling the slow demise of basic etiquette when it comes to responding to and attending engagements.

1. Ask for a response. Then keep a running count of the yesses, nos, and maybes. The type of response you get should correspond to the type of invitation: an e-mail is the expected response to an e-mail invitation; a phone call or a mailed reply card is appropriate for a written invitation.

2. Deflect the blame. Failure to respond to wedding and other formal invitations has serious consequences. A head count is needed; a caterer kept waiting makes everyone nervous. Seating plans must be finalized. If a response card is included in an invitation and doesn't get returned by the requested date, make a phone call. Don't frame the failure to respond in admonishing tones. Blame the caterer: "Hi, Barb. I know you must be swamped, but we're trying to get our final head count together for the wedding. The caterer is breathing down my neck. Anyhow, are you able to make it?"

15 How to Word a Last-Minute Invite

When you are planning a party and have a limited number of seats, you have to prioritize whom to invite. When the responses come in, and you have space to invite more people, how do you do so gracefully?

Last-minute invitations can be a sticky issue, but it helps to know who your friends are. If you have a friend who is easily offended or often feels slighted, it will probably save you some upset to not invite him or her on the fly. Instead, choose an easygoing friend, one who is not a big planner, or one who understands the trials and tribulations of hosting parties and extending last-minute invitations.

The best course of action for a last-minute invitation is a straightforward one. If you're having a small party, such as a dinner party or a game night, for which the guest list is organized around a set number of seats, and your last-minute invitation is the result of someone else canceling, honesty is the best policy: "I'm having a dinner party for a small group tomorrow evening and someone canceled. I would love to have you come and I think you'd really like everyone, besides which I've wanted to have you over for dinner for some time. I'm sorry it's last minute but I do hope you can come." As always, warmth and enthusiasm will make even a last-minute guest feel welcome and wanted.

If you're having a large party and honestly forgot to include your friend, say, in your warmest tone, "Oh, drat, you know, I'm having a party this Thursday and it suddenly strikes me that I failed to send you the invitation—I hope you can come." Apologize for its being last minute and understand that your friend may have other plans. You might suggest he or she come for part of the evening. These types of concessions will help express an A-list feeling for a B-list friend.

16   When the Answer Is No

Always be gracious and accommodating in the role of host, even when you receive regrets. Don't admonish your guests, or ask why they're unavailable. If they say they can't make it, or that they're not yet sure, don't seize the opportunity to remind them that they've been out of touch since meeting the new boyfriend or that they didn't mind getting a babysitter for dinner out with another friend two weeks ago. You might think these things, but never say them; it's impolite.

17   How to Keep Your Party Kid-Free

Where children are concerned, consideration from both parent and host is key. It's perfectly okay to throw kid-free parties; you need only state it gracefully and in advance. While most parents welcome an evening out on their own, some have more difficulty disentangling themselves from their children. Parents should not assume that their kids are invited to your cocktail or dinner party, but they might—especially if you have children as well. Find a casual but clear way to communicate that the event is kid-free, so your friends have time to find a sitter.

ETIQUETTE

---

18   How to Handle Uninvited Guests

The party's in full swing and one of your invited guests has just arrived with a friend who is not on the guest list. The only course of action now is to kick into full host mode and make the person feel welcome. Ask the invited guest to introduce his or her friend to others while you fix them drinks. If it's a sit-down dinner, you have no choice but to be gracious and squeeze in another chair and place setting and make all the portions a tad smaller. There's no point in getting upset, since your mission, once the party begins, is to have a good time and help guests do the same.

19   When a Guest Wants to Bring a Friend

Sometimes it's no big deal to add another guest. However, if it's a wedding or other structured event, even one more person might throw things off. You can head off trouble by being very clear on your party invitation and using the name of the guest(s) invited. Often a guest will take extenuating circumstances directly to the host. If you really can't accommodate an extra person, explain to your friend the financial and space limits of the situation and honestly say that, as much as you'd like to, you can't expand the guest list.

20 How to Make Them Mingle

Don't leave guests to awkwardly mingle at a party you're hosting. If it's a crowd filled with people that don't know one another, it's important to give people something to go on. When making introductions, try to jump-start the conversation—explain where you know each guest from, or bring up something they have in common—then break away once a conversation has been sparked.

21 How to Break Away from a Conversation

As the host, you've got a built-in exit strategy: "Please excuse me" followed by "I'd love to hear more about this later, but right now I'd better make sure that things are going as planned in the kitchen" or "I think I smell something burning" or "Sally just came in—I must go greet her." You get the idea.

22 How to Appear Calm, Cool, and Collected

The art of hosting is making it look effortless; this is easiest for hostesses who really love the pace and pressures of putting out a spread for friends. But even they know to ease this pace by planning parties for which most of the work can be done in advance.

The trickiest time is when your guests are arriving. You want to welcome them with open arms, but there are coats to put away, drinks to fetch, flowers to put in vases, and things in the kitchen to attend to. Keep your event running smoothly by making sure that your pre-party setup is complete before the first guests arrive. Transform anxiety into enthusiasm, both of which have an upbeat pace. Make a timeline for the evening in advance, mapping out when you'll clear the cocktail snacks, make last-minute sauces in the kitchen, let ice cream soften, open after-dinner drinks, et cetera. The timeline should be as detailed as possible, turning the evening into a well-choreographed dance. Preparedness helps make everything look effortless.

23   TIP: **Wear What You Want**

Certain practical considerations go out the window when you don't have to leave your front door. So wear those heels that you can barely walk a block in; you can just kick them off and go barefoot when they start to pinch. For that matter, you can host a party in ballet slippers, or forgo stockings even though it's cold out. If you're cooking, be practical; long, flowy sleeves will get in the way of your kitchen work, and skip the metallic necklaces if you'll be reaching into the oven.

24   How to Corral the Kids

When you invite children into your home, you're giving up some level of control. Make your peace ahead of time with the mess and the noise kids can make. If you haven't childproofed your home because your own toddler is a saint, be mindful that others might not be so placid. Hide the Swedish pottery, and place those carefully laid trays of nuts and olives out of reach. The clever host has kid-friendly snacks on hand and whips up Bambini Pasta (pasta with butter and grated Parmesan—the most universally appreciated dish among the younger set) for dinner. Don't be afraid to bribe kids: a fun dessert (preferably one that they can help decorate before serving) may help elicit their best behavior. Check with the parents first to see whether you might be able to let the kids watch a movie together in another room while the grown-ups have a leisurely meal. For larger parties, it may be worth it to hire a babysitter to watch the kids and keep them occupied. A word to the wise: Your own kids may be well behaved and enjoy asparagus, but you'll have to be very delicate about scolding your friends' children. Even if they're monsters, they're your guests, too.

25 Ten Jobs You Can Delegate

Relinquish your grip on some of the busywork. Adult children, spouses, and friends can really come in handy with the chores below.

1. Setting the table

2. Ironing and folding napkins

3. Cleaning wineglasses that have been gathering dust on a distant shelf

4. Setting up the bar

5. Slicing lemon and lime wedges for drinks

6. Buying ice and making ice buckets for the bar

7. Preparing water carafes

8. Slicing bread

9. Opening wine

10. Lighting candles

All Hands on Deck

Delegate tasks to family members; decide ahead of time which tasks would be well matched to which helpers, and let them know up front what you're expecting of them: "Honey, could you please make time to pick up the ice around four o'clock?" or "Kids, I really need your help today. I'm going to need this corn shucked by five o'clock." You get the idea. It's too late to ask for help when you're already "in the weeds" (that's restaurant talk for being in way over your head and too busy to see your way out). Refer to your handy prep list (see page 6) to find a suitable job for the helping hands.

Clear ample space for an extra person to be working, so he or she won't be underfoot. If you want help setting the table, pull the things you want to use out of cupboards and mark them with Post-its identifying what each piece is for, so you can easily point someone toward the job without having to stop what you are doing. You can also ask close friends to bring something or arrive early to pitch in. An efficient friend in the final hour before a party—crunch time—can be a lifesaver and a calming presence.

Calling for Backup

If you're having more than ten people, or if you are planning a plated sit-down dinner, consider hiring a helper or caterer to come over an hour or two before party time to help pull together last-minute details and review the menu with you. Every town has services that hire out help for such occasions, whether it's to wash dishes, serve hors d'oeuvres, restock a buffet, or assist in plating dishes for a more formal dinner party. Industrious high-school or college students are usually up to the job and are happy for the opportunity to put some extra cash in their pockets. Helpers are usually paid an hourly wage, often with a five-hour minimum, plus a gratuity, which should be 15 to 20 percent of the total. If you are using a staffing service or a catering company, there will probably be a surcharge in the form of a higher hourly rate or a separate fee. Having extra help will leave you more time to enjoy your party. There is nothing nicer than saying good-bye to your last guest and returning to a clean kitchen with the dishwasher humming.

28   How to Delegate to Hired Help

If you've hired helpers, make the most of it and know how you want them to contribute. When the help arrives, be ready to give them clear instructions so they can utilize the customary setup time most efficiently.

It is best to have staff arrive two hours before the party, giving them plenty of time to prepare. If tables and chairs need to be set up, sketch out where you would like them to go. Prepare a list ahead of tasks for the helpers, to reduce the number of questions they have for you during the party. These may include any cooking, heating, or serving instructions for food, which wines to serve when, how much time to allow between courses, which dishes to use for what, and where everything they need is located, including what to do with the garbage and recyclables at the end of the event.

29   TIP: **Take Five**

Schedule a small break in the action about an hour before your guests are due so you can change your clothes and perhaps wash the flour out of your hair. Chances are you'll be busy up to the last minute, but if you schedule a break, you can make sure you're not wearing your cooking sweats when guests arrive. It's okay to still be calmly fiddling in the kitchen at party time, but you want to be fresh and ready to greet guests.

30   Choosing a Caterer and Staying on Budget

If you need more than just a few extra hands during party time and want to hire a caterer for the whole soup-to-nuts deal, the first step is to find the right caterer for you. Recommendations from friends who have used caterers is a great place to start your search. Narrow it down to a few and then call at least two different companies to compare prices. This will also help you negotiate the price, if you find yourself liking one caterer more than another who charges less. Be sure to emphasize your budget when you describe the event. A good caterer will start with the budget and work backward to give you a realistic menu. Remember, it's not just the food that costs money; the biggest expenses in catering are often the staff and rentals. Ask the caterer if there are ways to adjust the menu or style of service to reduce the number of staff required. Ask if there is a way to reduce the rental fees for plates, glasses, and other serving items too. If you are inclined to prepare the food or some portion of the meal yourself, you can still use a caterer for some of the food and for serving; just make sure to discuss this in advance.

31 Three Things to Know Before Calling a Caterer

1. The total budget

2. How many guests are on the guest list

3. The time and date of the event

32 Twelve Questions to Ask a Prospective Caterer

1. Do you have a culinary specialty or a preferred serving style?

2. Can we have a tasting beforehand?

3. Do you have recent references I can call?

4. Is the company licensed? (This should include health department certification, liability insurance, and a liquor license if required by your state.)

5. Will you provide the liquor, or can I provide it myself? (You may be able to save money this way, as long as they don't charge a corkage or serving fee that will negate the difference.)

6. How involved do you get in decor (if I need help with that)?

7. Will you provide the rentals and staffing, or just the food?

8. Will adjustments be made to the price if I have fewer or more people than agreed upon?

9. How are staffing costs calculated? Is there a minimum number of hours I must pay for?

10. Will you supply a contract once we've agreed on the details?

11. What's the payment schedule? (Usually a deposit will be required up front, with the balance due at the end of the event.)

12. What's the cancellation policy?

33   TIP: **Rent Glasses and Plates**

If you're a bit overwhelmed by your party, a real lifesaver is renting the plates and glasses (and possibly tables, chairs, linens, and more). In addition to the obvious advantage of having access to however many matching sets of plates and glasses you need, renting the tableware means you won't have to wash anything. Party rental companies (sometimes listed under chair rentals on the Internet) deliver everything in boxes, and when your party is over, you send it all back, dirty. Just scrape, stack, and call it a night! If you are having a smaller party, be aware that some companies will impose minimums around the holidays or at other busy times of year. Make sure you research the minimums before you make a plan.

34 Ten Questions to Ask a Contracted Caterer

1. Will you be scheduling a walk-through ahead of time? (The caterer should, to determine in advance where and how everything will be set up.)

2. At what time will the staff arrive to set up, and how should I prepare for them?

3. What's the dress code for the staff? (This can range from Hawaiian shirts and chinos to full tuxedos, so discuss what's appropriate for your party.)

4. When will rentals be delivered and picked up, and where will they be stored?

5. Who will be in charge at the event, and is there someone off-site I can call in case something goes wrong?

6. How and when am I expected to feed the staff?

7. What happens to leftover food? (The staff should pack it up and put it in the fridge for you.)

8. Can unopened liquor be returned?

9. How will garbage removal be handled?

10. What is expected for gratuities for the staff, and how should they be paid? Can they be added to my final bill, or should I pay each staff member by cash or check at the end of the event?

35 TIP: An Apron Is Your Best Accessory

Aprons are crucial when you're all dressed up and putting the finishing touches on dinner, but greeting your guests in blood-spattered armor defeats the purpose. Invest in a cute, short apron to wear when serving drinks and snacks and retire the one you wore doing true dirty work.

36   Timing Is Everything

An inability to coordinate the timing of a meal can be the downfall of even the best cooks. We've all been to (or thrown) a dinner party where the main course didn't manage to make it to the table until eleven o'clock, or half the guests had finished their ravioli by the time the poor hostess got to sit down and join them. Getting all the components of a meal on the table at the same time, and at their peak of flavor and temperature, requires levelheaded multitasking, which is impossible without good planning. Timing should be on your mind from the get-go: when designing the menu, choose dishes that won't collide in the oven or on the stove, and balance items that require last-minute touches with those that can be made completely ahead of time. Experience is the best teacher, but there are some rules that can save you from those typical crunch-time pitfalls.

37   Timing and the Breakfast Lesson

You may not fancy yourself a master entertainer, but chances are you can pull breakfast together with some coordination. The most important meal of the day is also a perfect study in kitchen timing, because there are usually several elements that require last-minute preparation, and if any of them sit around for too long, they really suffer. When the eggs hit the frying pan, the bread had better be sliced and headed for the toaster. If you didn't make the coffee by the time you're pouring the batter onto the griddle for the first pancake, you're in trouble. After some time, these things become second nature, and knowing the order of operations makes all the difference. The same principles can be applied to cooking the more complex meals that you might be serving for a dinner party. The work may be spread out over a few days, and the proportions may be greater, but the same philosophy should always guide you. In that last hour or so before your guests arrive, the short-order cook in you will save the day every time.

Thinking Backward

When planning how to finish your tasks, make a list starting with the ones that must be done at the last minute, and work backward to those for which the timing is not as crucial. Make your list with the do-aheads at the top and the crucial items at the very bottom. This way, you'll clear the way so you can have ample time for the last-minute jobs.

For example, some dishes are better the next day, such as a braise that you want to let cool so you can skim the fat from the top before reheating and serving it. If you're baking a dessert, in most cases you will be able to get that out of the way the night before or first thing the morning of the party. When you write your menu, make sure to choose a few items that can (or must) be cooked ahead, and save as little as possible for the last minute. Allow yourself a time cushion for those little tasks that always seem to come up right before your guests ring the doorbell.

39 Don't Go Overboard

It's tempting to pull out all the stops and go a little crazy with your party, but this can backfire when you realize that you have bitten off more than you can chew. Even if you're a great cook, the bigger your party, the simpler your menu should be. One big communal dish like a pot of chili or hearty soup served from the stove can have just as much impact as a big spread. Mix up a pitcher of a signature cocktail rather than offer a full bar, or order dessert from your favorite bakery rather than make it yourself. Your guests will be just as happy.

TIP: **Don't Drink and Host**

Once your guests have arrived, of course, it's fine to sip some wine, and once the meal has been served, relax and have a couple of glasses. But when there are still guests to seat and cooking to be done and your nerves are acting up, a cocktail is not the cure. It will only result in more chaos and, possibly, last-minute blunders that can ruin hours of hard work.

41   How to Survive Crunch Time

The few hours before a party—when you're cooking up a storm and hiding your slippers under the bed—can (or should) be a bit like a ballet. Try to choreograph your movements by planning ahead so you can keep your cool. Don't get overwhelmed, and prioritize when time is running short. Nervous cooks sometimes make too much ahead of time, for fear that everything won't come out at the same time. Cooking ahead is recommended, but some things simply must be done *à la minute*, or at the last minute. Precooked pasta will be a gummy mess, for example, and delicate fish fillets will probably fall apart and/or dry out if you have to reheat them.

Anything that must be green and crisp, like green vegetables or a salad, should be saved for last. If you're steaming vegetables, prepare them and place them (and the water) in a steamer on the stove, but don't turn on the heat until you are almost ready to serve. Wash the greens and prepare the components for the salad (including the dressing), and even refrigerate them in the bowl you are going to serve in, but don't dress or toss the salad in advance.

Remember that all meat needs to rest after coming out of the oven, so plan to do other last-minute preparations during those 15 minutes or so. If you are serving something that must be eaten immediately, hot off the grill or the stove, make sure all the other components of the meal are completed first.

THE GIFTED HOSTESS

42   Six Worthy Investments

If you have the space to store them, having these items on hand will make entertaining so much easier, even if you use them only once a year.

1. **A case of wineglasses** (usually 36 to a box). Choose an all-purpose shape that can be used for red wine, white wine, or even soft drinks, and buy them cheaply at a restaurant supply store. Store them in the box they came in (they will need to be washed before using) or, better, in a plastic caddy specifically designed for the purpose that will keep them clean between uses.

2. **Cloth napkins.** Go with standard-issue restaurant ware; just aim for 100 percent cotton, since synthetic blends don't feel very nice against the skin, nor do they absorb liquids very well. Store clean, folded napkins in giant resealable plastic bags, so they're ready for use.

3. **Table linens.** These don't have to break the bank. Have on hand a few sturdy tablecloths, in sizes that cover your dining table and any other tables that you can press into service for a party, such as your kitchen table. White tablecloths are nice, but darker colors or prints and damasks won't show the inevitable stains the way white will. Depending on your space, you may want cloths that reach the floor so you can stash extra supplies underneath during your party.

4. **Extra serving utensils.** If you like throwing buffet parties, you would be wise to invest in some extra-large serving spoons, ladles, spatulas, forks, and tongs that are attractive enough to be on the table. Too often,

we use kitchen utensils that don't add much to the look of the table. Unwieldy serving utensils will also slow down your guests' progress through the buffet line. Try to choose implements that can be used easily with one hand, like scissor-style salad tongs, for instance, rather than a traditional two-piece salad server set. Stainless steel and wood are good choices and not too pricey.

5. Large platters and serving bowls. Every hostess needs extra platters for party time. White platters are the best default since everything looks good on white, and it lets the food shine. Go for a variety of sizes and shapes. These can become a decorative element in your home when not in use if you devote a wall of shelves or a glass-front cabinet to their storage.

6. Warming tray or chafing dish. A chafing dish is really the only way to keep food warm for an extended period of time. Chafing dishes are essential for buffet parties, cocktail parties, and stations, especially when your party is outdoors. There are many new and sleek chafing dishes for the modern hostess that won't call attention to themselves. Look for ones with clean lines and without a lot of unnecessary ornamental curlicues. At the same time, you don't want them to look as if they belong in the high-school cafeteria, either. Choose chafing dishes that go with your serving pieces and your decor.

43 *In Praise of* Paper Napkins

Using paper napkins is a reality for many of us when we throw a party, and there is absolutely nothing wrong with them. If you want to elevate your style above the standard-issue supermarket napkins, an array of beautiful choices is available in home stores and party stores and online in a variety of colors, sizes, and prints. Some are so nice you might think they were cloth; see Resources (page 274).

Aside from the usual *batterie de cuisine,* here are a few things that every successful hostess should have in her kitchen arsenal.

1. Cast-iron skillet. For searing and roasting meat, poultry, and fish, or making corn bread, crumbles, and cobblers that can be brought right to the table for a rustic presentation, cast iron is probably the best all-purpose pan around. If you like making desserts in a skillet, it's a good idea to reserve one for that purpose only, so your strawberry crisp doesn't taste like salmon.

2. Enameled Dutch oven. This oven-to-table staple is for braising meat stews, short ribs, or pork shoulders, or making a hearty soup. Available in an array of stylish colors, this is a pricey item, but one that will last a lifetime and lend a rustic beauty to your table. Enameled cast iron will retain its heat for a long time, which is a big plus for serving cold-weather meals.

3. Immersion blender. This is best for pureeing soups and sauces right in the pot, or blending a small batch of salad dressing. If you get one with a whisk attachment, you'll be able to make whipped cream quickly right before serving dessert.

4. Gratin dishes. Simple, attractive, oven-to-table baking dishes are wonderful for buffets or family-style meals. Cooking a dish in its serving vessel means one less thing to platter up at crunch time, and it keeps the food warm, too.

5. Kitchen tongs. A comfortable pair of tongs (make sure the spring is not too tight) will make you a faster and more facile cook. Tongs are not to be used for the most delicate items, like fish, but they should be an extension of your hand for just about everything else.

6. Fish spatula. This long, thin, angled spatula is a must for releasing and turning delicate fish fillets when pan-searing.

7. Instant-read thermometer. Unless you've been cooking so long that you've developed an unerring sixth sense about when meat is done, you shouldn't be without this tiny and inexpensive tool. It will save you a lot of stress and will prevent your having to apologize for overcooked (or undercooked) meat, poultry, and fish.

8. Offset spatula. These come in a variety of sizes, but I like the smallest ones best, since they do most jobs well. An offset spatula is absolutely necessary for icing a cake or spreading anything and is convenient for turning small items like blini or even removing a delicate cookie from a baking sheet.

9. Microplane grater. This versatile tool is perfect for finely grating nutmeg, lemon zest, and especially Parmesan cheese, which resembles freshly fallen snow when grated with a Microplane and sprinkled over pasta or salad.

10. Japanese mandoline. This handy item is inexpensive and is indispensable for making paper-thin slices of apples, fennel, radishes, carrots, celery, raw mushrooms, Parmesan cheese, and anything else that's firm and sliceable, for salads and garnishes. It's also indispensable for thinly slicing potatoes for a gratin.

SETTING
THE
SCENE

Taking the time to get your place party-ready is important in the overall impression that is made on your guests. You can create the mood you want by making considered choices when it comes to lighting, music, and a host of other details that all add up to a personal statement. Make choices that are right for you and your guests, being as formal or informal as you like.

45   How to Arrange Your Space

Whether your place is small or large, it's important to consider how people will be moving through the room(s): where they'll congregate, sit, stand, and linger. The key is to get people to spread out and keep moving as much as possible. If you've entertained before, you have some idea of where the bottlenecks naturally occur, so you have a head start on trying to prevent and avoid them. Place a large table in a central space away from any known bottlenecks. Remove the chairs from around the table and spread them throughout the house to give guests another place to sit and to provide easier access to the food. Float the table in the middle of a room rather than push it up against a wall, to allow guests to get to it from all sides. Try drawing a simple floor plan to see how your furniture might be arranged to create a good flow. Even if your drawing is not to scale, it's helpful to visualize the arrangement in two dimensions. It will also provide a visual guide if you have helpers assisting with the setup.

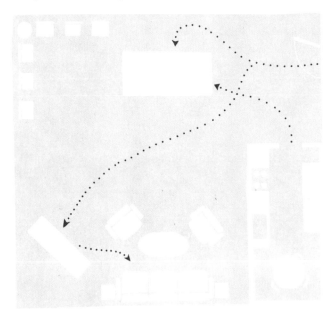

46   TIP: Spread the Love, in Snack Form

As we all know from personal experience as guests at a party, people tend to hang around the snack table, chatting and noshing. Even if you have one main buffet set up with food, place little dishes with nuts or any not-too-messy finger food around the room or rooms where you want your guests to linger. Also, make sure there are enough surfaces for them to place their drinks so they'll be comfortable away from the bar.

47   Where's the Bar?

Since the bar, like the snacks, will attract loiterers, it should be placed in an open, central location, away from high-traffic areas such as doorways and hallways or any narrow spaces around furniture. Placing the bar in a part of your home that tends to have less traffic during a party will draw your guests there and help prevent traffic jams. Of course you don't want it so far out of the way that it's isolated from other rooms, if you're hoping for people to spread out. It should also be convenient for you to replenish it. If you are planning a really large party (more than thirty people), consider a second bar, or a service bar behind the scenes from which drinks can be served to guests from trays.

48   How to Use Stations

Caterers create food stations for the flexibility they offer, and they come in handy for the amateur hostess as well. Creating stations, especially for a grazing cocktail party, means you spread the food out into distinct areas, say, with crudités and dips on a table in one room and sushi in another (or whatever type of station your heart desires). Stations make a party fun to explore and encourage guests to keep moving to different corners of your space, with the added benefit that they encounter new people to chat with. This keeps the traffic jams to a minimum. Stations also allow you to create mini themes, menu-wise. Each station should be self-sufficient, with all the accoutrements and utensils at hand. If you're hiring help, a staff person can do some minor cooking or serving at a station, like making blini (little yeast-raised pancakes) to serve with caviar and other toppings, opening clams and oysters on a raw bar, or carving a roast. Stations also can be self-serve, like a fondue, or a table set simply with sushi rolls or cheese and fruit.

49 TIP: Practice Makes Perfect (or Close to It)

As a hostess, you need to feel confident—about your home, your cooking skills, and your social skills. If you're not having fun, your guests won't be, either. It's helpful to master a few skills, some basic (such as opening a bottle of wine or champagne; see pages 169 and 213) and some more elaborate (such as making a soufflé; see page 224), that will impress your guests and create a bit of a performance. Just one small display of panache will give your guests something to remember about the party. These skills may take a little practice to master, so give them a dry run when there are no guests around.

TABLE SETTINGS

50 Do I Need to Use a Tablecloth or Place Mats?

If the table itself is great-looking and you don't want to hide it, use place mats rather than a tablecloth—just as you might go for an area rug to make your living room cozier but still show off the hardwood floors. If your table is not so gorgeous, use a pretty tablecloth to cover it up entirely (as you would use wall-to-wall carpeting to cover an unfinished floor). You should have some neutral tablecloths on hand, such as pale linen, but for festive occasions, go with colorful table linens or place mats to bring the party to life. Choose something that goes with the theme of the party and the food.

51   What's a Runner For?

A runner—a long, narrow piece of fabric that is usually centered down a rectangular table lengthwise—is a great way to dress up the table without being too formal. If you're serving dinner family-style, bowls and platters should be placed on the runner, with place settings on either side. While it is nice to show off a beautiful wood or marble table by leaving some of it uncovered, a runner can also be layered over a full tablecloth. Be sure both fabrics are smooth and not too thick, or you'll create a lumpy terrain. If your table is relatively wide, you can use two runners, kind of like extended place mats, running down the length of the table, leaving the middle exposed. A more modern treatment is to place two or more short runners across the width of the table, so they sit under the place settings in pairs, connecting people who are seated across from each other.

TIP: Use a Charger

A charger is a large, flat plate that sits underneath other dishes; traditionally, food is not served on it. Its purpose as part of a formal setting is as a placeholder, often with a napkin folded on top, and as a crumb or drip catcher for the plates that may be placed on top of it. A true charger is bigger than a dinner plate, but you can use a large dinner plate in a similar capacity, placing the first course on top of it and then (unless it's a very formal dinner) using it to plate the main course. Certain dishes should never be set directly on the table—foremost a soup bowl or a pasta bowl. A charger is provided as a place to rest the spoon and perhaps a piece of bread, and to protect the table from heat and sloshes.

53 A Place-Setting Cheat Sheet

Below are some basic table-setting rules. Think of each setting as a block of marble, to be chiseled away as the meal goes on. As we use our utensils and they are cleared from the table, the setting shrinks, from the outside in, until the final course is served.

• Forks on the left, knives on the right of the plate.

• Spoons on the right, with the knives.

• The silverware will be used from the outside in, so if you are serving a salad first, the salad fork should be the outermost utensil, and the next one in should be the one that will be used next—probably a large fork for the main course. If you are starting with soup, the soupspoon should be placed to the right of the knives.

• The napkin can be placed to the left of the plate, with the forks on it, or on the charger.

- The butter dish goes in the left-hand corner. If you have proper butter knives (which are small and short), they should be placed across the butter dishes. If you are using a regular knife for butter, place it to the right of the plate, on the outside, if the butter will be served at the beginning of the meal.

- Dessert utensils can be placed at the top of the setting, over the plate, or brought out when that course is served. It is customary to bring a fork and a spoon, unless the dessert can be eaten with only a spoon (for example, if you're serving pudding).

- The glasses go in the right-hand corner, starting with the water glass, which should be just above the knives.

- Wineglasses should be placed to the right of the water glass, in the order in which they will be used. So, if you're starting with white wine and then moving on to red, your glasses would be in this order, from left to right: water glass, white-wine glass, red-wine glass. They can also be arranged in a triangle, still with the water glass above the knife, and the first wineglass just to the right of it. If there is a second wineglass, place it behind those two.

- After-dinner glasses can be brought to the table at the end of the meal. If you are serving dessert wine, bring the glasses out with dessert.

- Coffee mugs or teacups should be brought to the table (or the living room, if your party migrates) with dessert. At a more casual party, you might ask how many of your guests would like to have one or the other. Teacups should be on saucers, with spoons for stirring in sugar.

54 TIP: Use Your Hands

Here's a "handy" way to remember that
the bread plate goes on the left and the
drinks go on the right. Your left hand
makes a *b* for bread. Your right hand
makes a *d* for drinks.

55 What Kind of Wineglasses Do I Need?

Here are the basics: The wider the mouth
of the glass, the greater the effect on the
wine of oxygen, which "relaxes" the flavors
and brings the aroma out. Generally, this
effect is more desirable with red wines and
full-bodied whites, like chardonnay. White-wine glasses have a narrower
opening, and red-wine glasses are more round. (Rosé is traditionally
drunk out of a tulip-shaped glass, but a white-wine glass is perfectly
acceptable.) At a formal dinner, different wines would be served in
different glasses, even if both wines are reds or whites.

Though there is a specific shape for every type of wine, using one
glass for red and one for white would suffice. If you don't have the
storage space or budget for two sets, then look for a glass with a shape
that accommodates any type of wine. It should be big enough for red,
but not so balloon-shaped that it can't work for a white. Rinse your
guests' glasses before refilling them with a new wine.

56 *In Praise of* Stemless Wineglasses

If you're entertaining a crowd or serving drinks outside, stemless glasses
are great because they're not as delicate as stemmed glasses and you can
fit a lot of them in the dishwasher at the end of the party without fear of
breaking them. Stemless wineglasses are available in the same shapes as

traditional stemmed glasses: rounder and
wider for red, more tapered and tall for
white wine, or an all-purpose shape, all
sans stem, of course.

57   What Kind of Salt Should I Serve?

For the table, flaky sea salt is a nice choice, because it can be crumbled
between one's fingers into something finer, or sprinkled lightly, the
crystals remaining somewhat intact until they hit the tongue. On hot
food, it will "melt," but not instantly. If you want to serve flavored salt,
such as truffle salt to enhance a mushroom dish or a spicy salt that will
add a little extra kick to barbecued ribs, make plain salt available as well.

58 To Shake or to Pinch

If you're serving kosher salt or regular-to-fine sea salt, use a regular saltshaker. But for flaky or coarse salt, only a little dish or bowl, also known as a saltcellar, will work, since the grains are too big to pass through the holes of a shaker. Using a saltcellar means you'll be faced with the finger conundrum. With good friends or family, you may not mind letting your guests use their fingers to pinch some salt for their plates, but you could also use a little spoon for scooping, especially if the crowd is not very intimate. If you have more than six people, particularly at a long table, put out two or more saltshakers, or dishes, for easy access. They don't necessarily have to match. If the occasion is formal, or if you happen to be a collector, you can provide a small dish or shaker for each person so there's no concern about using fingers.

59 Should I Put Pepper on the Table?

If you're serving black pepper, it should be freshly ground. Banish the preground stuff for cooking as well as at the table. A miniature pepper mill is a nice choice for the table, especially if you have a long table and want to put out a few. Another option is to grind the pepper yourself, right before the meal, and serve it in tiny bowls as you might serve salt and other seasonings, such as chili flakes. If the only grinder you have is not a good-looking one or one of those tall, showy grinders, this is the way to go.

ATMOSPHERE

60 Decorating Around a Cuisine

Use Mexican dish towels as place mats for a Cinco de Mayo party or a Moroccan jewelry box as a centerpiece for a tagine meal. If the menu is inspired by your travels, you might have some souvenirs that can be used

to decorate the table or dining room, evoking the special location. If you don't have souvenirs but are taking inspiration from a place, find an import store in your city or town where you can find a few inexpensive knickknacks that will evoke that place. Otherwise, look at some photos or Web sites for inspiration and get creative; a simple color scheme or type of flowers could be all you need to tastefully pull your theme together and flatter the food you serve.

61 Less Is Almost Always More

A few well-placed pops of color, and perhaps some candles, are often all that's needed to make a room sparkle. As with your menu, let the season be your guide, and bring some of the outdoors in. A few flowering branches are dramatic in the spring, unusual pumpkins and squashes are great in the fall, and simple greenery for the holidays is all you need to dress up your space.

62 *In Praise of* The Dimmer Switch

Soft lighting creates a warm and cozy evening atmosphere and flatters your guests, your home, and the food. A multitude of sins can be easily overlooked when people are basking in a warm glow. Create even more of a mood with candles (or go romantic and use *only* candles; if you use several there will be enough light, and you will be surprised at how quickly eyes adjust to low light). If you don't have dimmers, use 40-watt lightbulbs and play with the placement of lamps so the light isn't direct.

The best way to get people in a party mood is with the right music. With the help of laptops and MP3 players, it's never been easier to be your own deejay. Make a playlist with enough music to last for the whole party. Choose music that won't compete with conversation. Music, like lighting, has a big impact on the mood of an event—and is perhaps most successful when your guests barely notice it. So instead of throwing all your favorite songs together, decide what mood you're going for, and try to assemble a cohesive mix. Your list might also make a progression—say, from folk tunes during dinner to New Wave for the postmeal dance party that breaks out in the living room. If the music isn't conveying the mood that you expected, it's also easy to make adjustments mid-party and to take requests.

FOLKSY COCKTAIL HOUR TUNES
"Going Down the Road Feeling Bad" by Woody Guthrie
"Don't Think Twice, It's All Right" by Bob Dylan
"The Weight" by The Band
"Suzanne" by Leonard Cohen
"The Boxer" by Simon & Garfunkel
"Poncho & Lefty" by Townes Van Zandt
"All I Want" by Joni Mitchell
"Percy's Song" by Fairport Convention
"Harvest Moon" by Neil Young
"Wear Your Love Like Heaven" by Donovan

SOPHISTICATED LATIN AND JAZZ SONGS
"Só Danço Samba" by Antônio Carlos Jobim
"Agua de Beber" by Astrud Gilberto with Antônio Carlos Jobim
"Make Believe Mambo (Orisa)" by David Byrne
"De Camino a la Vereda" by Buena Vista Social Club
"Petit Pays" by Cesária Évora
"Quizás, Quizás, Quizás" by Rubén González
"Garota de Ipanema" by Stan Getz and João Gilberto
"My Favorite Things" by John Coltrane
"Blue Rondo à la Turk" by Dave Brubeck Quartet
"All Blues" by Miles Davis

"Black Coffee in Bed" by Squeeze
"Rudy, a Message to You" by Dandy Livingstone
"Cherry Oh Baby" by Eric Donaldson
"Mirror in the Bathroom" by The English Beat
"The Bed's Too Big Without You" by The Police
"Rat in Mi Kitchen" by UB40
"Police & Thieves" by The Clash
"The Tide Is High" by Blondie
"Watching the Detectives" by Elvis Costello
"Ghost Town" by The Specials

64   Five Candle Tips

1. Always start the evening with fresh candles so they don't burn out halfway through your party.

2. Do all your candle prep hours, or even days, ahead of time. Cleaning out old wax takes more time than you may think.

3. If you plan to spread votives around the room, place them on a single tray and light them all at once, right before the party starts. Then disperse them around the room (in safe spots, of course). This will save a lot of time running around lighting candles.

4. Invest in a long lighter (they're approximately $3), available in any supermarket or hardware store. There are even models especially designed for lighting candles, with a downward-pointing flame or a flexible neck.

5. Avoid using any kind of scented candle anywhere near food. The overwhelming scent will distract from the subtle smells of the food. Save scented candles for the bathroom.

SETTING THE SCENE

TIP: Clean Old Wax Out of Candleholders

The best method is preemptive. Do as waiters and waitresses in restaurants do and put a tiny bit of water into the empty glass votive holder before placing the new candle inside. This will eventually allow the old candle wax to pop right out with gentle prying. It may cause a little rust to form from the metal base of the wick, but it's unlikely to show when a fresh candle is in the holder. Pop the holders in the dishwasher now and then to freshen them up. If the wax is really stuck, put the votive holders in the freezer long enough to harden the wax. (This will make it easier to pop it out in one piece.) Place the votive on a sturdy cutting board and use an old butter knife to help pry out the wax, or crack the wax into a few large pieces for easy removal. Be careful not to use too much force, as the glass will be more brittle, too, from being in the freezer.

FLOWERS

66   How to Be Your Own Florist

If you live in a big city, locate a wholesale flower market and find out whether individual vendors sell to the public. Many do, and most likely you'll have to pay in cash. The flowers are less expensive and often fresher. That longevity will allow you to create your arrangements a day or two ahead of time. If you don't have access to a flower market, buy what's freshest from the local grocer or farmer's market. Choose individual bunches of a single type of bloom so you can mix and match as you want. Of course, if it's the right time of year, and you have a garden or a good friend who does, take full advantage of that.

TIP: When a Guest Brings You Cut Flowers

Cut flowers may not be the best hostess gift, because really, what hostess has the time to deal with making flower arrangements as guests are arriving? You would have already decorated with flowers if you wanted them, right? Nonetheless, it's inevitable that some guests will bring you fresh flowers rather than show up empty-handed. Depending on space and time, you have two choices: hand the guest an empty vase and cheerfully suggest that he or she arrange the buds, or just stick the flowers, as is, into some kind of vessel of water, put them in a corner of the kitchen, and worry about them the next day.

Nine Ways to Make Fresh Flowers Last Longer

1. Buy flowers that are not fully open, or are still in bud. These will last much longer than fully open blooms.

2. If cutting from your garden, condition the flowers before arranging them by placing them in a bucket filled one-third to one-half full with warm water for several hours or overnight.

3. Make sure containers are clean; bacteria will hasten the deterioration of your blooms.

4. Add a teaspoon of chlorine bleach, a teaspoon of sugar, and a tablespoon of lemon juice to a standard-size vase of water in place of commercial flower preservative.

5. Make sure to remove any leaves that sit below the waterline, as they will introduce bacteria to the water and cause flowers to rot more quickly.

6. Always make a fresh diagonal cut at the bottom of the stems. Certain woody-stemmed flowers, such as lilacs, should be smashed and split with a hammer to allow for maximum water absorption.

SETTING THE SCENE

7. Add water to vases each day to maintain the same level, and change the water if it looks murky.

8. Place arrangements in a cool room, basement, or garage overnight rather than leave them in a warm room.

9. Avoid placing flowers in direct sunlight or close to radiators.

69   No Vase? No Problem

Any container can be used to hold an arrangement, as long as it's watertight. Nontraditional vessels add a lot of charm. Keep your eyes peeled at flea markets and tag sales. An old pitcher could become your favorite vase. Here are a few great alternatives to the typical glass vase.

- Canning jars
- Teapots and pitchers
- Glass bottles
- Bowls
- Pumpkins
- A coffee can or an old jar
- Paper bags
- A French flower can or galvanized bucket
- An ice bucket

70   Centerpiece Dos and Don'ts

DOS	DON'TS
• DO use the centerpiece to tie your theme or color palette together. • DO use short candles. • DO decorate with short flowers or potted plants. • DO add cute, edible decorations, such as chocolates, that can be snacked on at the end of the meal. • DO think like a minimalist and keep it simple.	• DON'T use scented candles. • DON'T use tall candles. • DON'T use tall or overly fragrant flowers or plants. • DON'T crowd the table. • DON'T let your theme get too kitschy—unless you're going for tongue-in-cheek.

71   Five Ways to Decorate Without Flowers

1. Fruits and vegetables. A big bowl of peaches or tomatoes in August will evoke the season in a beautiful way. Gourds and small pumpkins in the fall will last for months. Decorative kale or cabbage in pretty pots looks great in fall, too.

2. Potted plants. Mini daffodils in the spring are charming: pop the plastic pots they come in into a slightly larger terra-cotta pot. Orchids are beautiful placed around a room or on the table. Fresh potted herbs in spring and summer are a lovely and fragrant way to decorate the table; combine a few different types in small pots in clusters on the table. Mini evergreens look festive around the Christmas holidays.

3. Foliage and greenery. These cost less and last longer than flowers. Think of using large leaves in a tall container placed on the floor, or plant wheatgrass in a simple container; it takes only a few days to grow, and it looks fresh and modern.

4. Branches. A wholesale flower market is a great place to find beautiful, decorative branches, including large ones that can be placed in a big pot on the floor or in an entryway. This is an excellent way to bring a little nature indoors without ever having to worry about watering or sunlight.

5. Eucalyptus. As a centerpiece, eucalyptus is far too fragrant, but it's perfect in the bathroom or a bedroom, and can be found at farmer's markets and flower shops in the fall. Even after the branches and leaves dry out, they're pretty and fragrant.

CLEANING

72   Pre-Party Decluttering

Make your home as uncluttered as possible when guests are coming over. Stash extraneous stuff in an extra bedroom or walk-in closet for the evening and close the door.

73   Start with a Clean Slate

For your own sanity, and to make after-party cleanup easier and faster, try to wash and put away as much as you possibly can before the party starts, which usually means cleaning as you go. Always start the party with an empty dishwasher, dish rack, trash can, and sink.

74　Pet Peeve

If you have pets, thoroughly vacuum all upholstered furniture a few hours before you expect company. Do a last-minute once-over with a tape roller or a 3M Scotch Fur Fighter (see Resources, page 274)—a fabulous tool for ridding your furniture of even the smallest and most deeply embedded hairs. This will keep little black dresses fur-free and will make any allergy sufferers more comfortable, too. If possible, send your dog off to a faraway room or to stay with a neighbor, especially if it is the mischievous type. Cats will usually hide when strangers come over, so you might not have to worry about them.

75　Invite Them, and They Will Spill

Let's face it, spills are inevitable, and the most dreaded is red wine. If you have a brand-new white (or nearly white) couch or carpet, just skip serving the red wine altogether to save yourself the stress. But there's no way to protect against all spills, so have a stain kit at the ready. Use a basket or a bucket as a container, and fill it with the following items.

- A roll of paper towels

- A soft, absorbent hand or dish towel for blotting up the spill

- A commercial red-wine stain remover such as Oxy carpet cleaner or Wine Away (a miracle product that will clean up any red-wine stain; see Resources, page 274)

- Club soda

- Basic kitchen salt

Club soda or salt will help to lift out any stain, whether it's a food stain on clothing or wine on the carpet. Simply pour salt on the stain or moisten it with club soda or a commercial stain remover. Let it work for a few minutes, and then blot up as much as you can. Repeat if necessary. This will keep the stain from setting if it doesn't remove it completely, and then you can deal with it later.

Here's the place you really need to make a good impression; it's the most personal of spaces, and suddenly friends and strangers have a chance to inspect it, all alone.

❑ Give the bathroom fixtures a once-over with a disposable cleaning cloth or a rag to make sure they're sparkling.

❑ Use a DustBuster or a Swiffer to make sure there are no unsightly hairs on the floor. Put your personal bath towels away, and leave clean hand towels on the towel bar. Providing disposable hand towels is a nice touch, but it's not necessary.

❑ Remove the bathroom rug or bath mat. It just gets in the way, and it will get dirty, too, from all those shoes.

❑ Remove anything very personal that you wouldn't want guests to see from the medicine chest. They shouldn't look inside, but they might.

❑ On the other hand, if you normally leave your toothbrush out, place it in the medicine chest.

❑ If you have a dimmer switch, lower the lights and leave them on. Add a lightly scented candle to a safe spot (not on the back of the toilet!) to make the bathroom cozy and inviting.

❑ If the bathroom door doesn't have a working lock, make a simple "occupied" sign to hang on the knob so guests won't feel vulnerable while they're using your bathroom.

❑ Close the shower curtain.

❑ Empty the trash.

❑ During the party, check the bathroom now and then to make sure there is plenty of toilet paper, empty the trash, change or replenish hand towels, and wipe up any messes.

77   Coat, Check

For most of us, a bed is the most likely makeshift coatroom when more than a few people come over. It's not the worst thing in the world, but there is often some confusion toward the end of the evening, since the first guests to arrive are usually the first to go, and have to start rummaging through the pile. Inevitably, all of the black coats start looking alike, keys start tumbling from pockets, and so on. Instead, consider investing in a collapsible metal coatrack. If you live in an apartment building, you may be able to put a coatrack in the hallway outside your door. In a house, there may be room for a coatrack in your foyer. In addition, clear your front closet: move your own coats to a bedroom closet for the evening.

78   Clean While You Party

You've got to maintain some sense of cleanliness and order during a party, so keep watch for abandoned glasses and plates, and scurry them into the kitchen whenever you can. If you have the counter space, scrape and stack like-size items into distinct areas, to make the real cleanup easier later. Try to keep the sink free for other tasks, and to make washing up easier. Why pile everything in the sink if you'll only have to empty it later in order to start the cleanup?

THE COCKTAIL HOUR

A cocktail party, which usually lasts about two hours (six to eight P.M. in most circles) and is held before dinner, gives you the opportunity to celebrate without having to feed your guests a full meal. You can go all out with a buffet full of cheese and salumi or pretty trays of quick hors d'oeuvres. Or you might decide to just serve snacks, which is an excellent idea, and your guests will be equally satisfied. Despite the moniker, you don't have to serve cocktails at a cocktail party; the bar can be as simple as wine and beer and pitchers of one "cocktail du jour" that fits the season and the mood of the party. If you're hiring a bartender, then go full-tilt and offer a bigger selection. Take advantage of the more flexible and spontaneous nature of the cocktail party. There are no rules, but there are some guidelines to follow to make yours stress-free and successful.

79 Putting Together the Perfect Spread

If you want to skip plates and silverware, make sure your snacks are bite-size and not too messy. When you are brainstorming about assembled hors d'oeuvres, begin with the vehicle—a piece of toast, a hollowed-out cherry tomato—and build from there. The ingredients that get piled into or on top of your base don't have to be fancy to make for a sophisticated spread. Try gussying up mayonnaise or sour cream with herbs and spices: something creamy can act as "glue" and complement other, stronger flavors, such as salty cured salmon or ham. In addition to a few composed hors d'oeuvres, you can offer a cheese plate, a salumi plate, or a crudité platter along with some nuts, olives, dips, crackers, and flatbreads. Depending on the size of your party and how long you expect people to stay, you might want to offer all these options, or just some cheese and bread to nibble on. Whatever you decide is most appropriate, remember that less is often more, and resist the urge to overdo. Leave yourself some time to make the offerings look beautiful, full, and inviting.

80 What's Wrong with This Menu?

> ### THE PASSED HORS D'OEUVRE MENU
> - Individual mac 'n' cheese in ramekins
> - Oysters on the half shell with mignonette sauce
> - Shrimp in escabeche
> - Giant mushroom caps stuffed with spinach
> - California rolls with soy dipping sauce
> - Baby lamb chops crusted with mint and garlic

It all sounds delicious, but if you plan to pass hors d'oeuvres from a tray, you have to keep in mind how your guests will be able to juggle their drink and the food you are serving them without dripping down the fronts of their dresses and ties, or dropping something on your rug. You want to make eating hors d'oeuvres a graceful experience for all. Individual mac 'n' cheese servings are great, but save this for a buffet, since no one can handle a fork, a dish, and a glass all at the same time. Oysters are tough to manage, especially with a drippy sauce, and where to put the shell? Shrimp is a crowd favorite and an old standby, but don't marinate them in an oily, drippy sauce; again, save that for when you're serving small plates. Mushroom caps can be a bit slippery to pick up off a tray. California rolls are well loved (and you can order them in from your favorite sushi joint), but the traditional soy dipping sauce is a recipe for disaster. Baby lamb chops are just the right size for a cocktail party, but your guests will be left searching for dental floss while they try to figure out what to do with the bone.

TRY THIS MENU INSTEAD

- Phyllo mushroom bundles
- Classic shrimp cocktail
- Cherry tomatoes stuffed with hummus
- Smoked salmon canapés
- Arancini (rice balls)
- Crab shiu mai

Why it works: This menu is focused on self-contained items. All can be eaten in one or two bites, and sauces, if any, are thick enough so that guests won't fear getting drips down their clothing.

THE COSTLY COCKTAIL MENU

- Smoked salmon and crème fraîche canapés
- Pâté of foie gras with fresh figs
- Prosciutto-wrapped jumbo shrimp
- Jumbo lump crab cakes with rémoulade sauce
- Truffled potato croquettes
- Cold filet of beef with horseradish sauce
- Buckwheat blini with sturgeon caviar

You might be happy to *attend* this party, but this book is for the hostess, and her wallet will be hurting after holding such a posh endeavor. Hors d'oeuvres can become very expensive without good planning. Even though you might be using smaller amounts of expensive ingredients than you would for a dinner, the cost quickly adds up. You can make sophisticated snacks with inexpensive ingredients—think of deviled eggs or a simple white bean spread on little toasts. Or make a statement and serve pigs in a blanket (your tongue need not be in your cheek; people love 'em!). You can still incorporate one or two pricier items into your menu—just pace the serving of those items, sending them out of the kitchen less frequently; and when they're gone, they're gone.

TRY THIS MENU INSTEAD

- Gougères (opposite)
- Mini vegetable calzones
- Pigs in a blanket
- Deviled eggs with smoked paprika
- White Bean and Tomato Toasts (page 64)
- Chicken satay
- Crispy chorizo coins

Why it works: Food doesn't have to be expensive to be good. All of these items are made with reasonably priced ingredients that won't break the bank. You can afford to have more of them—especially important if it is a heavy–hors d'oeuvre party that renders dinner unnecessary.

82   *In Praise of* The Passed Hors d'Oeuvre

Having one or two nibbles served from the kitchen is an awfully nice idea. Don't make it too tough on yourself, though. Choose something that can be done largely ahead of time, like the ever-popular gougères (see below), and walk around with a serving tray to make the offering to your guests. It's a wonderful and personal way to connect with them, and to really feel your hosting oats.

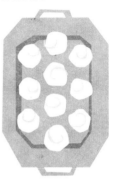

83   RECIPE: *Gougères* ·······································

This is a very versatile recipe in terms of timing. You can make them and serve them right away, or pipe out the batter and freeze on a baking sheet before transferring to a resealable plastic bag and storing in the freezer until ready to bake. You can also bake them right away, then cool and freeze them to be rewarmed before serving. Whichever way you choose, make an effort to serve these classic cheese puffs warm; they are irresistible with wine or cocktails. Change the flavor with different cheeses—the choice is yours—just keep the amount the same.

- If baking right away, preheat the oven to 400°F. Line two baking sheets with parchment or silicone baking mats.

- Combine **1 cup water; 6 tablespoons butter, cut into pats;** and **½ teaspoon coarse salt** in a small saucepan. Bring to a boil. As soon as the butter melts, add **1 cup flour,** all at once.

- Stir over low heat until a smooth dough forms and a film starts to form on the bottom of the pan, about 2 minutes.

- Transfer to an electric mixer fitted with the paddle attachment, and beat for a minute or so to cool the mixture slightly. Beat in 4 **eggs,** one at a time, making sure each one is completely incorporated before adding the next (you can also add the eggs by hand; it will just take a bit of muscle).

- Add **a dash of freshly grated nutmeg, a pinch of cayenne pepper,** and 1 **cup grated Gruyère cheese,** and beat to combine.

- Transfer to a piping bag (see page 68) fitted with a large plain tip, and pipe out the mixture into small mounds, about the size of a cherry tomato, about 2 inches apart. Sprinkle with **more grated cheese,** if desired, and bake for 20 to 25 minutes, until golden and puffed and not too moist inside (or they may collapse). Let cool in the oven for 5 minutes with the heat off and the door ajar. Serve immediately, or cool and freeze and then reheat in a 350° oven before serving.

84 ## Dips for the Chips

Artful and appetizing arrangements of good-quality store-bought dips will save you hours of work. The simple act of transferring hummus from the supermarket container into a pretty bowl and topping it with a little fresh chopped parsley and a drizzle of olive oil will score you all kinds of points with your guests. But don't stop at hummus. Even if all you have is a generic supermarket nearby, you should be able to find myriad suitable spreads to serve, such as baba ganoush, black bean dip, even thick Roquefort dressing for dipping veggies. If you are lucky enough to have access to a Middle Eastern, Indian, or other ethnic grocery, you will find even more offerings, including delectable freshly baked flatbreads to accompany the spreadable dips. Cut the bread into bite-size pieces, toast, and serve as dippers.

One thing that is always better when homemade is guacamole. We all know that avocados brown quickly, so any store-bought version will be full of preservatives or other greenish non-avocado ingredients and won't have the fresh, pure flavor of homemade. Guacamole is super simple to make, and it will keep for several hours in the fridge if necessary, even if you have to scrape the top before serving to remove any browning that might have occurred. If you have a *molcajete,* the traditional lava-rock mortar that is common in Mexico and Mexican restaurants, use it to both make and serve the guac. It's the ideal tool, since the rough texture of the mortar and the pestle grind the onion, jalapeño, cilantro, and salt into a fine paste that easily infuses the creamy spread with flavor. If you don't have a *molcajete,* use a regular mixing bowl, but try to emulate this grinding action when doing your chopping.

MAKES ABOUT 2½ CUPS

- In a medium bowl or *molcajete,* combine 1 **small white onion, finely minced;** 1 **medium jalapeño, finely chopped;** ¼ **cup chopped fresh cilantro;** and 1½ **teaspoons coarse salt.** Mix well, using a wooden spoon to combine thoroughly.

- Cut 3 ripe avocados in half lengthwise and remove and discard the pits. Remove the flesh and add to the other ingredients in the bowl.

- Use a large fork to mash the avocado, leaving some texture. Add the **juice of ½ lime** and 1 **medium tomato, seeded and chopped,** to the mixture. Adjust the seasonings with **salt, lime juice,** and **jalapeño,** and serve with tortilla chips.

NOTE: It pays to think ahead and buy avocados when they're rock-hard and green, 3 or 4 days before you need them. It's difficult to find avocados at the peak of ripeness at the store, and if they *are* ripe, they can be easily damaged on the way home. If they reach optimal ripeness before you're ready to use them, pop them in the fridge, where they will keep well for another day or two.

Write out your menu first, and then, working backward, figure out which things can be prepared, or partially prepared, ahead of time. Your list should end at the time you expect your first guests to arrive and should include last-minute tasks.

Break up the list by days first. Include shopping in your timeline so you can buy as much as possible all at once ahead of time, and re-shop only for those items that must be bought later. The more you can do ahead of time, the calmer you will be during the crunch. When plotting things out, don't forget to consider how much oven space you will have. As nice as it is to have everything fresh from the oven, there may not be enough hours in the day, so figure out what menu items can hold for a day, and make them ahead of time. Baked appetizers such as palmiers, which are made with puff pastry, or even cookies can be popped back into the oven for a few minutes before serving to soften up the butter and give them that just-baked taste and appearance.

HOLIDAY COCKTAIL SPREAD MENU

- Glazed Ham (page 108)
- Artisanal cheeses (see page 71) with *membrillo* (quince paste) and dried figs
- Assorted salumi (see page 78)
- Grapes
- Olives
- Marcona almonds
- Roasted Turkey (page 197)
- Cranberry chutney

- Crudités with Gorgonzola Dip (page 70)
- Parmesan Palmiers (page 83) and Cheese Straws (page 75)
- Pissaladière (page 80)
- Roasted Filet of Beef (page 146)
- Assorted bread and crackers
- Assorted mustards
- Cookies and brownies

HOW TO GET IT ALL ON THE TABLE

One week before:
- Shop for all nonperishables.
- Order any items that might not be readily available, such as a ham, a filet of beef, or a fresh turkey, from your butcher.
- Mail-order any items you may want to serve that you can't easily get where you live, such as cheese, special salumi, *membrillo,* or marcona almonds (see Resources, page 274).

Three to five days before:
- Make doughs for cookies and freeze or refrigerate.
- Prepare and refreeze the items made with puff pastry: the crust for the pissaladière, the palmiers, and the cheese straws.
- Pull out serving boards, platters, baskets, and bowls and arrange on the table with sticky notes assigning a menu item to each vessel.

Two days before:
- Make the dip for the crudité platter.
- Make caramelized onions for the pissaladière.
- Review and update the shopping list.

The day before:
- Pick up fresh meats, such as ham, turkey, and beef.
- Buy the cheeses and salumi.
- Buy the vegetables for the crudités and fruit for the table.
- Bake the cookies, palmiers, and cheese straws and wrap airtight after cooling.
- Roast the turkey and refrigerate.

The morning of:
- Buy fresh bread and any last-minute items.
- Cut up and blanch the vegetables for the crudités. Store in resealable plastic bags lined with damp paper towels and refrigerate until serving time.
- Bake the pissaladière.
- Roast the filet of beef and refrigerate when cool.

Several hours before:

- Cook the ham.
- Arrange the salumi on boards or platters, cover with plastic, and refrigerate.
- Arrange anything that will keep on serving trays or in bowls—nuts, olives, cookies, crackers, palmiers, cheese straws—cover with plastic wrap, and place on the table.
- Take the cheese out of the refrigerator and let it stand, wrapped, in a cool place.

Starting one hour before:

- Take the beef and the turkey out of the refrigerator.
- Slice the bread, cover with damp paper towels and plastic wrap, and place on the table.
- Unwrap the cheeses, arrange on serving boards or platters, and place on the table.
- Place the ham on a serving board or platter, garnish, if desired, and partially preslice. Place on the table.

- Arrange the crudités on a serving platter or in vessels (see page 69) and place on the table.
- Take the salumi out of the refrigerator and place on the table.
- Slice the beef thin and place on a platter; cover with plastic wrap and place on the table along with assorted mustards.
- Preslice the turkey and place on the table with carving implements so guests can continue slicing, or completely carve all the meat and place it on a platter.
- Cut the pissaladière into pieces and place it on the table along with any remaining items.
- Make sure all items that require serving implements have them, such as knives for cheese.
- Check the menu to make sure you have served everything, and prepare backups in the kitchen.
- Enjoy the party!

87   How Much Is Enough?

Figuring out how much food to prepare for a cocktail party is far from an exact science. Experience will teach you a lot, but there are some factors to take into consideration. How rich are the bites you plan to serve? Is this the main event for the evening, or will people be moving on to dinner? Where are they coming from—a big, late lunch or a long day at the office? What is the composition of your crowd? An all-woman group will generally eat less food than a group of hungry men. How long is the event?

Here are some rules of thumb that should help.

- Figure on six to eight bites per hour per person for a stand-alone cocktail party.

- For a cocktail hour preceding a meal, plan on six bites per person.

- People will eat more of the popular favorites, like shrimp or anything fried or cheesy, so plan for more of those items.

- The more options you have, the less you will need of each one.

- Always round your estimate up so that the food is plentiful. Leftovers can be incorporated into future meals and won't go to waste.

- Trust your judgment: no one knows your guests better than you.

- Keep a party journal or file with your notes so you can refer to it the next time. This way you can learn from your successes and failures.

WHAT TO EAT

88   Use Stations

You can take a page from the professional caterers' playbook and employ stations to serve a variety of mini menus at the same party. Though stations are often manned with chefs rolling sushi, making pasta to order, flipping blini, or opening oysters, you can use the same idea while keeping the food self-serve. Just make the stations abundant and beautiful. Use fruit, flowers, and props to fill every inch of your table to create a visual feast themed to the food that's being served on it.

89   Eight Ideas for Stations

1. Bruschetta and crostini. Set out a variety of toppings, such as the classic tomato and basil, eggplant caponata, or spicy greens; a few varieties of salumi with a few different kinds and sizes of toasted, grilled, or fried bread slices; and small plates so that guests can make their own. Bowls of grated cheeses, such as Parmesan and ricotta salata, and fresh herbs such as basil leaves, chopped Italian parsley, and even baby arugula can be used to top off the creations. Decorations for the table should be rustic Italian. Display fresh produce and add breadsticks for height.

2. Wine and cheese pairings. After consulting with your favorite wine and cheese merchants, come up with some pairings and set up a table that clearly shows which pairings to try. Use signage to help get the idea across. This is fun for guests and will get them talking and comparing notes.

3. Sushi. This one is easy: you can buy sushi from your favorite local restaurant and plate it attractively. Stick to vegetable-based sushi unless you are serving it immediately after buying it. Add a few Japanese-inspired salads and a tray holding cups of cold sake.

4. Sliders or burgers. You will need a chafing dish or a hot plate for this station. Keep precooked burgers of varying proteins—beef, turkey, lamb, or tuna—warm in a chafing dish with baskets of warm buns and all of the toppings and garnishes you can think of.

5. Panini. Make a variety of small sandwiches with Italian meats, cheeses, and spreads stacked neatly on trays covered with a clean dish

towel to keep them fresh. (Alternatively, you can let people assemble their own sandwiches, but this may be more of a challenge for some guests.) Set out an electric panini press, and encourage guests to grill their own sandwiches. Conversations will be sparked while people wait for their sandwiches to grill.

6. Quesadillas. Set out fresh flour and/or corn tortillas with a variety of fillings, such as fresh or cooked veggies, pulled chicken or pork, and cheese, toppings such as salsas and guacamole, and garnishes such as fresh cilantro, and let your guests cook their own quesadillas on an electric panini press or griddle.

7. Pan-Asian food. Here you can mix and mingle your favorite Asian tidbits: steamed or panfried dumplings (it's best if you can keep them warm in a chafing dish or a hot plate), cold noodle dishes, satays and yakitori (grilled skewered meats), summer rolls, and edamame.

8. Chocolate. This is a theme few people would find fault with. Just load up the table with all things chocolate, all of which you can buy. If you really want to wow your guests, and you have the budget, spring for a chocolate fountain (a little hokey, but fun!), which you can rent or buy, into which your guests can dip fruits for the ultimate fondue experience. Surround the fountain (or a regular fondue pot) with lots of skewered fruit, chocolate cakes, cupcakes, cookies, bonbons, other chocolates, and more.

90   RECIPE: *White Bean and Tomato Toasts*

This easy (and inexpensive) hors d'oeuvre is a variation on a classic Spanish tapa, *pan con tomate*, in which toasted bread is rubbed with garlic and a halved ripe tomato so that the tomato softens the crunchy exterior of the bread. Here a white-bean puree is added. The puree can be made one or two days ahead and kept in the fridge. Make sure to let it come to room temperature before serving.

SERVES 8 TO 10

- Position a rack in the middle of the oven and preheat the oven to 375°F. Slice 1 **crusty baguette** into ¼-inch-thick slices. Spread the slices out on a large rimmed baking sheet and bake until the edges are golden, 7 to 10 minutes. Set aside.

- Halve 1 **tomato** and chop one half into small pieces. Set the remaining half aside.

- Heat 2 **tablespoons extra-virgin olive oil** in a medium saucepan over medium heat. Add 1 **garlic clove, chopped,** and sauté until it begins to brown, about 3 minutes. Add **one 15½-ounce can white beans, drained and rinsed;** ½ **cup water;** ½ **teaspoon salt;** and **a dash of black pepper,** bring to a simmer, and cook until most of the liquid has evaporated, about 5 minutes. Add 1 **tablespoon red or white wine vinegar,** and mash the beans with a fork until roughly pureed. Remove from the heat.

- Rub the slices of bread with 1 **garlic clove, halved,** and then with the cut side of the remaining half tomato. Spoon about 1 tablespoon of the bean puree onto each slice and top with the chopped tomato. Drizzle with **extra-virgin olive oil** and serve.

1. Belgian endive petals with fresh fig, goat cheese, and chopped walnuts

2. Thick-cut potato chips with crème fraîche, smoked salmon, and dill

3. Cucumber cups with lime mayo and lump crabmeat, garnished with chile powder

4. Cherry tomatoes stuffed with hummus and topped with olive slivers

5. Toasted baguette topped with fresh mozzarella, cherry tomato, and pesto (can be served warm and melty or at room temperature)

WHAT'S A HOSTESS TO DO?

6. Celery boats filled with lemon mayo, Italian oil-packed tuna, and capers

7. Party rye triangles (toasted) with fresh turkey, herb mayo, and cranberry chutney

8. Melon balls or chunks wrapped with prosciutto

9. Wheat crackers topped with creamy pâté and sliced cornichon

10. Tortilla chips with guacamole and cooked shrimp, garnished with cilantro or salsa

In Praise of The Piping Bag

A piping bag, or pastry bag, is your best friend when you are filling cherry tomatoes with a creamy mixture, or when you need to make neat dollops of crème fraîche on forty crackers with smoked salmon. Forget the spoon-and-fingers routine. A piping bag makes these otherwise messy tasks a cinch. Canvas or plastic piping bags from a baking supply shop are great—they come with a variety of tips in different sizes. They aren't expensive, but a homemade version is perfectly good, too—no fancy tips required.

93

TIP: **Make Your Own Piping Bag**

If you find yourself in need of an efficient, neat way to dollop, spoon the topping into a resealable plastic sandwich bag, filling it no more than halfway; twist the open side closed; and keep it closed with your hand (or with a binder clip if you're not using it right away). Push the filling toward one corner, eliminating air bubbles as best you can. Then pinch that corner with your fingers to push the food away so that when you cut it, it doesn't pour right out of the tip of the bag. Snip the corner with a pair of scissors, making an opening as small or as large as you need, and simply pipe the filling by gently squeezing a bit of whatever creamy substance you are using.

Crudités: How to Class Up an Old Standby

Choose your veggies wisely, and make the tiny bit of effort to peel and cut regular carrots, rather than buy a bag of "baby" ones. By doing so, you've already classed up this old standby considerably. Browse the vegetable aisle for crunchy produce that appeals to you and makes for a variety of colors and flavors. Some great options are fennel, endive, colorful bell peppers, cucumbers (if you can find the seedless or "Persian" variety, they'll stay crunchy longer), asparagus spears, radishes, and summer squash. When it comes to presentation, experiment a little, making sure each spear or slice is easily accessible (you don't want to encourage more hands touching food than is necessary). Try standing the vegetables upright in glasses or glass jars, or offering a few different compatible dips.

95   TIP: **Make the First Cut**

When serving a whole cheese on a platter, make the first cut. Guests are often too timid to be the first, and the cheese may go uneaten. This is a good rule of thumb for an entire salami, too, or for anything whole that is meant for self-service and not display.

96 RECIPE: *Gorgonzola Dip*

Everyone loves their vegetables with a little fat. A crudité platter should be full of beautiful, crunchy, fresh veggies, which will do double duty as vehicles for a thick, creamy, tangy dip. This one's a real winner.

MAKES ABOUT 1½ CUPS

- Whisk together ¾ cup buttermilk or plain yogurt drink, ½ cup mayonnaise, ¼ cup plain low-fat yogurt, 1 teaspoon white wine vinegar, and 2 scallions, sliced, in a bowl. Stir in 6 ounces Gorgonzola, crumbled, and season to taste with salt and pepper. Refrigerate until ready to serve. The dip will keep, covered in the refrigerator, for 2 to 3 days.

97 How to Choose Cheese

- Get help. It's worth seeking out a place that specializes in cheese, since the cheeses there are more likely to be properly stored and taken care of, and the staff more helpful. Plus, the higher the turnover, the fresher the cheese.

- Get it cut up. In a good cheese store (or cheese department), each piece is cut to order, instead of being cut up who-knows-when and wrapped in plastic. When cheese is cut in advance—even if it's wrapped in plastic—it begins to lose flavor and dry out; it can also take on a plastic flavor if it languishes for long enough before being purchased. Cutting fresh pieces also goes hand in hand with getting a taste of the cheese, which is of course the best way to decide what to buy and how your selections will complement one another.

- Find a balance. You may love stinky blue cheeses more than any other, but to put out three different ones would be overkill. Try to balance your selection in terms of flavor and texture; make sure to offer a mild cheese and a more aggressively flavored cheese, as well as one firm cheese and one soft.

- **Don't be afraid of the basics.** It can be wonderful to introduce your guests to a very special cheese—something rare and local, or an imported cheese that they're unlikely to have encountered but that you love. However, especially if you are offering several cheeses, it can be just as eye-opening and enjoyable to have a really fabulous version of something familiar, like an aged Parmigiano-Reggiano or a local, artisan-made sharp Cheddar.

- **Take it to the 'net.** If your local options are limited, the Web sites listed in the Resources (see page 274) will help you learn more before buying. They are loaded with expert information from those who have tasted the cheeses. Aim for a variety of textures, flavors, colors, and types, and you will be sure to have something for everyone. Like wine, cheese offers a never-ending discovery process in which tasting and remembering what you like are the best ways to educate your palate.

98   How to Find the Best Cheese

If you really want to not only impress your guests but broaden your horizons and educate your taste buds, too, think ahead and order from one of the many excellent online sources for cheese (see Resources, page 274). Cheese travels well, so it's worth it to splurge if a beautiful cheese display is an important part of your party. Also find out if there is an artisan cheese-maker in your area. A lot of excellent cheese is being made in the United States; it's by no means necessary to buy imported stuff. Check out your local farmer's market. If you really are stuck with only your local supermarket, the situation is not hopeless. Most supermarkets these days carry at least a decent, if not a downright impressive, batch of cheeses. A small wheel of Camembert, a log of fresh goat cheese coated with ash or herbs, and a wedge of crumbly, extra-sharp Cheddar can be found most anywhere.

When putting together a cheese plate or platter, the key is balance. The specifics should reflect your personal taste, but be sure to present a variety of types of cheese—one that's hard and salty, another that's soft and buttery, and one that's more forward: stinky or tangy. Even if you strongly favor one style, try not to double up on any of the categories below. This way, there's something for everyone.

HARD CHEESE
(Parmigiano-Reggiano, aged Gouda)

Hard cheeses are often grated, but for a cheese plate they can be chiseled into bite-size chunks. Hard cheeses tend to be salty and granular and go well with honey and dried fruit.

FIRM CHEESE
(Manchego, Cheddar, Comté, Gruyère, Jarlsberg)

The longer a cheese is aged, the firmer it will be. Firm cheeses are ideal for slicing, so this category includes many sandwich favorites, but they deserve to be rediscovered in their own right on your grazing buffet.

SEMISOFT CHEESE
(Morbier, Fontina, Muenster, Provolone, Emmenthal)

These are good melting cheeses, with a consistency that falls between those of spreadable and grating cheeses. It's important to serve them at room temperature so their creaminess can be appreciated.

FRESH CHEESE
(Ricotta, Mozzarella, Fresh Chèvre, Boursin)

Because they haven't aged, these cheeses are
mild and moist. A fresh cheese can be a great
counterpoint to stronger flavors, and can
also be embellished with herbs for a simple
spread.

BLOOMY CHEESE
(Brie, Camembert, Robiola)

These are cheeses with white rinds (formed
from a mold growth that is completely edible)
and rich, creamy interiors.

WASHED-RIND CHEESE
(Taleggio, Tomme de Savoie, Époisses, Livarot)

Unlike the white rinds of bloomy cheeses,
washed rinds are orange or brown from being
bathed with beer, brine, brandy, or other liquids
that encourage bacteria to grow. The process,
unsurprisingly, makes for stinky cheese, but the
insides are often creamy, if forward.

BLUE CHEESE
*(Stilton, Gorgonzola, Roquefort, Cabrales,
Maytag Blue)*

The blue mold that runs in "veins"
throughout these crumbly, pungent cheeses
may turn off the faint of heart, but the funky,
salty flavor is more loved than not—at least
by adults.

100   How Much Cheese Do I Buy?

One of the advantages of shopping for cheese in person, rather than online, is that you can eyeball the wedges that are being cut. It can be difficult to conceptualize how big a half pound is going to be. A good rule of thumb is to assume each person will eat three or four ounces, but of course, there's a range. The amount of cheese you need depends on the rest of your menu: If you are serving a cheese course, get just enough for everyone to have a tiny taste of several different cheeses, especially if you have a small salad to the side. If you're putting the cheese out on a grazing buffet with other snacks, offer three different types, and make sure the wedges are generously sized. Even if you're ordering the cheese online, call first if you need guidance. All the cheesemongers listed in the Resources (page 274) will be able to help you make sure you don't spend more than necessary or run out of cheese before everyone has tasted his fair share. Tell them how many guests are coming and what role the cheese will play in your meal.

This is an easy recipe that every hostess should have in her repertoire. Store-bought puff pastry makes it simple, and you can vary the flavors by adding different cheeses, spices, herbs, or even sesame or poppy seeds to the mix.

MAKES ABOUT 24 STRAWS

- Roll out **one 14-ounce sheet thawed frozen puff pastry** on a floured surface to an even rectangle roughly 11 by 15 inches. Brush it with **1 egg, beaten with 1 tablespoon water.** Sprinkle **1 cup freshly grated Parmigiano-Reggiano** and **1 tablespoon chopped fresh rosemary** over the surface, and roll over the pastry with the rolling pin just to press the toppings into it.

- Use a pizza cutter or a knife to cut the pastry lengthwise into ½-inch-wide strips. Transfer 6 spirals to each of 4 parchment-lined baking sheets, twisting each strip into a tight spiral and placing them 1½ inches apart. Chill the straws until they're firm, about 15 minutes.

- Preheat the oven to 400°F. Bake the straws 2 sheets at a time for about 10 minutes, rotate the trays, and continue to bake for an additional 18 to 20 minutes, or until golden and crisp. Repeat with the remaining 2 trays.

THE COCKTAIL HOUR

For a casual cocktail party, cheese and crackers may suffice, but variety and abundance are the keys to making a simple spread of cheese into something special. Artisanal crackers and flatbreads will add interest to the always good and classic supermarket offerings like Carr's and Stoned Wheat Thins, and a few bowls of olives, marinated vegetables, or nuts (both salty and sweet) are always welcome. A good cheesemonger or gourmet shop can provide you with some of the more unusual items listed below.

- Quince paste. Manchego—and other salty, hard sheep's-milk cheeses—go wonderfully with quince paste, called *membrillo*. This is a classic Spanish pairing, but *membrillo* can complement any assertive aged cheese. Quince is a fruit related to apples and pears, and when cooked into a gelatinous pinkish paste, it provides a sweet, tangy counterpoint to a forward-tasting cheese.

- Apples. In the fall, take advantage of local apples. There's nothing quite like a crisp, sweet apple paired with cheese. The most tried-and-true pairing with apples is a sharp Cheddar, but apples also go beautifully with crumbly blue cheeses, such as Stilton or Roquefort.

- Mustard fruit. *Mostarda,* or mustard fruit, is an unusual Northern Italian condiment, made with a mixture of fruit, such as cherries, pears, apricots, and quinces, and a mustard-infused syrup, which preserves and candies the fruit and gives it a deep spicy flavor behind the sweetness and sourness. It is most traditionally eaten with *bollito misto,* or "mixed boiled meats," but it has become popular as part of a cheese plate. Mostarda works especially well at the end of a meal, to bridge the gap from savory to sweet.

- **Figs.** A favorite, especially served alongside a creamy, funky blue cheese such as Gorgonzola dolce, fresh figs are luscious: sweet and intense, with tiny, crunchy seeds in the center. Hors d'oeuvres can incorporate figs with prosciutto and cheese, or they can be grilled or macerated to become chutney-like and spreadable. Dried figs are delicious, too, but fresh ones are a real treat, especially at the end of a meal.

- **Dried fruit.** An assortment of dried fruit is a great standby when your cheese plate needs a little color and variety. Try to get beyond raisins and offer some combination of dried cherries, figs, apricots, prunes, plums, and so on. Include a few sweeter fruits (prunes) as well as some more tart ones (cherries).

103   TIP: **Prevent Cut Apples from Browning**

If you're going to be serving cut apples as part of a cheese plate, don't slice them until you're ready to serve, and then immediately toss them with a drizzle of lemon juice. The citric acid in the lemon will fight the browning enzymes in the oxygen. If you're serving a salad with apples in it, make sure to coat the pieces in the dressing right away.

104   *In Praise of* The Cheese Knife

For relatively soft cheeses, a normal butter knife or spreader will do fine, but in the case of harder cheeses, it will be easier for guests to use a knife designed for the job rather than hack away at a block of cheese, running the risk of slipping and

making a mess. Also, weaker knives can snap in two when used on a hard cheese, especially those cutesy ceramic-handled spreaders often set out next to a hunk of Parmigiano-Reggiano. Assign each cheese its own knife, and leave plenty of space on the platter for guests to maneuver.

105   Serving Charcuterie and Salumi

A selection of cured meats is the perfect accompaniment to wine and cheese. Both charcuterie (French) and salumi (Italian) refer generally to cured meats, and pork usually plays a big role. Salumi, such as prosciutto, salami, and speck, are very popular choices, as are the slightly more formal liver pâtés and terrines.

106   Shopping for Cured Meats

If there's a good gourmet shop in town—or a more old-school deli in an Italian neighborhood that sells imported salumi—you're set. Ask for tastes, and get a few things you like, making sure there's a variety. For example: a bit of spicy soppressata; a smoked meat, like speck; some prosciutto, because everyone loves it; and maybe a non-pork item, like bresaola, which is cured lean beef.

If you don't have access to top-notch imported meats, don't fret. Remember, these delicacies wouldn't exist but for the need to preserve food; they travel well and can be ordered online (see Resources, page 274). You may want to buy a few whole salamis, which you can slice yourself (the slices needn't be paper-thin), or if it is sliced, be sure to order the meat vacuum-sealed and have it sent overnight so it doesn't dry out on its way to you.

107   How to Present Charcuterie or Salumi

Cured meats are crowd-pleasers, and people will be glad to see them. It doesn't take much to make the distinction between good salami or

ham and the kind of cold cuts your guests might remember from the processed lunch meats back in the day. Buy your salumi as close to party time as possible, so the flavor is at its peak. Some meats, like prosciutto and bresaola, will dry out quickly; fattier meats, like salami, will keep longer. In any case, make sure to handle them while they are well chilled—the slices will be easier to arrange when cold. Just be sure to serve at room temperature.

With thinly sliced salumi, like prosciutto, take care to overlap (rather than stack), folding each slice so guests can easily pick it up. Arrange the folded slices of meat in groups, so that it's easy to see what is on offer. Use a cutting board or even a stone or marble slab; that sort of presentation is a little more interesting than a plain white plate, and it's perfectly in keeping with the rustic origins of the food. If you are serving any whole, hard salami, serve it on a wood cutting board and cut several rounds when you set the board out, so your guests will be encouraged to eat it and cut more. You can prepare the platter or board a few hours in advance and return it to the fridge, lightly covered in plastic wrap; remove it an hour before serving. Good salumi needs little accompaniment, but some good bread, olives, and crisp fennel slices will go nicely.

The best way to describe pissaladière is to say it is a French version of pizza, and it is the perfect accompaniment to drinks. Salty and warm, pissaladière fills the belly. It can easily be cut into bite-size pieces.

SERVES 8 TO 10

- Roll out **one 14-ounce sheet thawed frozen puff pastry** on a floured surface to an even thickness, roughly 12 by 15 inches. It should be a couple of inches larger than it was originally. Trim off a ½-inch strip of dough from all sides. Brush the edges sparingly with **a lightly beaten egg,** lay the strips of dough on top to make a crust around the border, and press gently. (Alternatively, stretch a **1-pound piece of thawed frozen pizza dough** into an oval about 10 by 13 inches; let it rest briefly if it's too springy to hold its shape.)

- Transfer the dough to a parchment-lined baking sheet and chill until needed.

- Make caramelized onions: Heat 1 **tablespoon extra-virgin olive oil** in a large skillet over high heat. Add **3 medium sweet onions, halved and thickly sliced,** and cook, stirring occasionally, until they begin to brown, about 8 minutes.

- Turn the heat down to low, add 1 **teaspoon thyme leaves** and **¼ cup water,** and continue cooking for about 10 minutes, or until the onions are meltingly soft.

- Add 1 **teaspoon anchovy paste, if desired,** and stir until completely combined.

- Season the onions with **salt and pepper** and let cool. (The onions can be made up to 2 days ahead and kept in the refrigerator until ready to use.)

- Preheat the oven to 400°F. Use a fork to prick the pastry all over. Spread the caramelized onions evenly over the dough, then scatter a **heaping ⅓ cup sliced pitted black olives** and **about 10 sliced**

grape tomatoes over the onions. Bake the pissaladière for 30 to 45 minutes, until it is uniformly golden brown and, if you're using puff pastry, has puffed up. Serve immediately.

NOTE: Thawing of pastry is best done overnight in the refrigerator, but it can also be left at room temperature until thawed, about 1 or 2 hours.

109   RECIPE: *Grape Schiacciata*

Schiacciata is an Italian regional variation on focaccia. In Tuscany, this delicious flatbread is often made with grapes during the wine grape harvest. This slightly unusual, not quite sweet or savory snack makes a rustic hors d'oeuvre to go with drinks.

SERVES 6 TO 8 AS AN HORS D'OEUVRE

- Preheat the oven to 400°F. Oil a baking sheet with **extra-virgin olive oil.** Stretch a **1-pound piece of thawed frozen pizza**

dough into a rough oval about 10 by 13 inches. If the dough is too springy, let it rest for a few minutes and then try again. Drizzle the dough with **olive oil** and let it rest for 15 minutes.

• Press your fingertips into the dough to make dimples all over the surface. Sprinkle with **kosher salt** and **1 tablespoon chopped fresh rosemary** and scatter **¾ cup halved black or red seedless grapes** over it.

• Bake the *schiacciata* for 30 minutes, or until the top is evenly golden and the bottom is browned and crisp. Cut into small pieces to serve.

Even easier to make than cheese straws, palmiers are a variation on that theme: store-bought puff pastry is layered with cheese and herbs, and then rolled up toward the center into a kind of double-barreled log and baked. Slicing the log yields many individual bites with little effort, and palmiers keep well for several days.

MAKES ABOUT 40 PALMIERS

- Roll out **one 14-ounce sheet thawed frozen puff pastry** on a floured surface into an even rectangle a few inches larger than it was originally, roughly 12 by 15 inches. Brush the surface with **1 egg, beaten with 1 tablespoon water;** set the egg wash aside. Sprinkle the pastry with **1 cup freshly grated Parmigiano-Reggiano** and **1 tablespoon thyme leaves.**

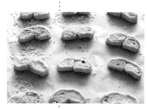

- Starting at one of the long sides of the rectangle, roll the pastry up (not too tightly) like a jelly roll, stopping at the center, then roll it up from the other side to meet in the middle. Use a sharp knife to cut into ¼-inch-wide slices (use your fingers to reshape any squashed pieces).

- Place the palmiers 1 inch apart on a parchment-lined baking sheet. Brush them again with egg wash, then sprinkle with **½ cup freshly grated Parmigiano-Reggiano** and **1 teaspoon thyme leaves.** Refrigerate for 30 minutes.

- Preheat the oven to 400°F. Bake the palmiers for 20 to 25 minutes, or until crisp and golden. Transfer to a cooling rack. When completely cool, store in an airtight container for 2 to 3 days.

111   The (Essential) Liquor List

The home bar should be streamlined and focused; stock the tried and true along with a few special touches. Plan to serve two wines, one red and one white; gin with mixers; and vodka with mixers. The following list outlines the basics that every prepared host should have.

- Vodka. The basis for many mixed drinks (including Bloody Marys, cosmopolitans, martinis, and the ever-popular vodka tonic).

- Gin. This grain-based alcohol flavored with juniper berries and botanicals is an aromatic, mild-flavored liquor. A gin and tonic with lime is a mainstay of the cocktail hour, particularly in warmer weather, so no home bar should be without the fixings. Have a fresh bottle of tonic water on hand. Tanqueray and Hendrick's are the top brands.

- Tequila. Made from the agave plant, the national drink of Mexico is smooth and complex. Good tequila is double-distilled and aged, and is to be sipped or mixed into a fantastic cocktail. Try Patrón or Sauza, in Silver, Gold, or Añejo for margaritas (page 91) or the Paloma (page 92).

- Rum. This sugarcane liquor is evocative of the Caribbean. Rum punch (page 261), or the stellar Dark and Stormy (dark rum combined with ginger beer), is a great warm-weather drink.

- Whiskey. Whiskey and bourbon drinkers are a dedicated bunch. They will wholeheartedly appreciate your including a good single-malt or small-batch artisanal in your bar setup. Scotch whisky, made in Scotland (where they omit the "e"), and bourbon, an American-made spirit, are usually served with ice and water on the side, over ice (on the rocks), or straight up. While a good bottle of whiskey can be expensive, it will usually last a long time.

112   *In Praise of* Ice

Unless you have a dedicated ice machine, or
bag up the ice from your freezer's ice-maker
for a few days in advance of your party, you
will need to buy ice. If a last-minute trip to
the nearest gas station isn't your style, then
call your local iceman in advance and inquire
about minimums and delivery fees, which will vary wildly from company
to company and depending on where you live. Bulk ice usually comes in
40-pound bags, which can be stashed in an extra freezer space, coolers, or,
if need be, the bathtub (still in the bags, of course). Arrange for delivery
an hour or two before the party so you can put it away and start chilling
the beverages.

The ice industry rule of thumb is 1 pound per person (since each
guest will typically have four drinks over the course of the evening:
4 cubes per drink equals 16 cubes, each about 1 ounce). In addition to
the ice to put in drinks, you will need some for chilling wine or beer;
the vessel you plan to use will dictate how much. If you are having an
outdoor gathering and the weather is warm, take this into consideration,
since you will lose a fair amount of ice due to melting. Offer ice in clean
ice buckets with tongs or scoops for self-service cocktails. Combine ice
and water in leak-proof coolers to chill wine and beer.

113   When and How to Hire a Bartender

A paid bartender allows the hostess more time to interact with her
guests, but it's only appropriate to hire help for a formal gathering or
when the guest list is big enough that serving the drinks or letting
people serve themselves would be unwieldy. Hiring a bartender (or a
bartending-school student) is easy and relatively inexpensive. Check
Internet job boards like craigslist.org or ask a bartender at your favorite
bar or restaurant if she is looking for extra work. Plan on paying at least
$100 for a few hours of bar coverage.

- Corkscrew. There are many types, both old-school and newfangled, but the choice often comes down to personal preference (see "Open Wine Like a Pro," entry 198).

- Jigger. Measures the amount of liquor to determine proportions (as in "1 part hooch to 3 parts mixer").

- Shot glass (with measurements). Available at kitchen stores and many airport gift shops (people collect them on their travels), a shot glass is a must-have for measuring a precise balance of alcohol to mixers.

- Juicer. Juice fruit ahead of time and store the juice in covered jars in the refrigerator. Take out as needed.

- The Boston shaker. The Boston shaker has a built-in strainer with a snug-fitting top; it's perfect for amateurs. The bartender's choice is a large glass topped with a stainless-steel tumbler. Shake, shake, shake and then pour into a cocktail glass, using the tumbler to hold back the ice.

- The Hawthorne strainer. With its springy coil, the strainer is held over the shaker while the drink is poured. The coil keeps even tiny shards of ice out of your drink.

- Long bar spoon. Although James Bond preferred his shaken, not stirred, most martini fans prefer theirs to be stirred, gently, if at all. Unless the drink contains clear ingredients only (spirits, vermouths, and the like), shaking creates cloudy air bubbles.

- A bartender bible. A comprehensive guide to classic and new drink recipes is essential for every amateur mixologist (see Resources, page 274).

- Cocktail napkins. Go for something small, in your signature color, or personalize them (available online) for an added touch. Figure on three napkins per guest per hour. Small square napkins should be placed at each drinks station and near snacks.

115 *In Praise of* The Cocktail Tray

A drinks tray is easy to put together, it protects furniture from spills, and it corrals many bar elements into one cohesive statement. Find a tray that is large enough to accommodate liquor and accessories (about 12 by 18 inches should do). Glasses can be set beside the tray on a linen cloth. The tray can be square, rectangular, or oval, but should have a lip. Bright lacquer trays are chic, silver trays polished to a bright shine are classic, and a wicker tray can be cute and casual.

116 TIP: **Cover Your Bar**

If you're turning a side table or a desk into a bar, protect it with a vinyl or plastic tablecloth designed for the outdoors, or with a couple of layers of plastic wrap hidden beneath a neat tablecloth. A table covered with a cloth that falls to the floor can do double duty, hiding the back stock of bottles. You can even keep a galvanized tub, cooler, or plastic jug filled with ice under the table for chilling beer, white wine, and champagne. Keep a small garbage can with a liner hidden from guests but convenient for trashing spent lemons, corks, and bottle tops.

How to Choose Your Mixers

If you are offering a full bar, you will need a full array of mixers to go with it. Start with the basics, and add the optional choices depending on what, if any, special cocktails you are serving. Even if you are only serving wine, it's nice to have some soft drinks on hand for those who don't imbibe.

BASIC
- Tonic
- Club soda or seltzer (San Pellegrino or other sparkling water is fine)
- Cola and diet cola
- Ginger ale

OPTIONAL
- Sour mix or fresh lemonade
- Freshly squeezed lime juice
- Cranberry juice
- Freshly squeezed orange juice
- Tomato juice or Bloody Mary mix
- Heavy cream or whipped cream (for winter drinks)

Choosing Wine and Beer

Most people go for wine and beer at a cocktail party, even if mixed drinks are available. Your strategy should be the same for both. Offer a few options that cover the most common tastes: one red and one white, and a few beers, including something light and refreshing, like a pilsner, and some more intensely flavored options, like an IPA (India Pale Ale) or a lager. In both cases (though especially with wine), shopping at a good store can be the key to your success. Explain to a knowledgeable salesperson that the drinks should be compatible with various snacks and not one particular dish. Your selections should all be crowd-pleasers and none too challenging or experimental, taste-wise.

119   TIP: **How to Save a Corked Wine**

It's a rare thing, but even an expensive wine from a reputable vineyard can be "corked," meaning the cork is spoiled and has tainted the wine itself with a musty, mildew-like smell and taste. The flavor is beyond personal taste discrepancies; a corked bottle of wine is undrinkable. In a restaurant, you would send it back and not be charged for the bottle. But at home, you can be your own hero in the face of such a disaster. Pour the wine into a bowl with a sheet of plastic wrap in it and let it sit for about five minutes. Use a funnel to pour the wine back into a decanter. Some say the molecular culprit will stick to the plastic wrap, which should be discarded. It might work, and it's worth a try to save a good bottle of wine.

120   A Bar on a Budget

Liquor is one of the biggest expenses of hosting a party. If you're operating on a tight budget, it's best to think about offering wine and beer only; there are many delicious inexpensive choices of both from all over the world, and inexpensive liquor is a much riskier proposition. A host should aim to have more than enough when it comes to beverages, so limiting your offerings to quality yet inexpensive wine or beer is a good solution.

One way to offer some booze without having a full bar is to choose just one mixed drink and make it the theme of the night. This is most natural when you're working with a theme already, like mint juleps for a Kentucky Derby viewing party, or margaritas with Mexican snacks.

121   Booze Clues: How Much Do You Need?

Calculating the amount of alcohol needed for a party is more of an art than a science. It's hard to know how many people will show up and whether they'll be throwing it back or sipping tamely. But here is some wisdom to start with.

- On average, assume your guests will have 2 drinks per hour (10 guests × 2 drinks × 2 hours = 40 drinks).

- There are approximately 5 glasses of wine per bottle.

- Most mixed drinks are made with a 1-ounce shot of liquor. A 1-liter bottle of liquor contains enough for 32 mixed drinks.

- Mixers are usually poured in 4-ounce portions. One liter of mixer will make 8 drinks.

122   Mixology Cheat Sheet

While the ingredients of a gin and tonic, a vodka and soda, or a rum and Coke are self-evident, the proportions and order of operations are not. The rule of thumb: 1 part alcohol to 3 parts mixer. Add ice, squeeze the lime wedge into the glass, add the wedge, and then stir or shake.

123   Five Great Cocktail Garnishes

1. Sugarcane, cut into skewers and served in tropical punches and rum drinks such as caipirinhas

2. Cucumber spears, especially for a Pimm's Cup (page 263) or any drink made with gin

3. Pineapple spears for rum punches

4. A few paper-thin slices of strawberries or peaches in prosecco or champagne

5. Spicy pickled green beans instead of celery for a Bloody Mary

RECIPE: *Three Cocktails Everyone Should Know*

MAKES 1

1. Martini

As one story goes, this drink was originally called the Martinez, for the California town where it was first mixed in the late 1800s. The martini is a perennial favorite, always glamorous and always served ice-cold. Keep the gin in the freezer, and the glasses, too.

- Combine **2 ounces gin** and **a dash of extra-dry vermouth** in an ice-filled cocktail shaker and shake or stir. Strain into a chilled martini glass and garnish with **an olive** or **a lemon twist.** A Dirty Martini includes **a dash of olive juice.**

2. Margarita

If you choose to make margaritas at home, commit to the following: freshly squeezed lime juice only, and Cointreau rather than Triple Sec. Your guests will thank you.

- Combine **2 ounces tequila, 1 ounce Cointreau,** and **2 tablespoons freshly squeezed lime juice** in an ice-filled cocktail shaker. Shake and serve straight up in a margarita glass. Salt the rims of the glasses or not as your guests prefer.

3. Cosmopolitan

It may be as overexposed as Samantha in *Sex and the City,* but, like the TV show, the cosmo, a pink combination of vodka, cranberry juice, and Triple Sec, is a crowd-pleaser and can't be ignored. It is often embellished with the flavor du jour.

- Combine **1½ ounces vodka, ½ ounce Triple Sec** or **Cointreau, 1 tablespoon cranberry juice,** and **the juice of ½ lime** in an ice-filled cocktail shaker. Shake and strain into a chilled martini glass.

THE COCKTAIL HOUR

MAKES 1

1. Negroni

Count Camillo Negroni always ordered an Americano made with gin at the Casoni Bar in Florence. The resulting classic was called the Negroni, and to some it is the essence of Italy.

• Combine **1 ounce Campari, 1 ounce gin, 1 ounce sweet vermouth,** and **a splash of soda water** (optional) in an ice-filled cocktail glass and stir well. Garnish with **an orange slice.**

2. Champagne Cocktail

Born in New York City, the champagne cocktail was the prizewinning drink in a bartenders' contest in 1889.

• Place **a sugar cube** in the bottom of a champagne glass. Soak with **2 dashes Angostura bitters,** and pour in chilled **champagne.**

3. The Paloma

The Paloma is a simple alternative to a margarita, and, as it's not overplayed, there's a feeling of discovery about it.

• Mix **½ cup grapefruit soda** (Mexican Jarritos or Jamaican Ting), **the juice of half a lime,** and **2 ounces tequila.** Serve over ice in a collins glass. Garnish with **a lime wedge.**

126   Flourish and Flair: How to Make a Twist

Using a paring knife, cut the skin of a lemon away from the pith in wide strips. Then cut the strips into ⅓-inch-wide pieces. Rub the rim of the glass with the lemon rind, coating it with the aromatic oils of the skin. Drop the skin into the glass as a garnish.

127   How to Cut Lemons and Limes

Rinse and dry the lemons and limes. Cut off both ends. Cut in half, and then slice each half into 4 wedges. For lemons, slice off the pithy edge where the seeds are, along with the seeds for clean slices. They should be squeezed into the glass and then dropped into the drink; don't sit the citrus on the rim of the glass.

128   RECIPE: *Two Classic Whiskey Cocktails* ·················

MAKES 1

1. The Manhattan

While stories about the origins of this drink vary, one thing is certain: it was created in New York City sometime in the mid-1800s. It can be served straight up (as below) or on the rocks in a highball glass.

- Combine **two 3-ounce shots rye or Canadian Club whiskey, one 1½-ounce shot sweet vermouth,** and **a dash of Angostura bitters** in an ice-filled cocktail shaker. Shake, and strain into a martini glass.

2. The Mint Julep

The mint julep has become synonymous with the Kentucky Derby. Spearmint is the mint of choice, and it should be very fresh and fragrant. Serving it in a silver cup is traditional, and makes a handsome presentation, but a glass tumbler is fine, too.

- Combine **5 or 6 mint leaves, 1 teaspoon superfine sugar,** and **1 tablespoon cold soda water** in a collins glass or julep cup. Muddle until the leaves and sugar are combined; the leaves will be bruised. Add ice and **two 3-ounce shots bourbon,** stir, and serve with **a mint sprig** for garnish and a straw.

THE
BUFFET

A buffet makes entertaining easier, whether a large group or a small one, especially if you don't have a lot of space at the table. A buffet will automatically invite your guests to make themselves at home, and with several dishes that guests can choose among and combine, everyone's dietary requirements can be met (vegetarian dishes can easily be served alongside dishes for meat lovers). Ask trusted friends to help out by contributing dishes; you can do so without the party becoming an all-out potluck. An "open house" party—at which people come and go over the course of a few hours—naturally lends itself to a buffet, since the hostess is free from timing the courses. Hosting a dessert buffet is a clever idea, too, and is a welcome way to wind down a busy evening.

129 What's Wrong with This Menu?

> **THE BUFFET MENU**
> - Mixed green salad with lemon vinaigrette
> - Peel 'n' eat shrimp
> - Sweet and sticky ribs
> - Spinach soufflé
> - Braised lamb shanks Moroccan style
> - Spaghetti and meatballs

While it's a fine idea to mix metaphors on a buffet, combining different styles of cooking and ethnic and regional influences, there are some problems with this menu. A mixed green salad is not the best choice, as it will wilt quickly; choose something with a little more staying power, such as a rice or grain salad, a raw kale salad, or green beans with vinaigrette. Things like peel 'n' eat shrimp and sticky ribs are fine for an outdoor barbecue, but for a more refined indoor affair, they are too messy and awkward to eat. Avoid items that won't hold up well at room temperature or will require too much of your attention in the kitchen, like spinach soufflé. When serving meat, braises are a great idea, but avoid large cuts like a lamb shank, and opt for an easy-to-eat stew instead. This way guests can just take a little taste rather than have to make a big commitment. Pasta is popular and easy for a buffet, but go for a baked pasta dish with a short shape that can be easily speared by a fork. Penne or cavatelli can be prepared in advance and kept hot on the buffet, and they won't lash your guests like sloppy long noodles would.

- Wild Rice Salad (page 257)
- Raw shredded kale salad
- Carnitas (page 98)
- Baked Orecchiette with Sausage and Broccoli Rabe (page 100)
- Roasted vegetables (see pages 155–156)
- Mixed Berry Crisp (page 117)

Why it works: This menu is made up of items that will look good and taste good even after sitting for a few hours on a buffet. They're easy to eat in small bites, too. Everything on this menu can be eaten with just a fork, which is essential for a party at which guests might be eating with their plates in their laps, or standing.

130 RECIPE: *Tomatillo Salsa*

This green hot sauce, or salsa verde, is a staple of Mexican cuisine, served alongside tacos or quesadillas and splashed onto meat and fish dishes. It goes perfectly with the Carnitas (page 98), and you'll want to keep a reserve in the fridge for any Mexican meal.

MAKES ABOUT 3 CUPS

- Preheat the broiler. Husk, rinse, and core **1½ pounds tomatillos (about 12)**. Put them on a baking sheet and broil until lightly charred, turning them over once, about 6 minutes. Let cool.

- In a blender, combine the tomatillos, **½ cup chopped onion, 1 garlic clove, 1 tablespoon freshly squeezed lime juice, 1 jalapeño, salt to taste,** and **a splash of extra-virgin olive oil.**

- Pulse until all the ingredients are combined, but some texture remains. Pulse in **½ cup cilantro leaves.**

THE BUFFET

Carnitas (literally, "little meats" in Spanish) might be your favorite filler for a taco, but it's about to become your greatest buffet hit. We're talking about pork that's braised until it falls apart. Serve the tender, flavorful meat with tortillas or rice and beans to soak up all the delicious juices. However you present it, your friends will go nuts. The best part is that you will have spent very little money and your oven will have done all the work for you.

SERVES 8 TO 10

- Have your butcher cut **a 4- to 5-pound pork butt** (which is actually cut from the shoulder and also called Boston butt) into 5-inch chunks.

- Preheat the oven to 350°F. Season the meat liberally with **salt**. In a large heavy-bottomed ovenproof pot, combine the meat with **the grated zest of 1 orange**; 1 yellow onion, chopped; 3 to 5 garlic cloves, chopped; 1 teaspoon ground cumin (preferably toasted and ground cumin seeds); 1 teaspoon dried oregano; 2 small bay leaves; 1 cinnamon stick; and ½ teaspoon peppercorns. Add 4 cups chicken stock and enough cold water to just cover the meat.

- Cook, uncovered, until the pork begins to fall apart, about 2½ hours. Remove the pork from the liquid and set aside until cool enough to handle. Discard the cooking liquid or strain it and

save it for another use, such as braising vegetables. Discard the
bay leaves, cinnamon stick, and peppercorns. Turn the oven up
to 400°F.

• Shred the pork with your hands, removing any large bits of fat,
and put it back in the pot. Cook the meat, stirring frequently, for
about 20 minutes, or until nicely browned and crispy. This dish
can be made ahead and reheated before serving.

132 RECIPE: *Mac 'n' Cheese*

Everyone loves mac 'n' cheese. Here's a foolproof recipe that you can use
as a base, adding meat or vegetables if you want more of a one-pot meal.

SERVES 10 TO 12 AS A SIDE DISH OR 5 TO 6 AS AN ENTRÉE

• Preheat the oven to 375°F. Bring a big pot of water to a boil.

• Meanwhile, melt **3 tablespoons butter.** Brush a 2-quart
casserole with 1 tablespoon of the melted butter. In a medium
bowl, combine **1 cup panko (Japanese bread crumbs)** and the
remaining 2 tablespoons melted butter, stirring to mix. Set aside.

• Add **a few big pinches of salt** to the boiling water, and then add
1 pound penne rigate (or whatever shape pasta you choose—
cavatappi works well, too). Cook for about 9 minutes, or until the
pasta is just shy of al dente. Drain and set aside in a big bowl.

• Meanwhile, make **Béchamel Sauce** (page 105). Once it's cooked,
turn off the heat and stir in **8 ounces sharp Cheddar, grated;
8 ounces Gruyère, grated;** and **½ cup freshly grated Parmigiano-
Reggiano.** Pour the cheese sauce over the pasta and mix well. Add
any other ingredients you choose (see next page). It may seem very
saucy, but it will thicken when you bake it and the pasta absorbs
the sauce. Transfer to the prepared baking dish and sprinkle the

top with panko and ¼ cup freshly grated Parmigiano-Reggiano. (You can let the dish cool to room temperature, cover it with plastic wrap, and refrigerate for 1 to 2 days or until you're ready to bake.)

- Bake for 30 minutes, or until the top is golden and the sauce is bubbling. (If you refrigerated it, it will take about an hour to heat.) Let cool for about 10 minutes before serving.

MAC 'N' CHEESE ADD-INS: 1 cup diced cooked ham, 2 ounces prosciutto, 1½ cups blanched broccoli florets, 1 to 2 cups sautéed mushrooms, or chopped herbs, such as thyme or rosemary.

133   RECIPE: *Baked Orecchiette with Sausage and Broccoli Rabe*

Broccoli rabe and sausage is a classic pairing, and here it's joined by tomatoes, cheese, and cream in a baked pasta dish that is as comforting as it is complex. This is great for a buffet, and a meal unto itself. The spicy sausage and bitter greens make this a dish for grown-ups.

SERVES 6

- Preheat the oven to 400°F. Butter a 3-quart casserole dish. Bring a large pot of water to a boil.

- Meanwhile, remove 1 **pound hot Italian sausages** from their casings and place the meat in a cold sauté pan, breaking it up with a wooden spoon. Turn the heat to medium-high and cook

the sausage until it begins to brown, about 7 minutes. Remove to paper towels to drain.

- Pour off the excess fat in the pan, add **1 tablespoon extra-virgin olive oil, a pinch of red pepper flakes,** and **2 garlic cloves, sliced,** and cook over medium heat until the garlic is golden. Add **1 bunch of broccoli rabe, thick stems removed, chopped,** sprinkle with **salt,** toss, cover, and cook for 1 to 2 minutes, until the greens wilt. Add **1 pint grape or cherry tomatoes** and cook until the tomatoes burst, 5 to 7 minutes. Add **1 cup Pomì brand strained tomatoes or tomato sauce** and **1½ cups heavy cream** and bring to a simmer. Add the sausage and stir well.

- Meanwhile, when the water comes to a boil, add **a few big pinches of salt** and **1 pound orecchiette** and cook for about 9 minutes, or until the pasta is just shy of al dente.

- Toss the pasta with the tomato sauce; **8 ounces Fontina, cut into ¼-inch cubes;** and **½ cup grated Pecorino.** Pour the mixture into the prepared baking dish. Sprinkle **½ cup grated Pecorino** on top, and bake for 20 to 25 minutes, or until golden and bubbling.

134   How to Maximize Your Fridge Space

Before you even start cooking for a big party, take a few minutes to assess your refrigerator's available real estate. Is it going to be stuffed to capacity by the end of the first day of prepping? If you're going to have a ham or a turkey in there, plus components of various side dishes and hors d'oeuvres, you may need to free up some space. This is the time to toss those leftovers that are slowly spoiling in the back corner, and consolidate the two open jars of mayonnaise.

135   TIP: Create Backup Refrigeration

Even a big fridge can be easily overwhelmed in the days preceding a big party. If you find yourself in need of extra cold-storage space, take advantage of a cooler to hold vegetables, eggs, cheese, condiments, and beverages, leaving meat, fish, and dairy in the fridge so you can be sure they are kept cold enough. Loose ice will quickly melt, so pack coolers with reuseable ice packs that can be repurposed for future picnics or trips to the beach. Use several ice packs and place them at the bottom of the cooler, piling the food on top. In the winter, you can make use of your porch, a fire escape, or even your car to stash food overnight. But be aware of the temperature: if it's below freezing, some delicate foods, such as vegetables and eggs, could be damaged, and anything in a glass bottle could explode.

RECIPE: *Lasagna with Ricotta and Mushrooms*

This creamy, meaty lasagna can be served as a one-dish meal with just a salad, or it can be the star of a buffet. It can be assembled ahead of time and left in the fridge until party time, and it holds up beautifully during a casual party where your friends help themselves (and they will come back for seconds). Béchamel Sauce (page 105) can replace the layers of ricotta if you prefer a more classic, slightly richer lasagna.

SERVES 6 TO 8

- Heat **2 tablespoons olive oil** in a large saucepan over medium heat and add **1 onion, minced; 3 garlic cloves, sliced; a pinch of red pepper flakes; 1 rib celery, minced;** and **1 carrot, minced.** Cook until the vegetables have softened, 5 to 7 minutes. Turn the heat to medium-high and add **1½ pounds ground beef or veal (or a combination).** Cook, breaking up the meat, until the liquid has evaporated and the meat begins to brown, about 5 minutes.

- Add **1 cup dry white wine, 1 cup whole milk, one 6-ounce can tomato paste, one 15-ounce can crushed tomatoes, one 15-ounce can full of water,** and **salt and pepper to taste** and bring to a boil. Cover, reduce the heat to low, and let the sauce simmer, stirring occasionally, for 45 minutes to 1 hour, until slightly thickened.

- Meanwhile, heat **1 tablespoon olive oil** in a large sauté pan over medium-high heat. Add **2 onions, sliced, and salt and pepper to taste** and cook until the onions are translucent, about 5 minutes. Add **8 ounces cremini mushrooms, sliced,** and cook until the liquid evaporates and the mushrooms begin to brown. Transfer to a bowl and set aside.

THE BUFFET

- In a large bowl, combine 2 **heaping cups whole-milk ricotta** (about 20 ounces); 6 ounces **mozzarella, shredded** (about 1½ cups); 2 **large eggs**; ⅓ cup chopped **fresh Italian parsley**; ½ cup freshly grated **Parmigiano-Reggiano**; and **salt and pepper to taste.** Stir to combine well and set aside.

- Preheat the oven to 350°F. Butter a 3-quart baking dish. Spread 1 cup of the sauce in the bottom of the baking dish. Follow with a layer of **no-boil lasagna noodles** (about 4 sheets per layer, depending on the size of the dish, overlapping if necessary), 1 cup sauce, and 2 cups of the ricotta mixture. Add another layer of pasta, 1 cup sauce, and half of the mushroom mixture, then a layer of pasta, 1 cup sauce, the remaining ricotta mixture, pasta, and the remaining sauce. Top with 6 **ounces mozzarella, shredded** (about 1½ cups); ½ cup freshly grated **Parmigiano-Reggiano;** and the remaining mushroom mixture. Cover the baking dish with greased foil. (The lasagna can be refrigerated for as long as overnight.) Put the baking dish on a baking sheet and bake for 45 minutes. (If you are baking straight from the refrigerator, bake for 1 hour covered and for 15 to 20 minutes more uncovered.) Remove the foil and bake until the top is golden, 15 to 20 minutes more. Let sit for at least 15 minutes before serving.

Béchamel is a white sauce in French and Italian cooking (*besciamella* in Italian), used in many lasagna dishes and as the base for lots of other sauces (in French cooking, béchamel is one of the "mother sauces"). Perhaps because it's French, people think it's very tricky, but the only trick is to stir it constantly so it doesn't get lumpy.

MAKES 4 CUPS

- Melt **4 tablespoons butter** in a saucepan over medium heat. Add **1 small onion, chopped,** and **1 garlic clove, minced,** and sauté until translucent, 6 to 8 minutes.

- Meanwhile, in a separate pot, heat **2 cups milk** just to warm it.

- Add **¼ cup all-purpose flour** to the onions and cook, stirring constantly, for about 3 minutes, or until the flour has absorbed the butter and the mixture has begun to thicken. Slowly pour in the warm milk, stirring constantly to prevent lumps from forming. Once the warm milk has been incorporated, stir in another **2 cups milk** and turn the heat up to medium-high. Add **1 teaspoon salt, a dash of cayenne pepper, a dash of black pepper,** and **a dash of freshly grated nutmeg** and cook, stirring constantly, until the sauce thickens, 8 to 10 minutes. Bring to a boil, then turn down to a bare simmer and cook for 10 minutes longer, stirring constantly to avoid scorching. If not using right away, transfer to a bowl or other container and rub **a piece of butter** over the top to prevent a skin from forming; refrigerate, covered, after the sauce has cooled off a bit.

A really good meat loaf will appeal to the kid in everyone, plus it's inexpensive to make and holds up beautifully on a buffet table. The leftovers, if there are any, are pretty good, too.

SERVES 8 TO 10

- In a large sauté pan over medium heat, sauté 1 **onion, finely chopped,** and 2 **garlic cloves, minced,** in 2 **tablespoons olive oil** until translucent, about 5 minutes. Remove from the heat and let cool. In a medium bowl, whisk together 2 **large eggs,** 2 tablespoons Dijon mustard, 2 tablespoons Worcestershire sauce, 2 teaspoons finely chopped fresh rosemary, ¼ teaspoon Tabasco sauce, ¼ cup ketchup, and ½ cup milk.

- Preheat the oven to 350°F. Line a rimmed baking sheet with aluminum foil.

- In a large bowl, combine ⅔ **pound each ground beef, veal, and pork (2 pounds total).** Pour the egg mixture over the meat and add ⅔ **cup crushed saltines, the onion-garlic mixture,** ¼ **cup chopped fresh Italian parsley, 1 teaspoon salt,** and 1 **teaspoon pepper.** Mix with your hands until all the liquid is incorporated and the ingredients are evenly distributed.

- Shape the meat into an oblong loaf on the prepared baking sheet. Bake for 30 minutes.

- Brush the top of the meat loaf with **a scant ½ cup ketchup.** Continue baking for another hour, or until the center of the loaf reaches 160°F. If you like, overlap **8 thin slices bacon** lengthwise on the loaf for the last hour.

RECIPE: *Baked Chicken*

with Apricots and Olives

With a complex balance of sweet (apricots and honey), salty (olives), and tart (balsamic vinegar and white wine), this is a killer dish. It's a great way to make chicken, that old standby, new and memorable. And, because the chicken is cut up, it's a perfect buffet dish: there's no carving to worry about, and your friends can help themselves to their favorite parts. They'll all be asking for the recipe.

SERVES 10 TO 12

- Pat dry **two 3½- to 4-pound chickens** and cut into 8 pieces each. Season on all sides with **plenty of salt and pepper.**

- In a large bowl, combine **4 to 6 garlic cloves, thinly sliced; 2 teaspoons dried thyme; ¼ cup balsamic vinegar; ¼ cup extra-virgin olive oil; 1 cup dried apricots; ½ cup pitted kalamata olives; 4 bay leaves; ½ cup honey; and ½ cup dry white wine.** Add the chicken to the marinade and turn the pieces over to make sure they're coated.

- Cover the bowl or transfer the chicken and marinade to doubled resealable bags and refrigerate for at least 2 hours, or overnight, turning occasionally.

- Preheat the oven to 350°F. Arrange the chicken, skin side up, in a single layer in a large roasting pan (or two smaller pans) lined with foil and spoon the marinade, apricots, and olives around and on top of it.

- Bake the chicken for 1 hour, basting twice during the second half hour. If the chicken is not golden brown, turn on the broiler and broil for a few minutes to brown the skin.

- Transfer the chicken, apricots, and olives to a serving platter. Discard the garlic, thyme, and bay leaves. Pour the cooking juices into a small saucepan, skim off the excess fat, and boil the liquid over medium-high heat until it thickens to a pourable sauce, 5 to 10 minutes.

- Pour the sauce over the chicken and serve. This dish is also great at room temperature.

140   RECIPE: *Glazed Ham*

A glazed baked ham is the quintessential buffet dish: traditional and always special. This recipe is foolproof and can be made well ahead of time if you want to serve the ham at room temperature. A tangy, sweet glaze of pomegranate molasses or honey and orange juice provides a perfect foil for the salty cured pork.

SERVES 12 TO 16 (OR MORE FOR GLAZING)

- Bring **a 10- to 15-pound, bone-in, fully cooked whole ham** to room temperature; this will take about 2 hours. Since it's fully cooked, this is not a health risk.

- Preheat the oven to 350°F. Place the ham in a shallow roasting pan lined with aluminum foil. Score the ham with the tip of a paring knife, cutting diagonal strips and then crossing them to form 1½-inch diamonds. If desired, stick **a whole clove** in the center of each diamond.

- Bake the ham until the internal temperature reaches 140°F, about 2 hours.

- While the ham is in the oven, make the glaze: Combine 1 **cup packed light brown sugar**, ¾ **cup grainy mustard**, ¼ **cup pomegranate molasses or honey, the juice of ½ orange**, and ½ **teaspoon cayenne pepper** in a bowl and whisk until well blended.

- Remove the ham from the oven and brush the glaze generously over the surface. Return the ham to the oven for about 1½ hours more, basting every 30 minutes or so, until the glaze is brown and crusty. Remove the ham from the oven and let it rest for at least 30 minutes before carving.

141   TIP: **Save Your Bones**

Bones—cooked or uncooked, from chicken, pork, beef, or any other meat—shouldn't go in the garbage can until you've rendered all you can from them. If the butcher removes meat from a bone for you, ask to take the bone home so you can make stock from it, or at least give it to the dog as a treat. Nothing could be easier than stock from scratch, and soup is also a great way to use other leftovers from the party, like vegetables from a crudité platter or the meat from a roasted chicken. Bones from a roasted chicken, a ham, or chops of any kind can be collected in the freezer for a rainy day when you have a few hours and a craving for soup.

142   Is a Good Ham Hard to Find?

This may seem like a silly question, until you start shopping for a ham. The ham we Americans are most familiar with—the one Mom always made for Christmas, studded with cloves and maybe even pineapple rings—is wet-cured (brined rather than rubbed with plain, dry salt, as are prosciutto and other European hams) and then smoked. In the supermarket, the ham will be labeled "fully cooked" or "ready to eat," because the smoking process cooks the ham enough to make it safely edible. (When we bake a ham, we do it just for the sake of the glaze, which adds flavor, and to heat the meat and melt the fat.) Hams that are labeled "water added" or "ham and water product" will have the most water and should be avoided. The percentage of water added is listed on the label; compare these percentages and buy the ham with the lowest water content. It's worth seeking out a butcher who specializes in smoking hams, or one who can order you a top-quality bone-in or semi-boneless ham. It's best to buy a ham with the bone in, because meat cooked on the bone is always juicier.

143   *Flourish and Flair:* How to Carve a Ham

Carve your ham shortly before you serve it, so it doesn't dry out. Do carve it, so your guests are spared the task of slicing at the buffet table.

You can carve and slice the ham right on the platter you plan to serve it on; your knife will not go through and damage the plate, because you are cutting the meat only down to the bone in the middle. The right knife will make things easier. If you have one, use a long, thin, but sturdy knife (most ham slicers are 10 inches long), not a chef's knife.

- Remove the cloves if you used them.

- A ham comes from the top of the pig's leg, and the leg bone that runs lengthwise through the meat is not perfectly straight; it dips down somewhere in the middle, where the joint is (picture a very shallow V or check mark). The key to carving is to find that bone. Start by cutting the top portion (the heftier side) of the ham free from it, scraping the knife gently along the bone so as not to veer away and waste any meat. You can leave the meat sitting right on top of the bone once it has been separated, and slice as thinly and evenly as you can. You'll have very large slices; if you want, you can cut through them in a perpendicular direction to make smaller pieces.

• If you think it's unlikely that your guests will eat the whole top side, you may want to leave some of it unsliced so it will fare better in its second life as leftovers (or in your freezer). If your crowd does make it through the whole top of the ham, don't worry; there's plenty more on the underside of the bone and along the sides. Bring the platter into the kitchen and carve off the "cheeks" of meat along the sides, then remove the bone and slice the meat underneath. Arrange the slices on the serving platter.

144   *In Praise of* The Spiral-Cut Ham

If you want to avoid the bother of having to slice the ham, and you don't mind sacrificing a little juiciness, you may want to consider a spiral-cut ham. This is already carved for you in the most amazing manner (by a machine, of course) in one continuous cut all the way around the ham. Guests can easily pull off a slice, and you might consider it a plus that the glaze can seep in a bit between the slices, adding even more flavor.

145   How to Present a Ham

A great big glazed ham is a gorgeous thing, and there are many ways to accessorize this crowd-pleaser. Mustard is de rigueur with ham, and it's a nice idea to serve a variety of them. Look for a few different flavors and textures: a grainy one, a honey mustard, a spicy one, and

always a smooth Dijon. There are even green (green peppercorn or tarragon) mustards and purple mustards (flavored and colored by grapes) to liven up your buffet. If they come in good-looking jars, and they generally do, you can put those out on the table, so people can see what each one is. If you have little wooden mustard spoons or knives, this is the time to break them out. Guests will get a kick out of choosing their mustard from a variety of interesting flavors. Cheese is another perfect partner for ham, especially a Cheddar or Gruyère. Serve a variety of breads as well, including anything from a sliced baguette and a rye or multigrain or a fruit and nut bread to freshly baked biscuits or little muffins.

To garnish the joint itself, you can gussy it up with a few well-placed pieces of seasonal fruit such as apples, pears, clementines, pomegranates, plums, or cherries, with some tufts of hardy herbs such as fresh bay leaves, rosemary, or thyme.

146 *In Praise of* The Salmon Platter

A salmon platter, which is a long, narrow oval, like a whole fish, is an incredibly flattering shape for serving many other foods as well. Anything that can be lined up, such as sliced meat, fish fillets, poached pears, or roasted vegetables, looks really elegant on a salmon platter.

147   Turn Your Buffet Table into a Dessert Buffet

When it's time to serve dessert, you may still be expecting new guests. This is a good time to consolidate and freshen the savory offerings on the buffet while clearing some space to add desserts to the table. Transfer savory foods to smaller dishes so they still look fresh, and clear anything that is decimated. Move the remaining dishes to one end of the table and set out the sweets, letting them take front and center.

148   RECIPE: *Strawberry-Rhubarb Lattice Pie*

For this recipe, you will need a double batch of No-Fail Piecrust (recipe follows). Use half of the dough to line the pie plate and the other half to form the lattice top. I've simplified the lattice by making the strips quite a bit larger than usual. The oversize weave looks modern, and it's easier and quicker to do.

SERVES 8 TO 10

- Preheat the oven to 375°F. In a large bowl, toss **1 quart strawberries, hulled and halved,** with **1 pound rhubarb, trimmed and cut into ¾-inch pieces; ½ cup sugar; 3 tablespoons all-purpose flour;** and (optional) **the grated zest of 1 orange.**

- Fill a prepared piecrust with the strawberry mixture.

To make a lattice top, roll out the second piece of dough and cut into 8 strips, 1½ inches wide, using a pizza or pastry cutter. Weave the lattice according to the illustration (see page 116). Put the pie on a rimmed baking sheet and bake until the crust is golden and the juices are thick and bubbling, about 1 hour.

149 RECISE: *No-Fail Piecrust*

Homemade piecrust is not nearly as intimidating as most people think. The trick to a flaky crust is cold butter—it's that simple. As long as you can resist fussing too much (your hands are warm and will warm up the dough), you can make a delectable crust. You can do it ahead of time, so that on the day of your party, the only work left is the same as if you had bought a premade pie shell.

MAKES ONE 9-INCH PIECRUST

- Combine **2 cups all-purpose flour, ½ teaspoon kosher salt,** and **1 teaspoon sugar** in a food processor and pulse a few times to blend. Add 14 **tablespoons (1¾ sticks) ice-cold unsalted butter, cut into 1-tablespoon pieces,** and pulse until the pieces are the size of peas. With the machine running, quickly pour in **¼ cup ice-cold water** and mix until just combined, about 30 seconds. The mixture should look dry and crumbly.

- Turn the mixture into a bowl and work the dough into a rough mass with your hands. Using the sides of the bowl, push the dough firmly and it will begin to come together. Don't overhandle the dough; it doesn't need to look perfect. More important is that the butter remain cold.

- Place the dough on a large sheet of plastic wrap and fold the edges over the top. Press down on the dough to form a disk about 1½ inches thick. Wrap the dough tightly in the plastic and refrigerate for at least 30 minutes. (The dough can be refrigerated for up to 3 days or frozen for a month or two.)

- Remove the dough from the refrigerator and allow to soften slightly, 15 to 30 minutes. Sprinkle the counter with a little flour, as well as the rolling pin and the top of the dough. It may need a few good whacks with the rolling pin to get it soft enough to roll. Starting from the center, roll outward; rotate the dough quarter turns, keeping a nice even circle. Keep the dough slightly floured so it doesn't stick, and check its thickness frequently to ensure an even crust; turn it over periodically, rolling it onto the pin to pick it up and lay it down on the opposite side.

- Brush off any excess flour using a dry pastry brush or your hand. Loosely roll the crust up around the rolling pin and transfer it to a 9-inch pie plate. Unroll it into the plate, center it if necessary, and trim to make a 1½-inch overhang. Roll the overhang under itself, crimp the edges as desired, and refrigerate until firm. If making a double-crust or lattice-top pie (see page 116), chill the bottom crust (in the pie plate, but untrimmed and uncrimped) while you prepare the top crust. Fill the chilled bottom shell, top with the top crust, and trim using scissors, leaving a 1½-inch overhang. Roll under and crimp as desired.

150   TIP: **Use a Turntable to Trim a Piecrust**

A simple plastic turntable, or a more official cake-decorating turntable, makes the job of trimming a piecrust simple and fast. Whether you are trimming a single-crust pie, a double-crust pie, or a lattice-top pie, you need to trim the crust to about a 1½-inch overhang. Using clean kitchen scissors while slowly spinning the turntable makes this job quick, neat, and easy.

Making a Wide Lattice

Cutting wide strips of dough for a lattice-top pie makes the job of "weaving" much easier, and it looks cute and modern. The top itself functions identically to a traditional lattice, which would be made with about twice as many pieces.

1. First, divide the No-Fail Piecrust (page 114) dough in half. Wrap one ball of dough and refrigerate it. Roll out the other half of the dough into the shape of a large circle. Place it in the pie plate, leaving a 1½-inch overhang. Set aside in the refrigerator to chill.

2. On a lightly floured surface, roll out the other half of the dough to the same thickness and diameter as the first half. Slide the dough onto a parchment-lined baking sheet and chill until firm, about 30 minutes.

3. Cut the dough into even strips, about 2 inches wide, using a pizza cutter, a small knife, or a pastry wheel. You will need 8 to 10 strips to cover the pie. Don't worry if some of them are shorter; you'll need a combination of short and long strips to make the lattice.

4. Pour the filling into the chilled pie shell. Lay 4 or 5 parallel strips on top of the filling, leaving about ½ inch of space in between.

5. Fold back every other strip.

6. Place one of the longer pieces perpendicular to the first strips in the center of the pie.

7. Unfold the folded strips over the perpendicular strip.

8. Now fold back the parallel strips that are underneath the perpendicular strip that you just placed.

9. Place a second perpendicular strip next to the first strip, leaving ½ inch of space in between.

10. Continue the process until the lattice is completely woven on top of the pie.

11. Using scissors, and a turntable if you have one, trim the edges of the dough so that there is ½ inch of overhang beyond the edge of the dish.

12. Roll the lattice dough up from the bottom inward, and gently press together with the bottom edge. Crimp as desired. Chill again until firm, about 30 minutes, before baking.

152   RECIPE: *Mixed Berry Crisp*

A warm berry crisp is sure to win over your guests with its irresistibly comforting flavor and rich aroma, and it is one of the easiest desserts to prepare. The topping can be made any time and stored in the freezer in a resealable plastic bag. This recipe is designed to be quick to prepare; there is absolutely no prep work for the fruit aside from washing the berries!

SERVES 6 TO 8

- To make the topping, combine **1 cup plus 2 tablespoons all-purpose flour** (if you are preparing individual ramekins, reduce the flour to 1 cup), **⅓ cup packed dark or light brown sugar, ½ cup granulated sugar, ¼ teaspoon ground cinnamon, ¼ teaspoon baking powder,** and **¼ teaspoon salt** in a food processor, and pulse to mix evenly. Add **8 tablespoons (1 stick) cold unsalted butter, cut into pieces,** and pulse until the mixture comes together and clumps. Chill in the refrigerator for 30 minutes.

- Preheat the oven to 375°F. To make the filling, in a large bowl, combine **6 cups mixed berries (raspberries, blueberries, and blackberries), ½ cup sugar, 3 tablespoons all-purpose flour, 1 teaspoon grated lemon zest,** and **the juice of ½ lemon.**

- Transfer the filling to a shallow 2-quart baking dish or divide it among individual ramekins placed on a rimmed baking sheet. Spoon the topping evenly over the filling. Bake for 35 to 45 minutes, for a large crisp, or about 25 minutes for individual crisps, until the topping is golden brown and the juices are thick and bubbling.

TIP: How to Revive Dried-Up Brown Sugar

It's inevitable in the life of an infrequent baker: the brown sugar, which you made sure you had in the pantry, has hardened into one unbreakable rock. To salvage it, cut a slice or a small hunk of moist white bread or a piece of an apple and put it and the sugar in a storage container, cover with a tight-fitting lid, and set aside for a few hours or up to one day. The sugar will absorb the moisture and magically soften, just like new.

Kids will go crazy for these, of course, but so will grown-ups, who will be reminded of malted milk shakes and their favorite childhood candies. You are likely to find yourself giving out this recipe, or receiving requests for the brownies at every potluck and bake sale in your future.

MAKES 16 LARGE OR 24 SMALL BROWNIES

- Preheat the oven to 300°F. Brush a 9-by-13-inch baking pan with **melted butter.** Line the bottom with parchment paper; set aside. Sift together **1 cup all-purpose flour, 1 cup malted milk powder (such as Ovaltine Malt or Carnation Malted Milk), ¼ cup unsweetened cocoa powder, ¼ teaspoon baking powder,** and **½ teaspoon salt;** set aside.

- Melt **8 ounces unsweetened chocolate, chopped,** with **½ pound (2 sticks) unsalted butter** in a medium saucepan over low heat, stirring frequently. Transfer the chocolate mixture to a large bowl.

- Stir **1 cup granulated sugar** and **1 cup packed dark brown sugar** into the chocolate mixture, using a wooden spoon. Add **1 teaspoon vanilla extract** and **4 large eggs** and mix well. Stir in the flour mixture until just incorporated. Let the batter cool for 5 minutes.

- Fold **1½ cups whole malted milk balls** into the batter. Pour the batter into the prepared pan. Spread with a spatula to distribute the batter and malted milk balls evenly. Bake until the center is firm and the surface looks dry, about 45 minutes, turning the pan around after 30 minutes. Let the brownies cool completely in the pan.

- When you're ready to serve, cut the brownies into squares.

155 How to Make a Buffet Look Beautiful

For a plentiful and colorful buffet that's easy to navigate:

- **Map it out.** Before the party, take a good look at the table and compose your buffet, placing empty platters and baskets on the table to see how everything fits. After you've worked it out, snap a photo or draw a diagram to follow later (especially if you have other people helping you out). It will be easier to remember where everything goes when the pressure is on, allowing for a swift setup of the table.

- **Think texture.** Mix things up by using a wooden cutting board, a marble pastry slab, or a small wicker tray for things like bread and fruit, or anything that won't be messy or wet. Here's your chance to use all of those one-off flea-market finds—variety, not uniformity, is the key to a sumptuous buffet.

- **Create levels.** A cake stand can come in handy to elevate one dish, making it more accessible, and making the buffet instantly look more bountiful since you can nudge other platters or bowls underneath it, close to the base. Feel free to improvise and set a platter on top of a shoe box or a dictionary—just cover the base with a tablecloth or a napkin. The effect should be seamless, though; the idea is to not have guests notice that something is being elevated, or what is elevating it, but to notice the food that's being elevated.

- **Fill in the holes.** Clutter is not the look you want, but nothing is sadder than a skimpy-looking spread. If you are left with some space at the end of a sideboard, for example, move a vase with flowers to that spot, or make a second bread basket. A bowl of fruit would work, too.

156 Seating Plan for Buffets

Although part of the motivation for having a buffet may be that you have more guests than can comfortably fit at your table for a sit-down, you still need to consider where guests will sit once they have their food. Bring any extra chairs into the room where people are congregating, setting them up in little groups along the edges of the room. Even a piano bench can provide a perch for a person or two. Depending on the pace of your party, everyone may not eat at once, which can be a blessing; but folks will find places to sit, and a few may end up standing, which is fine as long as you've followed one of the cardinal rules of buffet menu–planning and chosen foods that are easily managed with a fork or one hand.

1. **Prepare backups.** For large parties, it's helpful to have doubles, or at least comparable platters and bowls to use as "backups" in the kitchen; that way you can easily replenish the buffet without leaving a big hole on the table while you refill a platter. Simply swap a fresh platter for a depleted one to keep the buffet looking fresh and appetizing.

2. **Make shortages look intentional.** If you have only six matching plates and have to fill in with another set, try to use them in equal numbers, rather than put out just a couple of the other dishes, and integrate them into the stack. Just try to use plates that are roughly the same size. The mixed-up look can be charming.

3. **Place the silverware and napkins at the end of the buffet.** It may seem natural to put the dishes and silverware together at the beginning of the buffet, but remember that your guests will need a free hand to serve themselves as they progress down the line. Once they've filled their plates, they can pick up utensils and be on their way.

4. **Wrap the silverware in the napkins.** To avoid a traffic jam at the end of the buffet, have silverware and napkins bundled and ready to go. Even though a particular guest doesn't eat beef and therefore

doesn't need a knife, it's worthwhile to simplify things and provide everyone with a complete set. This is a job you can do well ahead of party time.

5. **Provide one-handed serving utensils.** Ideally, your friends won't have to set down their plates in order to fill them, or ask for help from the person next in line. Instead of a salad spoon-and-fork, put out tongs or one big spoon.

6. **Place accoutrements in obvious proximity to main dishes.** If you're serving a sauce with the fish, make sure to position it next to, or even directly on, the appropriate platter, so your guests don't plop the sauce on top of the asparagus instead.

7. **Think about travel time.** Food that is being kept warm in chafing dishes should be placed at the end of the buffet, so they don't have a chance to cool before your guests sit down to eat.

8. **Make your treasures last.** Place items that you are concerned about running out of, or that are more expensive and scarce, at the end of the buffet. People tend to be more conservative as their plates fill up, and they won't have as much room on their plates at the end. If you really are worried about running short of something, consider serving guests before yourself for the first round to make sure everyone gets a taste.

9. **Choose dishes with longevity.** When planning a buffet, avoid dishes that will suffer from sitting out, such as a delicate dressed salad that will become soggy. Ideally, you won't have to keep everything warm for the whole event. Try to include dishes that are at their best at room temperature, such as boiled potatoes dressed with olive oil and herbs rather than with a butter-based sauce that will congeal.

Platter Up!

SIZE MATTERS

Putting food on a large platter—one with lots of extra space around the food—will make it look less abundant. Yet sometimes the negative space can lend elegance to the meal and make it look more refined or "restaurant," so it all depends on the circumstances. Food should never be overflowing out of its bowl or plate. Remember, once a guest plunges a spoon into an already too-full bowl, the contents will spill over the sides.

CONSIDER COLOR

Solid white or cream-colored platters go with everything and flatter any food. Greens are also flattering, especially for vegetables. Blue is a tricky color for food, and you don't often see deep or bright solid blue serving platters, though a white and blue pattern can be pretty for dessert. Black serving pieces are certainly untraditional, but they can really make food "pop"; just stick to a more modern matte finish rather than something with a shiny glaze. If your taste is on the modern side and you're serving something colorful, especially food that's bright yellow, orange, or red, it could be a successful, bold move.

PATTERN POLICY

If you love pattern, then go with it, but if you're not sure, it's best to stay with solids, as patterned serving dishes can be distracting, and many are downright old-fashioned.

MATERIAL WORLD

Glazed ceramic bowls of every color and shape can really show off your food, and stone can give a great rustic look to a hearty meal. Stone bowls are great heat conductors, so if you want your dish to stay warm, be sure to begin with a warm bowl. Conversely, a cold stone bowl will suck the heat right out of your food. This is also true of enameled metal bowls. Wood vessels and boards are fine for foods that are not too wet.

IN GOOD SHAPE

Round, oval, square, rectangle . . . there are no bad shapes when it comes to serving food, but some will work better for certain types of dishes. A deep bowl will keep foods such as mashed potatoes warmer for longer, while food on a flat platter is exposed to more air and will come to room temperature pretty quickly. Wide platters are ideal for composed dishes, like a Niçoise salad, so you can attractively show off all of the different ingredients, and guests can easily access them. Sliced meat also looks best "shingled" on a wide, flat platter. It makes slices easier to pick up when guests are serving themselves.

NO FUSS, NO MUSS

In general, try to let food fall naturally into or onto its serving vessel, and make a few tweaks afterward if needed, rather than fussily arranging. No one wants to get the feeling that what he's about to eat has been poked and prodded and smooshed and shaped. Pile things like mashed potatoes or roasted Brussels sprouts loosely in bowls. Resist the urge to flatten, smooth, primp, and perfect. Don't worry if a roasted carrot is hanging off the edge of the platter—it adds character!

159

TIP: Flea-Market Finds

Shop at flea markets, antiques stores, and garage sales year-round and keep an eye out for lovely and unusual pieces that will work for your next party. Mid-century modern casseroles and accents, old English ironstone platters or pedestals, or American farmhouse wooden bowls and boards provide an interesting backdrop for your food and add the "wow" factor to your table.

THE DINNER PARTY

A few foolproof dishes, wine to match, and an easy dessert, and you've mastered the dinner party. The cooking need not be daunting to be impressive, especially when the food is plated with a stylist's eye for presentation or plattered attractively. Rustic is as appealing as refined; just make a decision about which way you want to go and stick with it. The whole idea is to cook good, simple food and present it in an appetizing way. Don't get caught up in performance cooking; make sure you spend more time than not at the table so you can focus on what's most important: good conversation and making it an evening to remember.

160   Planning a Dinner Party

Writing a menu may be the most important step in planning your party. First, take into account your guests' tastes: are there any "I don't eat red meat" people or "I don't like fish" types? It's easy enough to accommodate these requests, as long as you know in advance and can plan around them. Next, take the season into consideration. A heavy stew in August wouldn't be ideal, nor would a Caprese salad in January, when tomatoes are out of season. Go to the farmer's market or grocery store a week or so in advance of your party and see what looks good; it may just inspire your whole menu. Next, do some daydreaming about what you'd like to serve. Did you recently clip an intriguing recipe? Is there a theme or a concept that will help pull the party together? Your travels might inspire you, or a movie or a book. Find a hook, and then hang everything else on it. Put your ideas on paper, including as much detail as possible, so you can easily spot problems, such as clashes and repetitions, too many expensive ingredients, or timing disasters in the making. The most common mistake is setting yourself up for more work than you anticipated. Usually, the simpler the menu is, the more successful the meal will be, even for experienced cooks.

161   What's Wrong with These Menus?

Here are two examples of menus that may sound good but will set the hostess up for more trouble than success.

> **THE DINNER MENU**
> - Cheese soufflé
> - Braised lamb shanks
> - Potato gratin
> - Bibb salad with shallot vinaigrette
> - Chocolate mousse

Having a theme and making sure your flavors go well together is important, but this is a case of extreme repetition. Beginning with a cheese soufflé is a nice idea, but it's also a dish you will have to work around because having any additional egg or cheese on your menu will seem excessive. So instead of the gratin, plain buttered noodles would do nicely, and for dessert, a berry crumble or simple poached pears would lighten things up.

TRY THIS MENU INSTEAD

- Gougères (page 55)
- Boneless leg of lamb Provençal
- Roasted Fingerling Potatoes (page 153)
- Bibb salad with shallot vinaigrette
- Champagne-poached pears with chocolate sauce

Why it works: Instead of a heavy cheese soufflé, start the evening off on a French note by serving gougères, which is a fancy name for cheese puffs. These can be passed to your guests while they stand and sip an aperitif or wine. Follow with a well-balanced meat-and-potatoes menu that's not too heavy and doesn't repeat the richness of the gougères. A fruit dessert with a touch of luxury in the form of chocolate is the perfect finish.

ANOTHER DINNER MENU

- Warm onion focaccia
- Fennel and Parmigiano-Reggiano salad
- Twelve-hour pork shoulder roast with roasted Brussels sprouts and potatoes
- Apple crumble

Unless you're fortunate enough to have a professional range, or an extra oven, your kitchen can't make all this happen at once. Low-and-slow roasting is a great, inexpensive way to feed a crowd, and it requires very little hands-on work, but you have to plan around the fact that the meat will be dominating that oven all day. Since a roast like this requires a much lower cooking temperature than the other components in the meal, multitasking is going to be impossible. If you want to bake the dessert, choose something that will hold up better than a crumble, such as a cake, and make it the night before. For your side dishes, make use of your stovetop.

> **TRY THIS MENU INSTEAD**
> - Crudités with bagna cauda
> - Tuscan pot roast
> - Boiled Parsley Potatoes (page 154)
> - Lemon pots de crème

Why it works: Bagna cauda—literally, "warm bath"—is a nice way to liven up raw seasonal vegetables for a not-too-filling starter. Since it's a communal dish, you can serve it in the kitchen or living room before sitting down. The pot roast is even better if you make it the day before, and it anchors an elegant and homey fall or winter meal. Simple boiled potatoes look great on the side and are impossible to mess up. Lemon custards can be made ahead of time and just taken out of the fridge when it's time for dessert. With all that free oven space, you can throw in a last-minute roasted veggie or fruit, if you like.

162 Six Tips for the Budget-Conscious Cook

There are plenty of ways to serve comforting, soul-satisfying food without breaking the bank. You can coddle your guests and still stay within your budget. In fact, why not make it a challenge to stick to a budget? If you exceed it, you won't have to pack your knives and go, but at least you set some guidelines for yourself and saved some money in the process.

1. **Go with the grain.** When you eat out and plunk down $46 for a dry-aged rib eye, it feels like the restaurant must be making a killing. In fact, it's the $14 fettuccine dish you order that really makes the restaurateur happy. The price tag may be a lot less dramatic, but the profit is much greater, because pasta is so inexpensive. So, think like a chef—or better yet, a restaurant owner: rather than serve short ribs with noodles on the side, reverse the proportions and go for pasta with a short-rib ragù. Your guests won't feel cheated, that's for sure.

2. **Cheap meats are chic meats.** Luckily, many inexpensive cuts of meat, which are great for braising or slow roasting, have become very popular. In addition to being budget-friendly, cuts like oxtails, pork shoulder, and brisket require slow, long cooking, so they must be done in advance. That means that by the time the party starts, your work is done and you've saved a bundle.

3. **Tweak it, don't fake it.** If a dish calls for an expensive ingredient, there's often a way to alter it without resorting to inferior products. For example, Parmigiano-Reggiano is pricey, but the fake, pregrated stuff from the supermarket can truly bring down a dish. Instead, try to find Grana Padano (a less expensive hard, grainy cheese) or another authentic Italian cheese that will complement the flavors in whatever you're serving. It will alter the dish, but not for the worse.

4. **Let them bring wine.** When your friends ask if they can bring anything to your dinner party, say yes. Unless it's a formal dinner to impress your boss or celebrate your grandmother's birthday, let your guests contribute in small ways. If you can serve the wine they bring, you will save a lot of money. People like to contribute, and if you give them a little direction, everyone will be happy. If it's not appropriate or you don't want to mix different bottles, find a good wine store that will give you advice on an inexpensive bottle and a discount for buying a case.

5. **Time is money.** Small conveniences such as prewashed vegetables should be the first luxuries to go if you're determined to keep costs down. Just make sure to work these little chores into your schedule.

6. Special doesn't have to mean expensive. If you live in a city with interesting ethnic grocery stores, take advantage of ingredients that may be new and exciting to your friends, even if they're not fancy at all. For example, use labneh from a Middle Eastern store for a simple hors d'oeuvre, or build a salad around pickled watermelon rinds from a Russian market.

163   How to Break It Down

Break your menu down to a list of tasks. Rather than "Ropa Vieja with Roasted Peppers," think: marinate the beef, prep the peppers, and so on. List each component with equal weight; it's easy to underestimate how much time is required for small steps such as chopping parsley or making a vinaigrette. The sauce may very well require more hands-on attention and time than the main dish. Next, think about which things can be made fully ahead of time, and jot down a schedule for yourself, beginning with when to shop for your ingredients.

164   Three Tips to Keep You Sane

1. Make it ahead. Unless you're a very confident cook, avoid last-minute cooking at all costs. A frantic or absent chef does not put guests at ease. For many of us, salads and stews are saviors.

2. Cook what you know. The day of your party is not the time to practice something fancy you have never even tasted, let alone cooked. Your tried-and-true pot roast may not seem exciting to you, but a solid dish done well is always better than a flashy one gone awry.

3. Think like a chef (*mise en place*). Putting all of your ingredients in place before you start to cook (that's what *mise en place* means in French: "put in place") will keep your kitchen surfaces clean and neat and free for the next job, and will reduce your chances of making a mistake if you are following a recipe. Keep little bowls of everything you'll need, already chopped and measured, together on a plate or tray,

and all you have to do is add them in succession, not stop to read and measure—or worse, run to the store.

165 Making a Seating Arrangement

Unless the dining table is very small, people will most likely chat with those seated beside them. If it's up to us, we usually take a seat next to a friend or significant other, but it can be a wonderful thing to be gracefully nudged into getting acquainted with someone new. After all, countless romances and friendships date back to some distant dinner party. Creating a seating arrangement means having more control over (and therefore responsibility for) how the conversation flows at your party. A few ground rules can help you learn the art of matchmaking—romantic or not.

Start with yourself: If there is a head seat at the table, you should assume this position. If you're hosting the party with someone else, the two of you should anchor the table at opposite ends, not only because that's traditional but because you know all the guests and should be spread out in order to keep the conversation going. If there is no head or foot to the table, place yourself at a central position. If you'll need to leave the table several times to cook and serve, take that into consideration and take a seat that allows for smooth exits.

If there's a guest of honor, he or she should be seated next to one of the hosts. (At a traditional dinner hosted by a couple, the guest of honor would sit next to the host of the opposite sex.) It's not always necessary—or possible—to evenly integrate the sexes, but it is a good idea to avoid a cluster of men or women. This balancing act will give you the basic structure for the table; after that, it all depends on the individuals. It is traditional to separate couples, and the reasoning is the same: it gently forces people to talk to someone new. It is a particularly good idea when you are mixing couples with single friends, so the singles don't feel like third wheels. There are exceptions to the rule, and you'll have to judge for yourself when it's best to skip it, as in the case of a good friend bringing her boyfriend who doesn't know anyone else and might be shy, or even a couple who's been together forever but will be really annoyed to be separated; it just might not be worth the discomfort caused.

166   How to Let Guests Know Where to Sit

If you decide to use a seating arrangement, think of it as another opportunity for decorating the table. Pretty cards with your guests' names written in your best hand are always lovely. (A flat card can be propped between the tines of a dessert fork.) If you decide to use assigned seating at a casual gathering, have fun with it. If there's a theme to your event or meal, look for inspiration in that: for a summertime party at a beach house, or simply because you feel like serving clam chowder, write each guest's name on a shell or a stone, using a permanent marker. Seasonal fruit is another great base for a place card. Buy gift tags (or make them by punching holes in any card and running a ribbon through) and hang them on the stems of pears or apples. Name cards can also be incorporated into something edible, such as chocolates in a pouch or small box presented as a favor to take home. You needn't be exceedingly crafty to put together something cute. Just keep an open mind, and look for opportunities for personalizing the table.

167   *In Praise of* Menu Cards

Menu cards are a fun memento of an occasion and a meal, whether dashed off by hand on a nice piece of paper or typed on the computer and printed on heavy card stock or in letterpress, for very special occasions. Head off with the occasion (such as "Maya's Bridal Shower"), add the date, and then list each course. The language of

the menu should be simple and straightforward: "Corn Pudding with Blue Crab." Avoid pretentious restaurant-speak like "Flame-Licked Tomatoes" and "Free-Range [insert farm name here] Chicken." It's nice to give guests an idea of what's coming so they can pace themselves accordingly.

168 How to Ease the Way to Dinner: The Aperitif

A before-dinner drink, an aperitif is light and lively, with a low alcohol content (closer to that of wine than that of spirits) meant to whet the appetite and relax the palate for what's to come. An aperitif party can be easier on the hostess than a cocktail party is: aperitifs come ready to imbibe, no mix-mastering required.

Here are some of the most popular before-dinner drinks, along with simple serving directions. Most of the drinks hail from France and Italy, where aperitifs are a common way to start the meal. Aperitifs are less commonly served in the United States, but once you try them they may become part of your regular rotation.

- Lillet. A fortified, aromatized wine similar to vermouth but imbued with different aromatics. Serve chilled and poured into pretty little glasses over ice and garnished with a slice of orange. Lillet Blanc and Lillet Rouge are made in Bordeaux from the wines of the region. Combined with fruit liqueurs, they are especially pleasing in summer.

- Campari. The most continental of aperitifs, evoking Roman sidewalks and Sicilian sunsets. This simple and refreshing drink, with its bitter edge, is considered an acquired taste. Campari is often mixed into cocktails with soda water and ice.

- Cynar. An inky Italian libation somehow made from artichokes, but with a licorice bite. Cynar is poured over ice; top off with cola for the classic Cynar-cola if you like.

- Pernod. The quintessential French café aperitif. Pernod is poured over ice and combined with water (one part Pernod to five parts water). Absinthe, once banned for its wormwood, was the licorice-flavored inspiration for this French national drink.

THE DINNER PARTY

Five Dinner-Party Standby Menus

1. Tarragon Roasted Chicken (page 138) with blanched haricots verts (see page 162), Mashed Potatoes (page 152), and Peach Melba (page 172)

2. Lamb Tagine (page 140) with couscous and roasted carrots (see page 156), and Gelato with Chocolate Ganache (page 173)

3. Hoison-Glazed Salmon with Soba Noodles (page 142), snow peas (see page 157) with ginger and garlic, and Ambrosia Trifle (page 173)

4. Pork Tenderloin with Pomegranate Sauce (page 143) with braised fennel (see page 159), Potato Gratin (page 153), and Glazed Figs (page 173)

5. Roasted Filet of Beef (page 146) with Glazed Carrots (page 151), Sautéed Mushrooms (page 151), and Affogato (page 173)

How to Begin: The Art of the Salad

Starting your guests off with an appetite-whetting salad is a fairly standard approach to the dinner party, and it's also an easy, elegant way to show off your inner chef—no cooking required! Here are some sure crowd-pleasers. The dressing suggestions, given in italics, should be mixed at a ratio of 3 parts oil to 1 part acid, or closer to 2 to 1 if you like it acidic.

• Shaved fennel, baby arugula, grapefruit or orange segments, and pitted kalamata olives. *Citrus juice, extra-virgin olive oil, salt, and pepper.*

- Chopped escarole, thinly sliced radishes, and toasted rye croutons. *Dijon mustard, garlic, anchovy paste, freshly squeezed lemon juice, extra-virgin olive oil, salt, and pepper.*

- Shaved carrots and cucumbers, pea shoots, and dill sprigs. *Drizzle of vinegar, extra-virgin olive oil, salt, and pepper.*

- Sliced heirloom tomatoes, torn lettuce, shredded basil leaves, and sliced goat cheese. *Drizzle of extra-virgin olive oil, salt, and pepper.*

- Thinly sliced celery, celery leaves, sliced pickled or cooked beets, thinly sliced pear, chopped walnuts, and thinly sliced blue cheese. *Drizzle of extra-virgin olive oil, freshly squeezed lemon juice, salt, and pepper.*

- Shredded Brussels sprouts and cooked crumbled bacon. *Plain yogurt drink, red wine vinegar, chopped chives, salt, pepper, and extra-virgin olive oil.*

RECIPE: *Tarragon Roasted Chicken*

There is no better way to show your love than serving a delicious and fragrant roasted chicken, perfect for almost any occasion. A flavorful rub under the skin and a lovely pan gravy elevates roasted chicken from simple to special.

SERVES 6 TO 8

- Preheat the oven to 400°F. Rinse and dry **two 3½- to 4-pound chickens.** Remove and discard the giblets and any excess fat. Set the chickens aside.

- Combine **6 tablespoons (¾ stick) softened unsalted butter** with **¼ cup chopped fresh tarragon leaves; 1 shallot, finely minced; 1½ teaspoons salt;** and **½ teaspoon pepper** in a small bowl and mix well with a wooden spoon.

- Loosen the skin of the breast portion of the chickens by sliding your hands under it, from both ends. Smear the butter mixture all over the breast portion of each chicken, using half of it for each bird. Season the cavities liberally with **salt** and **pepper,** and place a **lemon half** in each one. Tie the legs together, and tuck the wing tips under the body. Rub **2 tablespoons softened butter** all over the skin, and season with **salt and pepper.** The chickens can be prepared to this point up to one day in advance and refrigerated.

- Slice **2 medium onions** into ½-inch-thick slices. In a large roasting pan, like the one you would use for a turkey, or two smaller roasting pans, create a "rack" for each chicken by arranging the onion slices close together for each chicken to sit on. If using one large roasting pan, evenly space the onion "racks" so the chickens will have plenty of space around them. Place a chicken on each "rack," their feet pointing in opposite directions.

- Place the chickens in the oven to roast. After 20 minutes, reduce the oven temperature to 350°F. Baste the chickens, and continue basting every 15 minutes or so, reversing the pan position each

time. Roast until an instant-read thermometer reads 165°F when inserted into the area where the leg meets the body, 1 hour and 15 minutes to 1 hour and 30 minutes. The legs should feel slightly loose, and the juices will run clear.

• Transfer the chickens to a platter to rest while you make the sauce. Pour off the fat from the roasting pan, keeping the onions in the pan. Use a paper towel to blot any additional grease from the pan. Place the roasting pan over one or two burners and turn the heat to medium. Pour in ¾ **cup white wine,** and bring to a boil. Scrape up the brown bits from the pan with a wooden spoon. Reduce by half, and add 1 **cup chicken stock.** Bring to a boil, and strain into a small saucepan, pressing down on the solids in the strainer before discarding them.

• Whisk in 1 **tablespoon Dijon mustard** and 2 **tablespoons heavy cream (optional).** Reduce over high heat until slightly thickened, about 10 minutes. Stir in 1 **tablespoon chopped tarragon,** and season to taste with **salt and pepper.**

• Carve the chicken into serving pieces and arrange on a warm platter. Serve the sauce on the side.

RECIPE: *Lamb Tagine*

Sometimes a slightly exotic dish makes perfect dinner-party fare. Lamb tagine fits the bill, and since it can easily be made a day or two ahead, it's easy on the hostess, too. Even if you don't own an earthenware tagine to serve it in, you can still put your guests in a Moroccan state of mind.

SERVES 8

- Preheat the oven to 325°F. Pat dry **3 pounds lamb stew meat.**

- In a small bowl, combine 1 **teaspoon ground coriander, 1 teaspoon ground cumin, ½ teaspoon paprika, 1 teaspoon salt,** and **½ teaspoon pepper.** Stir well and coat the meat with the spice mixture.

- Heat a Dutch oven over medium-high heat and add 1 **tablespoon olive oil.** Add half of the meat, and brown lightly on all sides,

5 to 7 minutes. Transfer to a plate and repeat with the remaining meat, using an additional 1 **tablespoon olive oil.**

- Return the first batch of meat to the Dutch oven. Thinly slice **2 medium onions** lengthwise, and add to the pot along with **2 cinnamon sticks, 2 teaspoons freshly grated ginger, a pinch of cayenne pepper, 1 large clove garlic, finely grated,** and **1 tablespoon tomato paste.**

- Add **3 to 4 cups water,** or enough to almost cover the meat, stir well, and bring to a simmer on top of the stove. Cover with a tight-fitting lid, and transfer to the oven.

- Cook for approximately 1½ hours, or until the meat yields to gentle pressure with a fork and feels completely tender. Gently scoop the meat and onions into a large bowl using a slotted spoon. Discard the cinnamon sticks. Degrease the liquid either by skimming with a ladle or pouring it into a fat separator and returning to the pot. Add 1 **cup dried apricots** to the liquid, and simmer over medium heat until slightly thickened, 10 to 12 minutes.

- Return the meat to the pot and coat the meat well with the sauce, heating it thoroughly. If making ahead of time, let cool and refrigerate until close to serving time. Reheat gently in the oven or on the stovetop over medium-low heat.

- Heat a small pan over medium-low heat. Add **2 teaspoons butter** and ½ **cup almonds, roughly chopped,** and cook, stirring frequently, until golden brown. Serve the tagine over cooked couscous with the almonds and **chopped fresh flat-leaf parsley** over top.

RECIPE: *Hoisin-Glazed Salmon with Soba Noodles* ·······························

If you know you're serving fish-eaters, salmon is a safe choice, since most people like it. Despite the simplicity of preparation, this dish will impress your guests.

SERVES 8

- Combine ½ cup hoisin sauce, 2 tablespoons freshly squeezed lime juice, 1 large clove garlic, finely grated, and 2 teaspoons honey in a small bowl. Combine thoroughly and set aside.

- Cook one 8-ounce package soba noodles according to package directions. Drain and rinse the noodles. Lightly dress with **toasted sesame oil** and **soy sauce**. Set aside.

- Preheat the oven to 425°F. Season **8 skinless salmon fillets** with **salt and pepper** and lightly coat with oil. Heat a large nonstick sauté pan over medium-high heat. Add **1 teaspoon vegetable or peanut oil** and arrange 4 salmon fillets in the pan. Sauté until golden, 2 to 3 minutes on each side. Transfer to a large rimmed baking sheet and repeat with the remaining salmon.

- Brush the hoisin glaze evenly over the salmon fillets. The salmon can be prepared ahead to this point. Store in the refrigerator until shortly before ready to cook.

- Place the salmon in the oven and cook for 10 to 12 minutes, or until the desired doneness is reached, basting with the glaze several times.

- Serve with room-temperature soba noodles and sautéed baby bok choy. Sprinkle toasted sesame seeds over the top.

174 RECIPE: *Pork Tenderloin with Pomegranate Sauce*

Pork tenderloin is an inexpensive cut of meat that is available everywhere, is easy and fast to cook, and dresses up nicely with ruby-red sauce made from pomegranate juice and demi-glace. Store-bought demi-glace or glace de viande is the best way to approximate the flavor of a restaurant sauce at home. It can be found in fancy food stores either as a thick concentrate or frozen. If you want to make this dish partially ahead of time, sear the meat as directed in the second step, then deglaze the pan and complete the sauce. Bring the meat back to room temperature for about 30 minutes before roasting and serving.

SERVES 8

- Preheat the oven to 375°F. Trim any excess fat and silverskin from 4 **pork tenderloins** (about 1 pound each) and tie them with butcher's twine, to hold their round shape during cooking. Season with **salt and pepper**.

- Bring 2 **cups pomegranate juice** to a simmer in a small saucepan over medium heat, and simmer until it is reduced to a syrupy consistency, about 20 minutes. Set the pan aside.

- Heat a large ovenproof skillet, preferably cast iron, over medium-high heat. Add 1 **tablespoon olive oil** and heat until hot. Place 2 of the tenderloins in the pan and sear well on all sides, about 10 minutes. Transfer to a rimmed baking sheet. Repeat with the remaining tenderloins, using an additional 1 **tablespoon oil.** Transfer to the baking sheet.

- Roast the meat in the oven until the internal temperature reaches 130°F, about 20 minutes. Transfer to a plate, loosely tented with foil, to rest while you finish the sauce.

- While the meat is resting, finish the sauce: add ½ **cup dry red wine** and 1 **minced shallot** to the skillet, bring to a simmer over high heat, stirring with a wooden spoon to loosen brown bits, and simmer until the wine is reduced by half, about 5 minutes. Add 1 **cup demi-glace** (1 tablespoon reconstituted with 1 cup water or 1 cup thawed) and 1 **sprig of thyme** and reduce until the mixture is thick and syrupy, about 8 minutes. Strain the sauce through a fine sieve into the pomegranate syrup. Season to taste with **salt and pepper** and bring to a boil. Remove from the heat and stir in 1 **to 2 tablespoons cold unsalted butter,** to give the sauce body.

- Slice the pork into 2-inch lengths. Stand 3 pieces of pork on end, closely touching, on each of 8 warm plates. Pour a bit of sauce over the meat, and top with a few **pomegranate seeds.** Serve immediately with Potato Gratin (page 153) and braised fennel (see page 159).

175 TIP: **Filet for the Masses**

Filet mignon is easy to cook and always pleases. Though it's pricey, a good deal can be had if you shop at a warehouse-style butcher. Remove the piece of very marbled meat called the "chain" that's attached, and any large pieces of fat, or the shiny "silverskin." Even after the trimming, you'll be paying less pound for pound than if you had bought from a custom butcher.

Once you've removed the chain, there are a number of things you can do with it, keeping in mind that it is a tougher piece of meat than the tenderloin itself. Trim out any large pieces of fat, and then grind it for burgers, cut it into small pieces and marinate it for a stir-fry, pound it thin and make Philly cheesesteaks, or braise it as a substitute for the short ribs in the recipe on page 215.

176 Always Let the Meat Rest

Letting meat rest after cooking it is very important. If you cut into it right after removing it from the heat, the juices will run out, and the meat will be much drier than if you waited about 10 minutes. Your patience will be rewarded as the juices thicken and the temperature of the meat evens out. (You can loosely cover it with aluminum foil if you're concerned about it staying hot.) So resist the urge to cut into a piece of meat in order to check its doneness. Use a meat thermometer (see page 27) or get familiar with how firm different types of meat should feel to the touch when they're cooked the way you like them.

As long as you have a carnivorous crowd, it's hard to go wrong serving a whole beef tenderloin. It's expensive, yes, but it's also incredibly easy and fast to cook—just be vigilant to avoid overcooking by using an instant-read thermometer (see page 27). Serve with simple Glazed Carrots (page 151) and Sautéed Mushrooms (page 151), and you'll have a classic pairing that always pleases.

SERVES 8

- Preheat the oven to 375°F. Rub **one 3-pound filet of beef** with **olive oil.** Season on all sides with **salt and pepper.**

- Heat a large ovenproof skillet, preferably cast iron, over high heat and sear the meat on all sides until well browned, about 10 minutes. Transfer the skillet to the oven and roast for 15 to 20 minutes, or until the internal temperature reaches 130°F for medium-rare. Transfer to a cutting board and let rest for 10 minutes.

- Meanwhile, sweat **2 shallots, minced,** and **1 thyme sprig** in **1 tablespoon butter** in a small saucepan over low heat until the shallots are translucent and tender. Add **½ cup dry red wine** and simmer until reduced by half. Strain through a fine sieve and return the sauce to the saucepan. Add **½ cup heavy cream** and simmer over low heat until reduced to a velvety sauce.

- Slice the meat and serve with the sauce drizzled over it.

A Menu Timeline: Timing Your Tasks

THE MENU

- Pork Tenderloin with Pomegranate Sauce (page 143)
- Braised fennel (see page 159)
- Potato Gratin (page 153)
- Glazed Figs (page 173)

HOW TO GET IT DONE

The morning of your party:
- Sear the pork and refrigerate. (Work through step 3 of Pork Tenderloin with Pomegranate Sauce.)
- Make the first part of the pomegranate sauce and refrigerate. (Work through step 2 of Pork Tenderloin with Pomegranate Sauce.)

One and a half hours before serving:
- Take the pork out of the refrigerator to return it to room temperature; this should take about 30 minutes.
- Prepare the Potato Gratin for baking.

One hour before serving:
- Put the gratin in the upper third of the oven to bake.

- After the gratin has been baking for 25 minutes, put the pork in the lower third of the oven to finish roasting.
- Meanwhile, make the braised fennel on top of the stove. When finished, cover the pan to keep it warm until serving time.
- When the gratin and pork are done, turn off the oven. Loosely cover the gratin and return to the oven to keep warm. Transfer the pork to a plate to rest at room temperature. Place the dinner plates in the oven to warm.

Ten minutes before serving:
- Finish the sauce for the pork. (Work through step 5 of Pork Tenderloin with Pomegranate Sauce.)
- Slice the figs and set out the dessert ingredients.
- Slice the pork and arrange plates as shown.

Ten minutes before you want to serve dessert:
- Broil the figs, make the sauce, and plate the dessert.

179   *Flourish and Flair*: Carve a Boneless Roast

Any boneless roast, whether it's a loin (or tenderloin) of pork or veal or a filet of beef, is easy to slice. First let the roast rest (don't forget this important step: after cooking, let the roast rest for 10 minutes, loosely tented with foil). Remove any twine used for trussing. Transfer the meat to a carving board with a well or a small edge to catch the juices, and carry it to the table along with your carving fork and knife. Hold the roast in place with the back of a carving fork or a regular fork (try not to actually pierce the meat) and begin slicing against the grain with long, even strokes, as if you were sawing something, or, more poetically, playing a violin. Don't think about pressing down; the back-and-forth motion and a sharp knife will result in effortless carving.

Knowing When the Meat Is Done

Use an instant-read thermometer to check for doneness, but don't check too often, as piercing will let the juices run out. Use your recipe as a guideline, and when you think it is approaching doneness, do the deed. Remember that the temperature will continue to rise as the meat rests—as much as 10°F—so always err on the underdone side. Use this handy chart as a guide.

MEAT	DONENESS	TEMPURATURE	DESCRIPTION
Beef, lamb, veal steaks, roasts, and chops	Rare	120 to 125°F	Cool, bright red center, pink near exterior, soft
	Medium rare	130 to 135°F	Warm red center, slightly brown toward exterior, firmer than rare
	Medium	140 to 145°F	Pink center, brown toward exterior, firm
	Medium well	150 to 155°F	Barely pink in center, very firm
	Well done	160°F and above	No pink in center, brown throughout
Chicken and turkey	Done	165°F	Juices run clear, legs will feel loose when wiggled
Pork roasts and chops	Medium (recommended)	145°F	Pale pink in center

TIP: **How to Unstick Food from a Pan**

We've all been there: ready to flip a fish fillet or a seared chicken thigh only to find its skin superglued to the surface of the hot pan. Jimmying your spatula under the food will most likely result in tearing the skin from the meat, or, depending on how delicate the item is, destroying it altogether. Usually, the answer is to let steam do the work for you. If you cover the pan and turn off the heat for a minute, moisture will get trapped around the food and help it release from the pan, undamaged. The same is true for starchy things like rice and even eggs. So, take a deep breath and back away from the stove.

182 How to Plan Side Dishes

Sides can be incredibly simple and straightforward and still complement the star player perfectly. Aim for providing contrasting flavors and textures, and color as well. Think of something cooling to counter something hot (fluffy jasmine rice with a spicy shrimp stir-fry), or something crunchy alongside something comfortingly soft (a green bean vinaigrette with a braised brisket). Also, for your own sake, plan to make only one labor-intensive dish (if any!), and balance that one with easy side-dish preparations to play the supporting role.

183 How to Serve Pasta as a Side Dish

Pasta can be served as a small first course, as in Italy, or as a more substantial entrée. (The Italian-American restaurant-style side of spaghetti with tomato sauce is outdated; unless your theme is "Little Italy," it's something to avoid.) But egg noodles or tiny pasta, such as orzo, simply buttered and sprinkled with parsley and maybe Parmigiano-Reggiano cheese, can be a great accompaniment, especially for saucy braised-meat dishes. Think of it as a stand-in for potatoes.

RECIPE: *Glazed Carrots* ···································

Bunched carrots are often sweeter and fresher than bagged carrots, but 6 to 8 thin bagged carrots can be used instead.

SERVES 8

- Peel and rinse **1 bunch of carrots.** Cut on the bias into 2-inch lengths and place in a small saucepan with **1 tablespoon butter, 2 teaspoons water,** and **salt and pepper.**

- Cover and cook over medium-low heat, stirring occasionally, until just tender when pierced with the tip of a paring knife, 8 to 10 minutes.

- Remove the cover, turn the heat to high, and cook until the liquid has evaporated, 1 to 2 minutes. Toss the carrots to glaze evenly, and serve.

RECIPE: *Sautéed Mushrooms* ···································

This simple preparation can be made with white button mushrooms instead of the creminis.

SERVES 8

- Wash and trim the stems from **10 ounces cremini mushrooms.** Cut the mushrooms in half.

- Heat a large sauté pan over high heat. Add **1 teaspoon olive oil** and **2 teaspoons butter.** Add the mushrooms, tossing to coat. Season with **salt and pepper,** and continue cooking until well browned all over, tossing frequently, 8 to 10 minutes.

THE DINNER PARTY

One Potato, Two Potato, Three Potato, Four

Here are four great classic potato dishes you shouldn't be without. If you're not sure what to pair with your main course, chances are one of these will be perfect. Think about what will best complement what you are serving. Pair the creamy gratin with something not too rich. Use mashed potatoes when there's a delicious, meaty sauce to catch. Parsley potatoes always look retro chic and are perfect with flaky white fish or a simple grilled steak. Roasted potatoes are a crowd-pleaser, and they go with almost anything; you can even serve them as an hors d'oeuvre accompanied by a spicy mayonnaise dip.

1. Mashed Potatoes

SERVES 4

- Cut 1¾ pounds Yukon Gold potatoes in half. Place them in a medium saucepan, add **water** to cover by 1 inch and 1 **teaspoon salt**, and bring to a boil over high heat. Reduce to a simmer and cook until the potatoes are easily pierced with a knife, about 20 minutes. Drain.

- As soon as the potatoes are cool enough to handle, peel them. Push the potatoes through a ricer or food mill back into the saucepan, or mash with a masher in the pan.

- Heat 1 **cup milk** in a small saucepan or in the microwave. Add **2 tablespoons unsalted butter**, ¾ **teaspoon salt (or to taste)**, and ¼ **teaspoon pepper** to the potatoes, then add as much of the milk as needed to create the desired consistency, stirring until well combined.

2. Potato Gratin

SERVES 6

- Preheat the oven to 375°F. Combine 1½ cups heavy cream, 1 sprig of thyme, and 2 garlic cloves in a small saucepan and bring to just under a boil. Remove from the heat.

- Thinly slice 2 pounds russet (baking) potatoes. Spread one third of the potatoes evenly in a buttered 2-quart gratin dish or 6 individual baking dishes. Dot the potatoes with butter, season with salt and pepper, and sprinkle with ¼ cup freshly grated Parmigiano-Reggiano (or divide the cheese evenly over the individual baking dishes).

- Repeat twice, to make 3 layers of potatoes. Pour the warm cream over the potatoes.

- Bake for 35 to 45 minutes, or until bubbling and brown.

3. Roasted Fingerling Potatoes

SERVES 4

- Preheat the oven to 425°F. Wash and dry 1½ pounds fingerling potatoes. Halve larger potatoes, and leave small ones whole, so they are uniform in size.

- In a large bowl, toss the potatoes with 1 tablespoon olive oil, ½ teaspoon salt, ¼ teaspoon pepper, 1 tablespoon chopped fresh rosemary, and 4 or 5 unpeeled garlic cloves.

• Spray a large rimmed baking sheet with **cooking spray** or coat it with **olive oil.** Spread the potatoes on the baking sheet, cut side down, and roast until tender and golden brown, about 20 minutes.

4. Boiled Parsley Potatoes

SERVES 4

• Wash **1½ pounds baby red potatoes.** Using a vegetable peeler or a paring knife, remove a strip of peel, like a belt, from each potato. Place the potatoes in a medium saucepan and add enough water to cover them by 1 inch. Add **1 teaspoon salt,** and bring to a boil over high heat. Reduce the heat and simmer the potatoes for 10 to 15 minutes, or until tender when pierced with a knife. Drain.

• Gently toss the potatoes with 2 **tablespoons unsalted butter,** 2 tablespoons finely chopped fresh flat-leaf parsley, and **salt and pepper to taste.**

A Guide to Roasting, Sautéing, Braising, and Blanching Veggies

These are the most basic techniques for cooking a variety of vegetables in the simplest, most optimal way. Use the suggestions following each entry to embellish as you see fit; just don't use all of them at once!

ROASTING

Starchy or fibrous vegetables are best for roasting. Because by nature they are drier than leafy vegetables, root vegetables are successfully cooked with dry heat, rather than steamed or boiled. Sautéing is tricky because they are so dense and require a long cooking time. In the oven, they can achieve the perfect balance of browned, even crisp, outsides and soft, creamy insides. Roasting is a very simple way to make very satisfying, beautiful side dishes. Be sure to turn the vegetables toward the end; they will be golden on all sides.

Preheat the oven to 425°F. Toss the vegetables with olive oil, salt, and pepper. A rimmed baking sheet (nonstick is a plus) is ideal for most roasting, but you can use a roasting pan or a cast-iron skillet. Large vegetables will cook much faster and have more caramelized surface area per bite if they are cut into smaller pieces, but be mindful to cut the pieces to a uniform size so they cook evenly. And don't crowd the pan, or you will create steam and end up with less brown and more mush. This is essential: there should be just one layer of vegetables with some space around each piece. The cut vegetables should be placed cut side down to start so they get nice and brown.

Baby Eggplant: To roast, cut small eggplant lengthwise in half, large ones into chunks. Cook for 13 to 15 minutes, cut side down, or until brown and tender. *Cook with* garlic. *Finish with* mint or parsley and tahini, or with Sriracha, sesame seeds, and sesame oil. *Serve with* Asian-style grilled marinated beef or lamb, or in a tomato sauce with pasta.

THE DINNER PARTY

Brussels Sprouts: To roast, cut in half if large. Cook for 20 to 25 minutes, turning after 15 minutes. *Cook with* shallots. *Finish with* walnut oil, toasted walnuts or pine nuts, and crisp crumbled bacon. *Serve with* turkey or chicken.

Cauliflower: To roast, cut into bite-size pieces. Cook for 20 to 25 minutes, gently stirring or flipping after 10 minutes. *Cook with* unpeeled garlic cloves. *Finish with* raisins, capers, bread crumbs, and freshly grated Parmigiano-Reggiano. *Serve with* pot roast, veal chops, or steak.

Celeriac and Turnips: To roast, cut into wedges. Cook for 30 minutes, turning after 20 minutes. Cook with garlic, thyme, and sliced onions. Finish with parsley. Serve with braised meat or chicken.

Parsnips and Carrots: To roast, peel and cut lengthwise in half. Cook for 30 minutes, gently stirring or turning after 20 minutes. *Cook with* fresh thyme sprigs. *Finish with* nutmeg. *Serve with* braised or roasted beef or lamb, or roasted chicken.

SAUTÉING

To sauté means to cook in a skillet with some fat. Most often, you sauté veggies that don't require an extended cooking time. Many vegetables will wilt, creating a bit of steam as they break down. Anything you sauté will pick up the flavor of whatever it's cooked with, such as the oil or butter you're using and any garlic, onions, or herbs you throw in the skillet.

The trick to sautéing is regulating the heat. A very hot skillet can get some color on your vegetables, which you may want in some cases—for example, if you're cooking small peppers that you want to stay crisp but become brown in some spots. Generally, though, your flame should be somewhere in the medium range. A very hot pan can burn your food before it cooks through, turn butter into a smoky disaster, or send grease flying dangerously. If the heat is too low, your vegetables may absorb a lot of fat without getting cooked. Taste things as you go, and stay involved, trusting your judgment to adjust the flame as needed.

Leafy greens such as spinach, kale, and chard will cook down to a fraction of their original volume. This means you should always make more than what looks like enough, and keep in mind that your

seasonings will be concentrated: a giant pinch of salt may look like the right amount when you begin but will result in overly salty greens.

Mushrooms: Depending on the type and size, slice them or quarter them. *Cook with* shallots or garlic, thyme or rosemary. *Finish with* tarragon, parsley, or chives. *Serve with* steak, mashed potatoes, chicken, or fettuccine with Parmigiano-Reggiano.

Snow Peas: Snip off the stem end. *Cook with* garlic, scallions, shallots, or sliced ginger. *Finish with* sesame oil, sesame seeds, grated lemon zest, and soy sauce. *Serve with* grilled fish, or chicken paillards.

Swiss Chard: Separate the leaves from the stems, chop the stems into 1-inch pieces, and roughly chop the leaves. Cook the stems a few minutes longer than the leaves. *Cook with* garlic and onions. *Finish with* crisp pancetta, freshly squeezed lemon juice, and red pepper flakes. *Serve with* pasta, roasted meat, fish—anything you would serve spinach with.

Yellow Squash and Zucchini: Slice into ¼-inch-thick half-moons. *Cook with* cherry tomatoes and basil or thyme. *Finish with* Parmigiano-Reggiano and toasted sliced almonds. *Serve with* grilled meat, chicken, fish, eggs, or pasta.

BRAISING

Although this is a method we most often associate with meat, braising—cooking at a relatively low temperature for a long time, covered and with liquid in the pot—makes for delectably saucy, tender vegetables. Braising is the wet counterpart to roasting, and, like roasting, is best for fibrous vegetables; but you should reserve this approach for veggies with some water content, such as cabbage and fennel. They do well in a steamy pan but require more cooking time than greens like spinach, which wilt immediately over heat.

Before adding the liquid, brown the vegetables over high heat on the stove, just as you would sear a beef roast before pouring the wine or tomatoes into the pot; your veggies will really shine if they get some color before the braise. Start with a large, heavy pan over medium-high heat. Melt 1 teaspoon butter with 1 teaspoon olive oil in the pan. Season the vegetables with salt and pepper and add them to the pan, placing them cut side down for maximum browning. Press them down gently with a spatula if necessary to ensure good contact with the hot pan.

When they have browned, turn the heat down and pour in the liquid. The vegetables shouldn't be submerged; the liquid should come about halfway up on the food. And the liquid should be at a simmer, not boiling. Cover the pan and let the braise begin.

As for the braising liquid, there's more room to play with the flavors: you can use any kind of stock, tomato puree, wine, or a combination of flavorful liquids, including some fruit juice—and the liquid you are left with in the end should by no means be wasted. If your veggies are finished cooking, lift them out of the pan with tongs or a slotted spoon and boil the remaining liquid, uncovered, to reduce it to a sauce. Keep in mind when seasoning that the flavors will become concentrated as the liquid cooks down.

Belgian Endive: To braise, cut 2 endives lengthwise in half. Brown, cut side down, for about 5 minutes. Flip and repeat on the round side, about 2 minutes. Add ½ cup chicken or vegetable stock, cover, and cook for about 20 minutes. *Cook with* orange juice, balsamic vinegar, or chicken or vegetable stock. *Finish with* grated orange zest, bacon, hazelnuts, nut oil, Parmigiano-Reggiano, or parsley. *Serve with* roasted chicken, roasted fish (such as halibut), or grilled salmon.

Fennel: To braise, trim 3 medium fennel bulbs and cut lengthwise into quarters, keeping the core intact so the wedges stay whole. Brown on all sides for 2 to 3 minutes per side. Add ½ cup chicken or vegetable stock, cover, and simmer for 20 to 25 minutes. *Cook with* sliced shallots, garlic, orange juice, and chestnuts (fresh or from a jar). *Finish with* shaved Parmigiano-Reggiano, fennel fronds, or parsley. *Serve with* sausages or fish, such as whole branzino.

Leeks: To braise, trim the roots and dark green portions off 3 leeks. Cut lengthwise in half and wash. Brown the leeks cut side down, in olive oil, in a skillet, for about 4 minutes. Flip and brown for about 2 minutes. Add ½ cup stock, lower the heat to a simmer, cover, and cook for 9 to 12 minutes, or until the leeks are tender and the liquid has thickened to a glaze. *Cook with* bacon or thyme. *Serve with* goat cheese, roasted tomatoes, shrimp, lobster, clams, eggs, or pork tenderloin.

Savoy Cabbage: To braise, trim any tough or dark outer leaves from 1 head of cabbage and cut into 6 to 8 wedges. Brown for 2 minutes on each cut side. Add ½ cup stock and simmer, covered, for 9 to 12 minutes, or until tender. *Cook with* pickling spices (tied in cheesecloth), bacon lardons, star anise, and soy sauce. *Finish with* crumbled bacon, thinly sliced apples, or butter. *Serve with* corned beef, braised meat, pork chops, or ham.

BLANCHING

Blanching, which is boiling vegetables very briefly in salted water, is an important technique. Blanching is generally useful for hardy, fibrous vegetables that would take a long time to sauté from raw or that you want to leave crisp. Blanching brings out the vibrant green of broccoli or string beans but leaves them firm and crisp enough to go into a sauté pan, where they will get more flavor, or into a salad, to be simply dressed with a vinaigrette.

The keys to successful blanching are to salt the water generously and to have an ice bath ready to "shock" the veggies. Fill a bowl with ice and cold water and leave it in the sink, waiting while you blanch. When the veggies are done, drain them and submerge them quickly in the ice water. This will stop them from cooking (or overcooking) and ensure that the bright green color doesn't fade to gray. Keep in mind that you'll want some time to dry the vegetables before throwing them into a salad or a hot skillet. But blanching and shocking can be done ahead of time, so the clever hostess has only to worry about the finishing flavors at the last minute.

Asparagus: To blanch, snap off the tough bottoms and boil the spears for 1 to 3 minutes, depending on thickness. Shock in an ice bath. *Finish with* lemon juice and/or grated zest, chopped almonds, butter, parsley, or truffle oil. *Serve with* lamb or grilled fish or in salads or risotto.

Broccoli Rabe: To blanch, trim the thickest stems and boil for 2 to 3 minutes; shock in an ice bath. *Sauté with* garlic, olive oil, red pepper flakes, and caramelized onions. *Serve with* sausages, or in pasta with ricotta and Parmigiano-Reggiano.

Broccoli Florets: To blanch, boil for 1 to 2 minutes; shock in an ice bath. *Finish with* ground cumin, garlic, red pepper flakes, soy sauce, or sesame seeds. *Serve in* salads or pasta dishes, or on crudité platters.

Haricots Verts or Green Beans:
To blanch, boil haricots verts (thin French beans) for 1 minute, and thick string beans for 2 minutes. Shock in an ice bath. *Finish with* caramelized shallots, sautéed garlic, vinaigrette, lemon and olive oil, parsley, crumbled blue cheese, chopped walnuts, walnut oil, or pesto. *Serve with* salmon, roasted chicken, or boiled potatoes, or in pasta salads.

188 How to Use Frozen Vegetables

In the right way, and at the right time, there is absolutely nothing wrong with using certain frozen vegetables, and they can save a lot of time, space, and money without sacrificing flavor.

- Peas. Unless you buy and cook fresh peas (just-picked from a farmer's market) the same day, you're better off using frozen. Their sugar starts converting to starch the moment they are picked, which is why frozen peas are so consistently and reliably sweet and tender—any time of year. Shelling peas is also one of the more time-consuming tasks in the kitchen, with a pretty low yield for the amount of time you put in. Shelled frozen peas should be cooked only briefly; they shrivel and lose color and flavor quickly.

- Spinach. Frozen spinach is sometimes more practical than fresh, like when making a Greek spinach pie, a spinach lasagna, or a spinach soufflé. You would need a whole refrigerator full of fresh spinach for some of these dishes because it cooks down so dramatically. Not only do you lose a lot of volume during cooking, but you then have to squeeze all the liquid out after it is cooked, turning an armload of fresh spinach into a fistful! The best way to use frozen spinach in a recipe is to defrost it, not cook it, and then set it in a colander to drain. Squeeze the liquid out before using.

189 *In Praise of* The Spider

A spider, traditionally used in Chinese dumpling houses to retrieve dumplings from hot oil baths without taking the molten fat with them, is a cross between a slotted spoon and a mesh strainer. Spiders come in handy for myriad tasks and often eliminate the step of straining. Short pastas can be scooped from boiling water and tossed directly into a pan with sauce; and blanched greens can be transferred straight to an ice bath, leaving the boiling water in the pot for the next batch.

190 Cooking Vegetables *en Papillote*

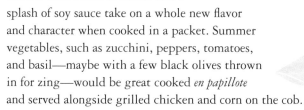

This cooking method, which translates to "in parchment," simply means to steam food inside a little package, either alone or in enticing mixtures, and it is a great way to prepare vegetables as well as fish (see page 223). Mushrooms cooked with a hint of butter and a splash of soy sauce take on a whole new flavor and character when cooked in a packet. Summer vegetables, such as zucchini, peppers, tomatoes, and basil—maybe with a few black olives thrown in for zing—would be great cooked *en papillote* and served alongside grilled chicken and corn on the cob. Just keep in mind that some vegetables will cook faster than others. If you're combining different veggies, choose ones that will cook at similar rates, or cut those hardier items smaller to even out the timing. Always include something aromatic in the packet, such as herbs, shallots, garlic, or olives, so the flavors can be suffused throughout. When the packet has puffed up and you can hear a sizzle, it's done.

191 How to Flatter the Food

The best-dressed people in the world don't just follow fashion trends; they have an individual look that suits them. The same is true when it comes to a great hostess and the way she serves food. It's not about spending a lot of money; more expensive platters don't guarantee that the food will look beautiful. Sure, you might invest in some special pieces, like a silver bowl or fancy glassware, but all that matters is that the food look enticing and inviting, which can be achieved with even the humblest serving pieces. Put the bread in a basket you found for a nickel at a tag sale, lined with a cute napkin that belonged to your mother, and the whole thing could look great. Your platters don't have to match one another, either. In fact, using mismatched china can be quite charming. If it looks great to you, try it out, and if it's not working, keep experimenting. If you entertain often, collect serving pieces that strike your fancy over the years—whether it's vintage ironstone from a flea market or a mother-of-pearl caviar spoon from the fanciest boutique in town—and bring them out when you entertain.

192 Plating vs. Family-Style

At a modern dinner party, there are no strict rules about when to plate the food and when to pass serving platters around the table. Generally, if your party is meant to feel more formal, you should plate the food and take each course to the table, but remember that this will take you away from the table before each course to do the plating and then again to deliver all the plates to the guests (this may be a good reason to enlist outside help; see "Calling for Backup," entry 27). If you want to wow your guests with a beautiful plate but a more casual atmosphere is what you're going for, then serving family-style will be just the ticket. To serve family-style, consider logistics: Is there room on the table for the serving platters without crowding your guests? Are you serving something from a hot or heavy vessel that will be difficult for folks to pass? Often, a combination of plating and passing works best. Try plating a first course, especially one that is to be served cold or at room temperature (which means you can get it done ahead of time). Then serve the rest of the meal family-style, to strike a balance between informality and artful presentation.

193 Plating the Food for a Formal Dinner Party

Here are some guidelines to follow.

PLACEMENT
If you're serving a traditional main course, with meat or fish as the main component and starch and vegetables to the side, place the protein at the bottom center of the plate (six o'clock, from the perspective of the eater). This may not be a rule most people would consciously recognize, but it is the natural—and customary—place.

THE PLATE
When choosing which plate to use, think of it as a canvas. A dainty appetizer can look elegant placed right in the center of the dish, with some space around it. For a main course, though, the plates should look abundant, without being sloppy. Avoid a lot of negative space between different elements of the meal.

ASSEMBLY LINE
If there are several finishing touches to your meal, or a lot of plates to make up, enlist a friend or a family member to help you get everything out to the table in a timely manner. One person might heap the linguine into the bowls while the other makes sure each serving has roughly the same number of clams and a pinch of parsley, and wipes the edges of the bowl with a towel if necessary. Perhaps the most important part of plating is to make it happen quickly, so everyone receives his or her food within a minute of one another, and at the right temperature. Save the least attractive (or skimpiest) plate for yourself.

DOS	DON'TS
DO add color. Especially when you're garnishing a cooked dish (a stew, for example, as opposed to a salad) in which the colors might not be very vibrant, a nice big pinch of chopped raw parsley can bring life to the plate and make something that may not otherwise look as delicious as it is become irresistible.	**DON'T use inedible garnishes.** Always avoid garnishes that can't be eaten and those that are technically edible but not really appealing. A pineapple top decorating a fruit salad is just ridiculous. And don't throw a sprig of mint onto a dessert just because it looks pretty, even though you've probably seen this done in restaurants. You want to avoid that moment when your guests have to remove the garnish obstacle, at a loss for its purpose, before they can get to the point: eating.
DO repeat flavors. If there is basil in the tomato sauce you made, throw some more on top when the pasta is plated. Aside from adding color and a great aroma, it lets your guests know what they're about to dig into. Incorporating raw and cooked versions of the same ingredient in a dish is a wonderful way to layer the flavors.	**DON'T garnish ahead.** Always wait to garnish with fresh herbs, so their aromas are maximized, and especially so the more delicate herbs don't wilt. Wilted herbs are worse than no garnish any day!
DO think seasonal. If garnishing a large item such as a ham or a turkey, you will need something beautiful to adorn the platter. Use small edible whole fruit, such as clementines, lady apples, or Seckel pears, and tuck sprigs of herbs in between. For grilled pork chops in the summer, throw some halved peaches on the grill to surround the meat.	**DON'T use curly parsley.** These days, flat-leaf, or "Italian," parsley is available in most supermarkets around the country, and its flavor and texture are superior to those of the dark, curly variety, which tends to be aggressively flavored— sometimes even bitter—and very thick and fibrous.

195 Don't Forget the Water

Include a water glass at every setting and fill the glasses before seating your guests. In addition, put carafes, pitchers, or glass bottles of water on the table. Whether to serve regular tap water, bottled flat water, or bubbly water is up to you; providing options is above and beyond expectations. If you're serving bottled water and the bottles are plastic, transfer the water to a glass pitcher or bottle; those plastic bottles are an eyesore. If you're serving tap water or water from your own filter system, again, use a glass pitcher or fill a glass bottle for the table. To find a good-looking glass bottle, try used wine or liquor bottles with the labels removed (think neighborhood bistro: it's a charming look). You can put a small ice bucket out, but it's not necessary. Just chill the water in the fridge beforehand, and be sure to have backups.

196 Should I Put Bread on the Table?

It's not always necessary to serve bread. However, a cheese course calls for some bread, and many soups are best enjoyed with some buttered bread for dipping. Bread can be good served alongside a salad, especially if it's simple and light. In fact, if you're concerned that a dish is so light that it's veering toward skimpy, bread can help satisfy your guests' appetites. Bread is particularly satisfying with saucy, wet dishes that beg to be sopped up (such as steamed mussels and braised meats). Bread should not be served with a very starchy dish, such as pasta or a stew with lots of potatoes. More is sometimes too much, and too much bread will just leave your guests feeling stuffed.

Buy freshly baked bread from a good bakery. Presliced loaves begin to dry out very quickly, so buy loaves whole and slice them a few minutes before they'll be served.

If you're serving French food, you might want to go with a classic baguette. With Italian, go with a crusty, Tuscan-style loaf. If you get into something more intensely flavored, such as a dark rye or an olive bread—which (respectively) could go great with ham or a salumi spread—provide a more plain option as well. Of course, if you like to bake, homemade bread is a real treat.

197 Wine Pairing 101

- Light-bodied whites (Muscadet, Pinot Grigio, Sauvignon Blanc): Nuts, fried foods, shellfish, light-fleshed fish

- Medium-bodied whites (White Bordeaux, French Chenin Blanc, Gewürztraminer): Shellfish, fatty fish, chicken or turkey

- Full-bodied whites (Chardonnay, White Burgundy, Pinot Gris, Viognier): Cheeses, creamy pastas and soups, shellfish, pork and veal

- Light-bodied reds (Beaujolais, Sangiovese, rosés): Creamy pastas and soups, fatty fish, chicken or turkey

- Medium-bodied reds (Bordeaux, Red Burgundy, Dolcetto, Barbera, Chianti, Cabernet Franc, Pinot Noir, Rioja): Creamy pastas and soups, chicken or turkey, pork and veal

- Full-bodied reds (Barbaresco, Barolo, Rhônes, Cabernet Sauvignon, Syrah, Shiraz, Malbec, Zinfandel): Pork and veal, lamb, beef, duck, game birds

Flourish and Flair: Open Wine Like a Pro

Waiters and sommeliers carry a basic waiter-style or stainless-steel wing corkscrew. With no moving parts, these last forever and offer a swift and smooth pop of a cork. From the inexpensive (about $10) to the lavish French-made Laguiole waiter-style corkscrew with heavy, carved handles, there's one of these to fit every budget.

To open any wine bottle, first cut the foil away from the top (the Laguiole corkscrew has an attached blade for doing this). Or use a foil-cutter, a little device with two mini blades that spins around the bottle top and cleanly removes the foil top.

For an easier method, look for the Rabbit wine opener or another screw-pull product. These are pricey cork removers, but they're worth it. After two or three practice runs with either one, you'll be able to open wine in rapid-fire succession, bottle after bottle. A great gadget for the frequent host, a Rabbit wine opener makes quick work of opening copious amounts of wine.

AFTER DINNER

199   Moving the Crowd

After a few hours of drinking and eating and talking, you should hope that even the most buttoned-up guests feel relaxed. This is the time to get the crowd to migrate to the living room, where there might be after-dinner drinks, dessert, or even a roaring fire waiting. After two hours of sitting upright in a chair, talking to the same two people, your guests will appreciate a change of scenery and seating, especially if the evening has been going well and they want to linger. It gives people a chance to talk to someone who was sitting at the other end of the table, and the change of room can feel like a whole new party. If you anticipate it, you can factor the move into your menu planning; serve a dessert that won't be too messy to eat off laps, such as cookies or a cake that requires only a fork.

200 Clearing the Table: Dos and Don'ts

DOS	DON'TS
• **DO** make sure every last person has completely finished eating before you begin to gather plates.	• **DON'T** ever scrape the food at the table, even with the most intimate of company. It's just gross.
• **DO** clear plates from the right of each seat.	• **DON'T** stack the plates at the table if it's a fancy occasion.
• **DO** take away the salt and pepper and condiments before putting dessert on the table.	• **DON'T** separate out the silverware if you are stacking plates to carry them from the table. Keep them between layers and do not stack so many that it becomes unwieldy.
• DO let a pre-designated guest help with the clearing.	• **DON'T** encourage guests to help with cleanup; urge them to sit and keep the conversation going.

201   Cheese to End the Meal

A cheese course is best at the end of a meal that's not too heavy or rich. If you're serving anything cheesy, such as a gratin or a salad with Gorgonzola, skip the cheese course and go straight to dessert; too much of a good thing will make people feel unpleasantly stuffed. A cheese course can range from a few bites and some good bread to something more ambitious. And it can be followed by sweets, or served, perhaps with some fruit, in lieu of dessert. Since cheese is best at room temperature, you can set up a tray or individual plates ahead of time. Supplement the selection of cheeses (three to five should be sufficient) with any or all of the following: nutty bread, dried fruit, fresh fruit, mustard fruit, nuts, quince paste, honey, fig and almond cake, and after-dinner drinks such as grappa or port.

202   How to Choose One Special Cheese

If you're serving one cheese with a salad before dessert, go for something ripe and runny, and perhaps a bit stinky. The best—and most enjoyable— way to pick which cheese to serve is to taste a few, with some guidance from a knowledgeable cheesemonger, but here are a few suggestions.

Washed-rind cheeses (kind of pinkish-yellow-orange) self-contained in their own wooden boxes, like **Époisses or Affidélice,** can be easily passed in their original packaging, and are about the right size for a party of eight or ten. These types of cheeses are usually so ripe they are served with a spoon, making them a decadent conversation piece. Serve with a fresh warm baguette and a simple green salad.

A true **Muenster**—not the square stuff sliced at the deli, but a washed-rind cheese that comes in a flat wheel about 8 inches across—is also an excellent choice, and you'll have the pleasure of re-introducing your guests to a fabulous cheese that has gotten a bad name because of poor commercial imitations.

Another immensely pleasurable cheese that shows the best of what American cheese-makers have learned from the Europeans is **Humboldt Fog,** from California. This goat's-milk cheese has become an instant classic and is great with a salad course, or any time. It's beautiful to look at, with a layer of vegetable ash through the center (similar to Morbier in this way) and around the outside edge, which is encased in a pure white, bloomy rind. As the cheese ripens, it becomes more gooey and complex in flavor, starting just under the rind and moving to the center over time. Be sure to serve it at room temperature so it oozes enticingly.

203   Ten Great Assembled Desserts

A great time-saver is to serve an assembled dessert: one that doesn't require baking or a lot of cooking or making much of a mess at all but is simply put together from various store-bought components (see following). As long as the ingredients you buy are good and fresh and you put some thought into the presentation, it is possible to pull off a fabulous dessert without measuring a single cup of flour.

1. Peach Melba. For each serving, slice 1 **peach** into thin wedges, put in a bowl or glass, and sprinkle with 1 **teaspoon sugar** and 1 **teaspoon freshly squeezed lemon juice.** Let sit for 5 minutes. Top with **a scoop of vanilla ice cream** and **a handful of raspberries.**

2. Greek Yogurt Parfait. Place 1 **cup dried apricots** and ½ **cup dried sour cherries** in a saucepan, add 1 **tablespoon honey,** and pour in enough **dry red wine** to cover. Simmer until the fruit is plump and most of the liquid is gone. Let the fruit cool, then spoon it over **thick Greek yogurt** in a pretty goblet or tumbler and top with **toasted walnut halves.** This sauce makes enough for 4 servings.

3. Glazed Figs. Slice **figs** lengthwise in half, sprinkle with **dark brown sugar,** and broil to melt the sugar and warm the fruit. Melt **raspberry jam** in a small saucepan or in the microwave, adding a tablespoon or two of water if needed to create a sauce. Place **a dollop of ricotta cheese** on each plate, arrange the figs alongside, and drizzle with the sauce.

4. Gelato with Chocolate Ganache. Bring **¼ cup heavy cream** to a boil and pour it over **3 ounces semisweet chocolate, finely chopped,** in a bowl. Stir until smooth. Spoon over **gelato,** and serve with **biscotti.** This sauce makes enough for 4 servings.

5. Affogato. Serve bowls of vanilla or dulce de leche ice cream with a double shot of hot espresso on the side to pour over. Eat immediately.

6. Ambrosia Trifle. Slice **angel food cake** and toast in a 400°F oven until golden. Peel and cut **1 orange** into sections. In a 350°F oven, toast **shredded coconut** until golden and **pecans** until fragrant. Sweeten **crème fraîche to taste** with **confectioners' sugar.** Layer the ingredients in clear dessert glasses. (These can be assembled in advance and stored in the fridge.)

7. Fresh Apricots with Mascarpone. Combine 1 **teaspoon butter** and 1 **tablespoon sugar** in a small frying pan and set over high heat. Cook for 2 minutes, swirling. Add 1 **halved fresh apricot,** cut side down, and 1 **teaspoon lemon juice** to the pan and reduce the heat slightly. Cook for 2 minutes on each side and transfer to a plate to cool slightly. Serve with **a dollop of mascarpone** and 3 to 4 **crumbled mini amaretti cookies.**

8. Sautéed Bananas with Caramel Sauce. Slice 2 **bananas** into ¾-inch rounds. Sauté in 1 **tablespoon unsalted butter** with 1 **tablespoon light brown sugar** until glazed and brown. Serve over **vanilla ice cream,** with store-bought **caramel sauce.**

9. Ice Cream Sandwiches. For each sandwich, place **a scoop of ice cream** on a **chocolate chip cookie** (try Tate's brand or another thin, crisp cookie). Top with **another cookie** and press down gently. Place on a rimmed baking sheet and set in the freezer. Wrap individually after they've hardened, and freeze until ready to serve.

10. Nutella Sandwiches. Toast **thinly sliced brioche bread,** spread with **Nutella,** and sprinkle with **confectioners' sugar.** Serve warm.

204 How to Serve Perfect, Pre-scooped Ice Cream

Before the party, take your ice cream out of the freezer and give it a few minutes to soften. Use a scooper to make nice, round balls, and place them on a rimmed baking sheet. Work quickly so they don't melt before you slide the baking sheet into the freezer. When dessert time rolls around, your scoops will be waiting to be plopped into bowls and served, picture perfect.

205 RECIPE: *Meringue-Sorbet Layer Cake*

You don't need to bake this cake; it can be assembled with store-bought ingredients to make a fruity and crunchy layered dessert. Use three sorbet flavors that go well together, such as coconut, passion fruit, and raspberry. You can find the little meringue cookies in most good grocery stores; they're usually sold in plastic tubs in the bakery section.

SERVES 6 TO 8

- Line an 8-inch springform pan with enough plastic wrap to create an ample overhang. Use heavy-duty aluminum foil to build a collar inside the pan at the top, making the pan taller by 2 inches.

- Sprinkle 1¼ **cups crushed meringue (about 7 cookies)** into the bottom of the pan. Spread 1 **pint fruit sorbet, softened,** evenly

THE DINNER PARTY

over the meringue layer, making sure to reach the edges. Repeat these steps twice to make three layers, using **2 more pints of sorbet** (use different sorbet flavors for each layer) and **an additional 2½ cups crushed meringue.** Top the cake with **another 1¼ cups crushed meringue.**

• Cover the cake with the overhanging plastic wrap and freeze until ready to serve. When ready to serve, remove the outer ring of the springform, remove the foil collar and the plastic wrap, and transfer the cake to a serving plate. Let soften for 10 minutes, slice into wedges, and serve with whipped cream, if desired.

You can vary this recipe with different kinds of fruit, depending on what is in season. Apples, peaches, pears, or apricots would work just as well. Cut fruit into medium-thin wedges and pile into the center of the pastry.

MAKES 4 INDIVIDUAL TARTS

- Roll out **one 14-ounce sheet thawed frozen puff pastry** on a floured work surface into a square about 13 by 13 inches. Using a bowl or a plate as a guide, cut out four 6-inch circles. Place the pastry rounds on a parchment-lined baking sheet. Chill them in the refrigerator until ready to bake, up to 1 day, or freeze them for up to 1 week.

- Toss **one 6-ounce container each of blueberries, raspberries, and blackberries** with **⅓ cup sugar, 1 tablespoon all-purpose flour,** and **the grated zest and juice of ¼ lemon.** Use a fork to prick the pastry circles. Divide the berry mixture evenly among the four pieces of dough, leaving a ½-inch border. Fold the edges of the dough over the fruit, cupping your hands over it and pressing down lightly to secure the shape. Refrigerate the tarts until they're firm again, 15 to 30 minutes.

- Preheat the oven to 400°F. Bake the tarts for 30 minutes, or until the pastry is puffed and golden. Serve warm.

THE DINNER PARTY

HOLIDAYS AND OTHER SPECIAL DAYS

Although any day is a good day to throw a party, there are certain times, and we all know what they are, that just call for entertaining. Whether it's a holiday brunch or lunch, Thanksgiving, New Year's Eve, or a special birthday, having a few simple but impressive recipes in your arsenal will help you look like a star without sweating too much. Holidays are not the time for spontaneity, however. Careful advance planning will smooth your way to successful celebrations. Pick a holiday, and make it your annual party. You'll get better at hosting it every year.

Parties can take on a whole new flair when you entertain in the daylight hours. Brunch can be an intimate, laid-back affair, and lunch can stretch out into an afternoon of hanging out, if you want it to. And you still have your night free to catch a movie.

207   What's Wrong with This Brunch Menu?

- Omelets with Gruyère, caramelized onions, and pancetta
- Tomato salad
- Home fries
- Pancakes with blueberry sauce

Brunch at home is very different from brunch out. It's great to cover sweet and savory tastes, but there's just too much going on here. If you want to make pancakes, let the egg dish be a simple one, such as scrambled eggs with some herbs. (And of course, most people want bacon with that.) If the eggs play the starring role and you want them to be more substantial, a frittata or a quiche will make your life a lot easier than individual omelets for each guest. Even if omelets are your specialty, take into consideration the difficulty of timing. Individual ramekins with baked eggs are another solution. They can be assembled just before your guests arrive and then popped into the oven all at once. A fruit salad at the end of the meal will round it out perfectly.

- Layered Frittata (page 183)
- A Bunch of Bacon (page 184)
- Tuscan Parmesan toast
- Melon salad with mint syrup
- Apple cinnamon mini muffins

Why it works: The layered frittata can be completed shortly before guests arrive and kept warm in the oven. Bacon can be cooked with very little attention. Thick slices of rustic bread get a crunchy sprinkle of Parmesan. The sweet side of the meal is represented by a gussied-up fruit salad, and little muffins provide a dessert-like touch.

208 What's Wrong with This Lunch Menu?

- Fried baby artichokes
- Pan-fried skate wing with brown butter
- Pan-fried fingerling potatoes
- Sautéed Swiss chard
- Individual molten chocolate cakes

Though the cooking here isn't complicated, every one of these dishes requires last-minute preparation, so the hostess will be absent from the table—and, most likely, pretty frazzled—for much of her own party. With a few tweaks, though, this could be a very successful lunch. First, save the skate wings for a romantic dinner for two, not a big gathering, because they're so delicate and will probably overwhelm your stovetop and create a real challenge in terms of getting each plate out at the same time. The potatoes can be roasted instead of fried, and if you really want to minimize the pressure, replace the Swiss chard with a crunchy salad. For dessert, avoid last-minute fussing and make something that can be prepared in the morning or even the day before.

> **TRY THIS MENU INSTEAD**
>
> - Simple pea puree soup
> - Snapper *en papillote* (see page 223)
> - Roasted potatoes (see page 153)
> - Haricots verts with vinaigrette (see page 162)
> - Flourless chocolate cake

Why it works: A little cup of a smooth and creamy soup, which can be served hot or cold, depending on the season, is a great way to start off any meal and can be made completely in advance. Pass it around in tiny teacups or espresso cups before even sitting at the table. Snapper baked in parchment can be assembled ahead of time and popped into the oven shortly before serving. Roasted potatoes can be cooked before the snapper and reheated just before serving. A crunchy salad of delicate haricots verts need only be splashed with dressing at the last minute, and a chocolate cake from your own oven or your favorite bakery can be baked or bought a day ahead of time.

209 Do I Have to Make Eggs for a Brunch?

If you don't like eggs or hate cooking them, you can certainly skip them and focus on the sweeter elements of a traditional brunch, such as pancakes or crepes; but it is nice to offer something savory as well. You might consider an eggy dish like a quiche rather than straight-up scrambled or fried eggs, or skip the eggs altogether and go with a bagel spread and some fruit instead.

If you're serving a larger crowd, simply increase the number of eggs. Add a minute or two to the cooking time for each egg you add. You can substitute different vegetables or make two or three more layers as well.

SERVES 10 TO 12

- Preheat the oven to 200°F. Trim the tough ends of 1 **pound asparagus,** and cut into 1½-inch pieces. Heat 1 **teaspoon olive oil** in a large skillet over medium heat. Add the asparagus and sauté until tender, about 5 minutes. Set aside to cool.

- Trim the dark green portions and roots of 2 **small leeks** and cut them lengthwise in half. Rinse thoroughly under cold water, pat

dry, and slice into ¼-inch half-moons. Heat 1 **teaspoon olive oil** in a large skillet over medium heat. Add the leeks and sauté until softened, about 5 minutes. Set aside to cool.

- Cut 1 **cup grape tomatoes** lengthwise in half and set them aside.

- For the first layer: whisk 7 **large eggs** with ½ **teaspoon salt** and **a dash of pepper** in a bowl. Stir in the asparagus.

- In a 10-inch frying pan with a lid, melt 1 **tablespoon butter** over medium heat. Pour in the egg mixture and cook, using a spatula to pull the uncooked eggs into the middle of the pan, until the eggs begin to set, about 2 minutes. Smooth the top, cover the pan, reduce the heat to low, and cook for 6 to 8 minutes, until the frittata is completely set.

- Shake the pan to loosen the frittata, and slide it onto an ovenproof serving plate. Crumble **3 ounces goat cheese** over the top and keep warm in the oven.

- For the second frittata, follow the method just described, using another 7 large eggs and the leeks. When the frittata is set, slide it onto the asparagus frittata and crumble **3 ounces goat cheese** over the top, then return to the oven.

- For the third layer, follow the same method, using another 7 large eggs and the grape tomatoes, and adding 1 **tablespoon chopped chervil** and 1 **tablespoon chopped tarragon** to the eggs. When the frittata is set, lay it on top of the others.

- Leave in the oven for 10 minutes. Sprinkle the top with **shaved Parmesan** and **chopped herbs, such as parsley, basil, or mint.** Cut into wedges and serve.

211   RECIPE: *A Bunch of Bacon*

If you're cooking brunch, let the bacon cook itself while you get other things done.

SERVES 8 TO 10

- Preheat the oven to 350°F. Arrange **1½ pounds thick-sliced bacon** on 2 wire racks set on 2 rimmed baking sheets (to catch the fat). Bake for about 30 minutes, until crisp (slightly less if using thin-sliced bacon).

212 Should I Serve Dessert at Brunch or Lunch?

A dessert course isn't necessary at brunch; the fun of the meal is to have sweet and savory foods together. If you're serving a more savory brunch, such as baked eggs, and nothing very sweet such as French toast, you might put out some pastries or a coffee cake as well, or just a fruit salad, which people can integrate into the main course or snack on at the end of the meal. For a seated lunch, you should offer something sweet at the end, but in most cases, it should be a lighter and more casual dessert than you would serve after dinner. Again, it could be fruit, but it could also be a tart or some cookies or brownies.

213 How to Put Together a Bagel Spread

A New York–style bagel and lox feast is a great way to please a crowd for brunch, and there's no cooking involved, unless you want to offer softly scrambled eggs on the side (they complement the saltiness of smoked salmon perfectly). Good sliced smoked salmon is available in vacuum-sealed packages at many supermarkets and on the Internet (see Resources, page 274), and it ships well. If you have access to a gourmet store or a Jewish market with good smoked fish, buy a few different kinds, such as sable, sturgeon, or whitefish salad as well as the salmon. (If it's being cut to order, you should be able to try each one.) Likewise, get an assortment of very fresh bagels, and serve thinly sliced cucumber, tomato, and red onion on the side to counterbalance the fattiness and saltiness of the fish. In addition to regular plain cream cheese, whipped or not, you may want to add a scallion variety and a low-fat version. Lemon wedges are a nice addition for those who may be making a plate and not a sandwich.

214 How to Serve Warm Bagels

Preheat your oven for about 10 minutes at 350°F, and meanwhile, cut the bagels in half. Place them on a baking sheet (or two if necessary), reassembled with the tops sitting on the bottoms. Warming them up this way makes for a slightly steamy inside, just like a fresh-baked bagel—and spares your fingers from having to slice hot bagels. Of course, you can also leave them open for toasty, browned cut sides. Serve the bagels in a basket with a napkin to cover and keep them warm.

215   TIP: **Know Your Lox**

If you find yourself in an old-school Jewish appetizing store, keep in mind that "lox," which is often used to describe smoked salmon in general, actually refers to an especially fatty cut of salmon (from the belly), which is not smoked at all but is cured in a very salty brine. This may not be to your taste unless you were reared on it. "Nova," as most Jewish-style smoked salmon is called, is not as salty, and will be lightly flavored with smoke. Scottish salmon has an even more pronounced wood-smoke taste. All will be fairly silky in texture, and naturally oily. If it's not prepackaged, ask for a taste, or buy a variety for guests to try.

216   RECIPE: *Three Brunch Drinks* ·······························

SERVES 1

1. Bloody Mary

The exact balance of flavors is subjective, so add the ingredients judiciously and then balance to taste.

• Combine 1 **cup tomato juice, ½ teaspoon horseradish, 1 tablespoon freshly squeezed lemon juice, ¼ teaspoon Worcestershire, ¼ teaspoon celery salt, 6 dashes Tabasco sauce, ¼ teaspoon pickle brine, ¼ teaspoon salt,** and freshly ground black pepper. Stir well and add **2 ounces vodka** to the mixture. Fill a large glass with ice and pour in mixture. Garnish with **a cucumber spear** or **a celery stalk** and **a wedge of lemon.**

2. Ramos Fizz

This old-school cocktail, originally called the New Orleans Fizz for the city where it was invented in 1886, deserves a comeback. Introduce it to your friends, and take them back to the days when this sweet, refreshingly frothy drink was a brunch standby. Use pasteurized egg whites to give the drink its trademark foam without any health worries.

• Combine **2 ounces gin, ½ teaspoon orange blossom water, 3 tablespoons pasteurized egg white, 1 tablespoon heavy cream, 1 tablespoon freshly squeezed lemon juice, 1 tablespoon freshly squeezed lime juice,** and **1 tablespoon simple syrup** in a cocktail shaker filled with ice and shake well for about 30 seconds. Strain into a tall glass.

• Pour **¼ cup seltzer** into the shaker and swish it around to collect the froth that remains, then pour the frothy seltzer into the glass. Garnish with **grated nutmeg** and serve.

NOTE: To make simple syrup, combine 1 cup water and 1 cup sugar in a small saucepan. Bring to a boil and simmer until the sugar is dissolved. Let cool, then pour into a container, cover, and store in the refrigerator until needed, up to 1 month.

3. Bellini

One of many lovely sparkling cocktails suitable for brunch, the elegant Bellini is made with white peach puree and prosecco, the Italian wine.

- Put 1 **tablespoon peach puree** in a chilled champagne flute and fill halfway with **prosecco**. Stir well, allow the froth to subside, and then top up with prosecco. For a Mimosa, follow the same proportions, substituting **freshly squeezed orange juice** for the peach puree and **champagne** for the prosecco. Blood oranges, when in season, can be used for added color.

NOTE: When fresh white peaches are in season, you can make your own puree: Blanch **ripe peaches** in boiling water for 1 minute to loosen the skins. Peel, and cut the flesh from the pits. Puree in a blender with **a splash of freshly squeezed lemon juice**. Refrigerate or freeze. You can also puree frozen yellow peaches for a similar effect.

217   RECIPE: *Savory Bread Pudding*

This is French toast for those who lack a sweet tooth at the brunch table. It can be assembled in advance, even refrigerated overnight, for truly stress-free hosting. Just be sure to remove it from the fridge about 20 minutes before baking to bring it to room temperature.

SERVES 10 TO 12

- Preheat the oven to 325°F. Butter a 9-by-13-inch casserole. Heat **2 tablespoons butter** in a large skillet over medium heat. Add **1 bunch of leeks**, white and pale green parts only, halved lengthwise, sliced into ¼-inch half moons, and rinsed

and patted dry, and cook until soft, about 5 minutes. Season with **salt and pepper** and transfer into a bowl.

- Melt 1 **tablespoon butter** in the same pan, add **5 cups packed baby spinach,** and cook just until wilted, about 3 minutes. Transfer to the bowl with the leeks.

- In a large bowl, whisk **8 large eggs** together with 4 **cups milk** and **salt and pepper** to taste.

- Layer ten ½-inch-thick slices **brioche or challah, 6 ounces thinly sliced ham,** the leeks and spinach, **2 tablespoons thyme leaves,** and **2 cups grated Gruyère (about 8 ounces)** in a buttered casserole. Arrange the bread slices like shingles, slightly overlapping, tucking the leeks, ham, spinach mixture, and cheese between the slices. Pour the egg mixture over the ingredients. (The casserole can be refrigerated for as long as overnight; bring to room temperature before baking.)

- Press the bread down gently to help it absorb the egg mixture. Bake for about 1 hour, until golden brown and set in the center. Tent the casserole with foil if the top of the pudding is becoming darker than golden brown. Cut into squares or simply scoop out with a spoon to serve.

RECIPE: *Baked French Toast*

Here's a way to make French toast without slaving over a hot stove: take the same ingredients, layer them in a dish like a bread pudding, and bake! You will be able to sit down and eat with your guests, which is the whole point of inviting them over! You can even let this dish sit, assembled, in the fridge overnight before baking.

SERVES 8 TO 10

• Preheat the oven to 350°F. Grease a 3-quart baking dish with **3 tablespoons melted butter.** Cut **one 1-pound loaf challah** into 1-inch-thick slices and lay them in the dish, overlapping them like shingles.

• Whisk together **6 large eggs, 1½ cups milk, 2 tablespoons sugar,** **¼ cup maple syrup, ½ teaspoon vanilla extract, a pinch of salt,** and **a pinch of freshly grated nutmeg** in a large bowl. Ladle this mixture over the bread, making sure it goes in between the slices. Let it sit for 5 minutes so the bread absorbs the liquid. (The French toast can be covered and refrigerated overnight. Let it sit at room temperature for 20 minutes before baking.)

• Bake for 40 to 50 minutes, until the top is golden brown. Sprinkle with **confectioners' sugar** and scatter **1 cup raspberries** on top. Serve with **maple syrup.**

A beautifully composed big salad can be assembled ahead and dressed just before serving. Classics like the Cobb and Niçoise are room-temperature equivalents of one-pot meals: protein, carbs, and colorful fresh vegetables working together to dazzle and satisfy your guests. The dressing suggestions, given in italics, should be mixed in a ratio of 3 parts oil to 1 part acid, or closer to 2 to 1 if you like it acidic.

SERVES 6 TO 8

1. *Cobb Salad:* Chopped Boston lettuce, chopped tomatoes, chopped English cucumbers, cubed avocado, crumbled bacon, chopped hard-boiled eggs, crumbled blue cheese, and sliced grilled, roasted, or poached chicken breast. *Red wine vinegar, extra-virgin olive oil, salt, and pepper.*

2. *Italian Chicken Salad:* Sliced grilled chicken breast, sliced roasted red peppers, pitted oil-cured black olives, thinly sliced fennel, freshly shaved Parmigiano-Reggiano, artichoke hearts, canned white beans and/or borlotti (cranberry) beans (drained and rinsed), and greens. *Extra-virgin olive oil, freshly squeezed lemon juice or vinegar, salt, and pepper.*

HOLIDAYS AND OTHER SPECIAL DAYS

3. *Salade Niçoise:* Hard-boiled eggs, cucumber, cherry tomatoes, blanched asparagus, blanched haricots verts, cooked and quartered red potatoes, canned tuna, sliced red, yellow, and/or orange bell peppers, Niçoise olives, and scallions. *Red wine vinegar, anchovy paste, extra-virgin olive oil, salt, and pepper.*

4. *Thai Beef Salad:* Pan-seared or grilled filet mignon (or any steak you like), red leaf lettuce, julienne carrots, julienne red bell peppers, sliced scallions, cooked rice sticks or vermicelli noodles, peanuts, mint leaves, cilantro leaves, and blanched snow peas. *Canola oil, fish sauce, freshly squeezed lime juice, and Sriracha.*

5. *Mexican Shrimp Salad:* Large shrimp (sprinkled with chili powder, salt, and pepper and sautéed), pickled red onion, cherry tomatoes, sliced avocado, canned black beans (drained and rinsed), cooked corn, cilantro leaves, toasted corn tortilla strips, and romaine lettuce with lime wedges on the side. *Cilantro, garlic, freshly squeezed lime juice, olive oil, a pinch of sugar, salt, and pepper pureed in a blender or food processor.*

220   TIP: **Present a Salad Untossed**

When serving a big salad from a bowl, leave it untossed until the
last minute, so that heavier ingredients, such as beets, tomatoes,
or olives, which are colorful and lovely to see, don't fall to the
bottom of the bowl before your guests have a chance to lust after
them. Dress and toss the salad when you're ready to serve it, and
be sure to distribute the different elements evenly, so everyone
gets some of everything.

THANKSGIVING

People tend to be very attached to whatever traditions they grew up with.
That means your aunt may give you hell if there are no candied yams,
or your boyfriend if there's no corn-bread stuffing on your Thanksgiving
menu. But ultimately, it's your party and you should serve what excites
you and what you feel confident preparing. Just balance this unusually
high-carb meal with an ample selection of vegetables.

Organization and planning are absolutely key to pulling off a
successful Thanksgiving feast. Enlisting plenty of help is also a good
idea, so ask those closest to you to bring a side dish or a dessert to help
minimize the stress. Less shopping, less prep work, and less cooking
means you can concentrate on that beautiful bird.

221   Thanksgiving Menu Planner

Knowing that guests will be putting a little bit of everything on their
plates, try to offer the greatest variety of textures, colors, and flavors,
while still keeping it all harmonious. Avoid overly rich or creamy dishes

and filling appetizers that will leave guests groaning. But offer a few extra green vegetables, simply prepared, or even a salad. This cheat sheet can help with your menu planning.

APPETIZERS
(choose 1 to 3)
Olives
Nuts
Shrimp cocktail
Crudités and dip
Stuffed mushrooms

STARCHES
(choose at least 2)
Some kind of white potatoes
Some kind of sweet potatoes
Stuffing or dressing

GREEN VEGETABLES
(choose at least 1)
Green beans
Brussels sprouts
Leafy greens
Broccoli

OTHER SEASONAL VEGETABLES
(choose at least 1)
Cauliflower
Fennel
Squash
Onions or leeks
Root vegetables

GARNISHES
Cranberry sauce or relish
Gravy

DESSERTS
(choose at least 3, depending on the number of guests)
Pumpkin pie
Apple pie
Pecan pie
Lemon meringue pie
Chocolate ganache tart
Chocolate or gingerbread ice cream roll
Berry cobbler
Poached pears
Apple bread pudding

222 How to Prep Any Turkey

Regardless of the cooking method you choose for your turkey, there are some basic preparations you'll need to do. First, remove the giblets from the cavity of the bird. ("Giblets" is a blanket term referring to the internal organs left when poultry is cleaned, like the heart and liver.) Don't forget to reach into the neck cavity and remove the neck, and save all the parts for making your gravy. Then rinse the bird inside and out with cold tap water, and pat it dry with paper towels.

223 Roasting or Grilling Turkey, Piece by Piece

The problem with cooking any whole bird is that the legs and breasts cook at different rates: the breast meat is done before the dark meat, and therefore is usually overcooked and dry by the time the dark meat is cooked through. It won't look as dramatic as bringing a whole cooked turkey to the table, but cooking the bird in parts, rather than whole, is the best way to ensure even doneness.

Order in advance, so your butcher can cut the turkey into quarters for you.

SERVES 8 TO 10

- Preheat the oven to 400°F.

- Place the legs of **one 12-pound fresh turkey, cut into 4 pieces**, in a large roasting pan. Season all the pieces with **salt and pepper** and **2 rosemary sprigs, chopped**. Drizzle with **olive oil**. Add **2 carrots, cut into chunks; 2 celery ribs, cut into chunks; and 2 onions, cut into quarters,** to the roasting pan with the legs.

- Roast the legs for 10 minutes. Add the breasts to the pan and continue roasting for 1 hour, basting occasionally with the pan drippings; add water to the pan if necessary to keep them from scorching. Check the internal temperatures: the legs should reach 180°F, the breasts 165°F in the thickest part.

Roasting the Whole Bird

For most of us, the moment when the glorious and fragrant bird is brought to the table is a little like watching fireworks on the Fourth of July. It just wouldn't be the holiday without it. There are other methods that might result in a more even cooking of the bird and a shorter time in the oven (see page 195), but if it's all about that Norman Rockwell moment, then you have to roast your turkey whole. After you present your whole-roasted turkey, slice the breast meat and ladle some gravy or stock over it right away to keep it moist. (See Tip, page 200.)

226 RECIPE: *Roasted Turkey*

One thing that will ease your way to cooking a delicious bird is a good roasting pan; even if you use it just once a year, it is worth the investment. You will have a pan to deglaze for a flavorful gravy base, and it will be much sturdier than a disposable foil pan.

SERVES 8 TO 10

- Preheat the oven to 375°F. Remove the neck and giblets (save them for the gravy) from **one 10- to 12-pound fresh turkey** and pat the turkey dry, inside and out. Rub all over with about 4 **tablespoons soft butter.** Season inside and out with **salt and pepper** and 3 **tablespoons chopped fresh rosemary.** Stuff 1 **head of garlic (unpeeled)** and 1 **handful of thyme sprigs** into the cavity. Place the turkey on a rack in a roasting pan.

- In a saucepan, melt **8 tablespoons (1 stick) unsalted butter** with 1 **cup dry white wine.** Cut a piece of cheesecloth long enough to cover the breast four times, about 16 inches, and soak it in the butter-wine mixture. Fold the cheesecloth into quarters and drape over the turkey breast.

- Pour **¾ cup dry white wine** and **¾ cup water** into the roasting pan, place in the oven, and roast for 2 hours. Baste the turkey every

half hour with the liquid in the pan. Add more water if the pan is dry. Keep the cheesecloth moist.

- Remove the cheesecloth after 2 hours and continue cooking for 1 more hour until an internal thermometer reads 165°F. Let the bird rest for 10 to 15 minutes before carving.

227   The Truth about Trussing

You do not need to truss your turkey, or any bird you roast. Trussing, which can refer to simply tying the legs together or to much fussier tasks, such as sewing the cavity of the turkey shut, is mainly an effort toward presentation. So, if you like the more formal, old-fashioned look of a gussied-up bird, go for it. But this is one chore you can skip without any loss. In fact, leaving the legs open to allow heat to hit the dark meat more directly, since that is the part of the bird that requires more cooking time, is a better cooking method.

TIMING FOR FRESH TURKEYS	
Unstuffed	
8 to 12 pounds	2¾ to 3 hours
12 to 14 pounds	3 to 3¾ hours
14 to 18 pounds	3¾ to 4¼ hours
18 to 20 pounds	4¼ to 4½ hours
20 to 24 pounds	4½ to 5 hours
Stuffed	
8 to 12 pounds	3 to 3½ hours
12 to 14 pounds	3½ to 4 hours
14 to 18 pounds	4 to 4½ hours
18 to 20 pounds	4½ to 5 hours
20 to 24 pounds	4¾ to 5¼ hours

Here are some simple guidelines for how long to cook a turkey. Keep in mind that there will be plenty of discrepancies from oven to oven, and other variables include how often you open the oven and even how moist the particular bird is. You can use a thermometer, either the kind you leave in while roasting or an instant-read (see page 27), to make sure the meat has reached a safe temperature of 165° all over, including at the center of the stuffing (if you've stuffed the cavity of the bird).

229   TIP: **Conserve the Heat in Your Oven**

Opening an oven door lets heat out, so it's important to resist peering in more often than necessary. When the oven heat level drops and then has to climb back up, the cooking time is prolonged and the meat you're cooking is more likely to dry out. If you are basting the turkey periodically, quickly remove the whole pan and close the oven door. Do your basting outside the oven and then quickly put the roast back inside. Of course, it's good to keep an eye on things as you near the finish line, but keep door opening to a minimum, and make use of your oven light to look through the window to check on the browning and bubbling.

HOLIDAYS AND OTHER SPECIAL DAYS

230   TIP: **How to Rescue Dry White Meat**

The breast meat on any bird is highly susceptible to drying out, because it's lean. Especially when the bird is cooked whole, this is nearly unavoidable, since the thigh meat requires more cooking time. It's best to accept a little dryness and fix it after the fact. When the turkey or chicken is finished cooking, let it rest for at least ten minutes before carving. Then slice the breast meat and ladle some of your gravy base—the pan drippings before you have reduced and thickened the liquid, or simply chicken or turkey stock—over the meat. Cover the meat with aluminum foil, keep it warm in the oven, and it will absorb the flavorful juices. The concept is as simple as drinking water when you're thirsty, or moisturizing your skin when it's dry.

231   *Flourish and Flair:* How to Carve a Turkey

Whether you're carving behind the scenes or at the table, it's essential to have the right tools. Use a very sharp long, thin, slightly flexible kitchen knife and a long-handled meat fork. Do your carving on a carving board with a well to catch the juices, or on a cutting board set inside a large serving platter for the same purpose. Have a damp dishcloth nearby to wipe your hands or the knife if things are getting slippery. If you carve the meat at the table, have a stack of warm plates ready and take requests for white meat, a wing, and so on, as you go. If you're plating the meat for a buffet, group the dark meat and white meat separately so your guests can clearly distinguish them.

1. Remove the wings by inserting the tip of the knife into the joint and then slicing through. The joint should be pretty loose.

2. Start slicing the breast at the outermost part, keeping the skin attached to the slice you are cutting. Use the fork to help lift the slices and transfer them to the platter. An alternative method, usually saved for kitchen carving, is to run your knife straight down against the breastbone, removing the entire breast. Lay it on the board and cut across the grain, as thin or as thick as you like it, keeping the slices together and the breast intact. Then slide the knife under the sliced breast and transfer to the platter.

3. Gently pull the entire leg and thigh away from the body and, with your knife, find the hip joint. Separate the joint by working the knife in between the two parts. You don't need to cut through any bones.

4. Do the same thing to separate the drumstick from the thigh: find the joint and separate the two parts, keeping the skin intact.

232   To Brine or Not to Brine

Brining—soaking meat in a flavored saltwater solution for a day or so before cooking—has some great effects, such as adding flavor to the meat and increasing juiciness. But there are downsides as well. You'll have to weigh the pros and cons and decide on your priorities.

PROS	CONS
• Flavor. The salt in a brine will bring out the natural flavor of the bird, and you can add your choice of herbs and spices to the solution for more flavor, which will penetrate the meat as it is absorbed. Think of it as deep-tissue marinating. • Juiciness. As it soaks, your bird will absorb a lot of liquid (it will be heavier than it was originally), and the meat will be noticeably juicier. The salt increases the water-holding capabilities in the meat, just as salt causes our bodies to retain more water. As the turkey cooks, it loses moisture, as is always the case, but the brine adds enough liquid to prevent it from drying out. • Tenderness. Another magical effect of salt: it breaks down some of the muscle and protein structures in the meat, which means the meat emerges a lot more tender.	• Real estate. Especially when you're preparing for a big holiday feast, fridge space might be a concern. Brining a big turkey requires a lot of space in the fridge, since it needs to sit in a vessel large enough to hold both it and the brine. Brining bags will help solve this particular problem. • Time. Brining isn't difficult, but it is somewhat time-consuming and requires good planning in advance. Not only will you need a day for the soaking of the bird, but when it is finished brining, you should leave plenty of time to let the skin dry out before you begin cooking it. If you go right from brining to roasting when the skin is still moist, it will not brown and crisp up as nicely. • The great gravy sacrifice. This is the biggest potential deal-breaker for most cooks who consider brining. The pan drippings from a roasting bird that's been brined are extremely salty—too salty to use as a base for gravy.

233 One Turkey or Two?

When you're hosting Thanksgiving for a big crowd, you may want to make two smaller turkeys, rather than one enormous one. If presentation is not very important to you, and your great-aunt isn't fixated on snagging a dinosaur-size drumstick, two smaller birds is a great way to go. You'll taste the difference. Smaller birds are more tender. Very large turkeys (over 18 pounds) tend to be tough. Keep in mind that two birds will take up more oven space, but if your oven can accommodate two turkeys, try it. If you value the tradition of presenting a big, stately bird to your awed guests, then you'll probably stick with one big turkey, but consider roasting an extra breast to supplement—especially if your crowd favors white meat. This way you can get a slightly smaller bird, which will be more tender.

234 RECIPE: *Turkey Pan Gravy*

If you have lots of brown bits left behind in your roasting pan, the easiest and fastest way to make a flavorful gravy is to do so right in the pan. Be careful not to let the drippings burn while the turkey is roasting. Add small amounts of liquid—either water or stock—to prevent burning. To boost the flavor of your gravy, while the turkey cooks, make a turkey stock using the neck and giblets (except for the liver) and aromatics such as celery, carrots, onions, and herbs.

MAKES 2 CUPS

- Remove the turkey from the roasting pan and place on a platter or carving board to rest, tented with foil to keep it warm. Pour off any liquid that may have accumulated in the pan into a fat separator, reserving both the liquid and the fat. If there is no liquid in the roasting pan, pour off all but about **2 tablespoons fat** from the pan. If you had a lot of liquid, and there is no fat left in the pan, return 2 tablespoons of the reserved fat to the pan.

- Set the roasting pan over 2 burners on your stovetop and turn the heat to medium high. Sprinkle in **2 tablespoons all-purpose flour** and stir with a whisk, loosening the brown bits on the bottom of the pan. Cook for 3 to 5 minutes, stirring, until the flour browns a bit and the mixture sizzles.

- Slowly add **2 cups reserved cooking liquid, turkey stock, or chicken stock,** stirring all the while.

- Add **1 to 2 teaspoons chopped fresh herbs,** such as rosemary or thyme, if desired, and simmer for a few more minutes. Season to taste with **salt and pepper.**

235   How to Prepare Stuffing

Stuffing is endlessly variable. The same basic technique is used to make stuffing (or dressing, as it is known if it's cooked outside the bird), no matter what flavor combination you choose.

Start with the **aromatics.** Use some kind of onion (1 or 2 large ones for an average batch of stuffing), celery, and/or fennel, and whatever other aromatic ingredients you choose. Sauté with as much **butter** and/or **olive oil** as you want to use. You can use as little as a tablespoon or two if you want to keep it lean, and as much as a stick of butter if you like it rich. Then add any **vegetables** you'd like to use and sauté briefly. Season lightly as you go. Add some **cooking liquid,** and bring to a boil to combine the flavors. (You can add more liquid later if the stuffing isn't moist enough, so use about 2 cups to start.) Pour over the **bread,** which should be cubed and dried out or toasted, in a big bowl. Add whatever **fruits, cooked meat,** and **nuts** you'd like to use, and toss well. Taste for seasoning, and adjust with **salt** and plenty of **black pepper.** You can add some more herbs at this point, if you like, and an **egg** or two, but you don't need to. Squeeze some of the stuffing in your hand. If it doesn't quite hold together, add more liquid until it does. Refrigerate until needed.

Use this chart for inspiration and then experiment with your own creation.

AROMATICS
(choose 1 to 3)
Carrots, celery, onions, garlic, fennel, thyme, rosemary, sage, parsley, marjoram, oregano, orange zest

VEGETABLES
(choose 1 to 3)
Turnips, celeriac, bell peppers, kale, squash, mushrooms, corn

COOKING LIQUID
(choose 1)
Vegetable stock, chicken or turkey stock, veal stock, orange juice, water, sherry

BREAD
(choose 1)
Corn bread; white, wheat, or sourdough bread; ciabatta; focaccia; baguette; rye

FRUIT
(choose 1 or 2)
Fresh or dried cranberries, raisins, dried apricots, apples, pears, grapes, dried currants

COOKED MEAT
(choose 1)
Pork or turkey sausage (removed from the casing), bacon or pancetta, ground beef

NUTS
(choose 1)
Hazelnuts, walnuts, pecans, pine nuts, chestnuts

If you want to stuff the bird, stuff it loosely just before roasting, and bake any remaining dressing on the side in a shallow baking dish. Or bake it all on the side, dotted with butter if you like a crunchier top. Bake at 350°F or 375°F for 30 to 40 minutes, until piping hot and golden brown on top.

236 Tips for Making Stuffing Even Better

There are a few rules of thumb that will improve any stuffing.

- If you're using meat, such as sausage or giblets, be sure to cook it before combining it with the other ingredients, whether you plan to stuff the bird or cook the stuffing or "dressing" in its own pan. This way you can be sure you avoid any contamination from undercooked meat.

- For the same reason, don't stuff your bird until just before cooking it. You can make the stuffing well in advance, but keep it stored separately in the fridge.

- Make your own bread crumbs, and use day-old bread—or several days old if you like your stuffing on the dry side. (The amount of broth you add and whether you toast the bread also depend on your preferences for a softer, wetter stuffing or a looser version with more texture.) To make your own bread crumbs, you can also cut a fresh loaf of bread and leave it out to dry overnight or in a warm oven.

- Regardless of the type of bread or the degree of dryness, the "crumbs" should really be chunks. Don't grind the bread down to a crumble, or you'll end up with a dense, pasty stuffing.

- If you use a store-bought product, choose croutons rather than bread crumbs, and increase the amount of liquid you add because they'll be very dry.

237 *Flourish and Flair:* When to Break Out the Fancy Silverware

If you have sterling silver flatware, platters, or bowls, use them! Even if they are hand-me-downs that your own mother brought out only once a year, or a wedding gift from your most proper great-aunt, you needn't treat them like museum pieces. What's the use of having them if they're hidden away? If you clean and store your silver properly (see page 270), you won't even have to do any polishing. Ever. In fact, the more you use your silver, the less likely it is that tarnish will build up.

New Year's Eve is a fun night to host a party at home; you don't have to brave the crowded streets yourself or make reservations for disappointing and expensive dinners months in advance. You don't have to throw a raging house party, either. New Year's is a great night to have a small but decadent, cozy late-night dinner party. It's an excuse to get dressed up and drink champagne, or not—and if you're at home, you can kick off your heels when they start to pinch. Your menu will depend on your budget and how many people you're serving. Because some of the most traditional elements (caviar, champagne) are pricey, you might want to offer your home for the party but ask that everyone contribute something. No need to follow tradition, though; any delicious menu will thrill your guests, as they'll be so grateful for a good party to attend!

238 The New Year's Eve Menu

MENU
NEW YEAR'S EVE
tuesday, december 31

lobster salad
mushroom risotto
braised short ribs
chocolate soufflé

New Year's Eve is a night for sexy, sophisticated presentation. Some simple, pretty hors d'oeuvres (whether you spring for caviar or not) are a perfect way to begin the night, with champagne as well, of course. For a plated first course, start with seafood, such as a lobster salad (see page 208) or seared scallops, and then move on to something more rich and filling (it is winter, after all), but still special, such as osso buco or Braised Short Ribs (page 215). For dessert, anything goes, and you might want to leave the table to watch the ball drop on TV by this point, in which case think of something that transports easily and perhaps doesn't require silverware, like cookies or fancy chocolates.

RECITE: *Avocado, Grapefruit, and Lobster Salad* ⋯⋯⋯⋯⋯⋯⋯⋯⋯⋯⋯⋯⋯⋯⋯⋯⋯⋯⋯⋯⋯⋯⋯⋯

Most good fish markets sell cooked and chilled lobsters. The meat tends to be in better condition and less expensive than shelled lobster meat; you just have to do some of the work yourself. Ask the fishmonger to crack the claws for you, since this can be a bit messy to do at home. Two 1¼-pound lobsters will yield about 8 ounces of meat.

SERVES 4

- Pull off and crack the claws of **2 cooked small lobsters** and remove the meat. Cut the underside of each lobster tail down the middle with kitchen shears to expose the meat. Pull the meat out and cut it into large chunks.

- Slice off the top and bottom of **1 grapefruit** to expose the flesh. Stand the grapefruit up and remove the peel and white with a sharp knife by running it down the sides in sections. You'll be left with a naked grapefruit. Now you can remove each segment without any of the membrane by slicing between the segments.

- Arrange 1 **head of Boston lettuce, separated into leaves,** among 4 salad plates. Distribute the grapefruit segments, 1 **avocado, pitted, peeled, and sliced,** and pieces of lobster evenly among the plates.

- Whisk together **the juice of 1 lemon, 6 to 8 tablespoons extra-virgin olive oil,** and **salt and pepper to taste.** Drizzle the dressing over the salads and garnish with **chopped fresh chives.**

240   TIP: **Buy Cooked Lobster**

If you're serving lobster in a composed dish, such as the Avocado, Grapefruit, and Lobster Salad opposite, you can save yourself a lot of time and trouble (but not money) by buying them already cooked and shelled. Most fishmongers will steam them for you and remove all the meat from the shell, so you can just cut it up and combine it with your other ingredients. Keep in mind that this time-saver is best in cases when no additional cooking is required. If you need to simply heat the lobster at the last minute, talk to your fishmonger and ask him to undercook it slightly.

241   RECIPE: *Home-Cured Gravlax*

This is a great way to impress your friends with zero cooking and very little effort at all, aside from measuring some salt and spices and letting them work their magic on a slab of salmon. Curing a side of salmon doesn't take long; depending on how salty you want the exterior to be, it can sit packed in salt (in a sealed container in your fridge) for as few as six hours, if it has already been skinned. Take it out of the fridge at least an hour before you're ready to serve it, so it can come up to room temperature, and brush off all the excess salt. Then slice it as thin as you can and use it in an hors d'oeuvre, such as inside blini with crème fraîche or sour cream, or just let your guests pile it onto buttered bread.

- Mix **1 cup coarse salt** with **1 cup sugar, 2 tablespoons coarsely cracked peppercorns,** and **2 tablespoons cracked coriander seeds.**

- Use a pair of needle-nose pliers to remove the small bones from a **2-pound piece of skinless salmon fillet** (see note).

- Line a glass or ceramic baking dish with plastic wrap, leaving plenty of overhang, and sprinkle about half of the salt mixture in the dish. Lay a the **salmon fillet** on top, and cover with the remaining salt mixture.

- Very roughly chop **1 bunch of fresh dill** and place on top of the fish. Wrap tightly in the plastic wrap, and rewrap with another piece of plastic wrap.

- Place in the refrigerator, and put something heavy on top to weight it, such as a small cutting board topped with some heavy cans. Cure for 2 or 3 days, turning the fish occasionally.

- When ready to serve, wipe the salt mixture from the fish and discard. Slice the fish on the diagonal, across the grain, as thin as possible.

- Serve with crème fraîche, black bread, capers, red onions, and lemon slices.

NOTE: The small pin bones will look like a row of white dots running along the fatter side of the fillet (not the side with the belly flap) near the center line. Run your fingertip along the flesh against the direction of the bones so you can feel where they are and pull them out, firmly gripping them with the needle-nose pliers.

242 Serving Caviar: Let the Eggs Shine

When serving caviar, keep it simple. You don't want to splurge on something so special just to cover up the flavor and texture of it with a lot of bells and whistles. Caviar is intensely flavorful, and it shines beautifully against a mellow, fatty backdrop such as crème fraîche or sour cream and blini, small boiled potatoes, hard- or soft-boiled eggs, buttered noodles, or seafood. Caviar can be used almost like a precious garnish, which can also be a fantastic way to stretch out a small amount of it. You can also just pass it around the table with blini and sour cream. Of course, if you let guests help themselves, it may disappear quickly, but don't sweat it. As long as there's enough for everyone to have a taste, you've given them a very special food experience, and when it's gone, it's gone. Just pour some more champagne!

Three Ways to Keep Caviar at Its Best

1. Keep it cool. When you bring caviar home, refrigerate it immediately in its tin in the coldest part of your refrigerator (usually the back of the deli drawer). If you're making hors d'oeuvres, be sure to work quickly and serve them immediately, or put the finished snacks back in the fridge so the eggs aren't sitting out. If you're serving it straight up, place the tin itself or the caviar in another bowl over crushed ice. The caviar needn't be freezing cold, but it should be kept cool so the eggs hold their shape and freshness.

2. Don't metal. The most important rule with caviar is not to let it come into contact with reactive metal, which can impart a metallic taste. This means using your beautiful silver bowl or spoon is out. Traditionally, a mother-of-pearl spoon is used to serve caviar, but you can also use plastic (a takeout spoon or fork is perfect for behind-the-scenes arranging). Wood, ceramic, and glass utensils all work, too. Don't pass a thick or heavy spoon around with it: you'll only increase the caviar casualties. You want those eggs to burst in your mouth—not in the serving dish. (But refrain from lecturing your friends on how to handle the stuff—a micromanaging hostess is the only thing worse than busted caviar.)

3. Make it last. In the miraculous and luxurious case of leftover caviar, don't throw it out or freeze it. Eat some more the next day. Toss it with buttered noodles or put a blob on your scrambled eggs. It should last in your fridge for about a week.

Champagne 101: The Pour

Champagne is drunk out of a flute, which is a tall, stemmed glass. If you don't have flutes and you don't want to invest much, you can find inexpensive ones or even good-quality plastic flutes. You can also get away with using white-wine glasses with champagne. A water glass really won't do, because without the stem to hold it by, the heat from your hands will warm the liquid quickly. Champagne and other sparkling wines are best drunk very cold, so keep the open bottle in an ice bucket, unless it's emptied very quickly. When you fill each glass, stop halfway, because the bubbles will keep climbing. After you've gone around and filled each glass halfway, go back and top them off.

245   How to Shop for Champagne

A sparkling wine of some sort is absolutely necessary if you're sticking with tradition, but champagne, technically, isn't the only option. Americans generally refer to sparkling wine as "Champagne," but it's only technically Champagne with a capital "C" if it comes from the Champagne region of France. There are other French sparkling wines, Italian ones (like prosecco), German ones (some Rieslings, Gewürztraminer), and lots of American varieties. There are sparkling reds and rosés as well. What you choose for your party should be whatever crowd-pleaser fits your budget. Good wine stores often hold tastings in the days leading up to New Year's, which can help you navigate all the options. Some sparkling wines are much sweeter than others, or drier, and so on. Shop at a wine store with variety (bigger stores also tend to offer more competitive prices), and ask for recommendations. In a good shop, you should be able to get honest advice about the best bottle in your price range, and you very well might find that it's one they would recommend even if you were willing to spend more. Don't be intimidated into overspending.

246   *Flourish and Flair:* Popping the Cork

The flying cork and frothing overflow of wine so popular in movies are dramatic, but that cork could take an eye out and that booze isn't cheap, so it's time to learn the grown-up way to open a bottle. It's not nearly as tricky as it looks, though sometimes it requires a little muscle. First, remove the cage that surrounds the cork. Keep your thumb pressed gently against the cork in case it should pop prematurely. Loosely cover the top of the bottle with a clean dish towel, so you can catch the cork and any bubbling wine. Next, firmly grasp the cork and twist the bottle. Though it may seem more natural to twist the cork, you will have more leverage by twisting the bottle. The pressure from the air that gets into the bottle will push the cork out, and you're done!

247 How to Serve Bubbly on a Budget

For a New Year's Eve dinner party, champagne (or any sparkling wine) could be poured at the beginning of the evening or just at midnight. If your budget doesn't allow many bottles of a quality champagne, serve the bubbly just for a special toast. Filling in with less expensive wine throughout the night is a fine plan. In fact, you shouldn't assume that everyone wants to drink champagne all night, especially if you're serving meat as your main course (in which case, you'll want to serve a red). A great way to make up for not-great champagne is to serve champagne cocktails, such as a Kir Royale, which incorporates a splash of crème de cassis.

248 *Flourish and Flair:* A Toast from the Host

Some people have a knack for giving a toast; they can make you tear up and then burst into hysterics a minute later, and then spin the whole thing on a poignant-yet-celebratory note that you remember for years. But this takes practice. Most of us fear we'll be too nervous to make any sense at all. If you tend more toward the latter, here are a few golden rules to follow: First, be prepared. Don't assume that a few glasses of wine will turn you into some kind of poet and try to wing it. (In fact, don't get too tipsy before the toasting time comes!) Begin with an anecdote that isn't too long or complicated and that illustrates the holiday or person you're celebrating with a little humor. Practice in front of a close friend with whom you're comfortable and whom you can trust for an honest critique. Jot down a few key themes on a note card so you have the structure of your talk down and don't forget anything, but don't read whole sentences. Most important, keep it short and simple, and speak from your heart. If you're really uncomfortable, it's fine to raise a glass and say something as simple as "I'm so glad to have the family together to celebrate the New Year" or "Here's to Joe's return from London!" If the cook is someone other than you, it's always nice to raise a glass in his or her direction.

249 TIP: If You're the One Being Toasted

If it's your birthday or engagement party, graduation celebration, or any other occasion when you're the one being toasted, tradition says you're to keep your drink on the table while everyone else clinks and drinks. Raising your glass is something like clapping when receiving a round of applause. Most likely, your crowd isn't so attached to such rules, but at a formal occasion, keep this in mind.

250 RECIPE: *Braised Short Ribs*

Short ribs are extraordinarily rich, so serve what might seem like a smallish portion, and with the exception of creamy mashed potatoes, keep the rest of the menu on the light side. A raw kale salad or a cold green bean salad will help cut the richness of the meat. Make sure to buy the right kind of short ribs for this recipe—the choices can be confusing. Short ribs that are cut parallel to the bone are known as English-style or English-cut short ribs. When the short ribs are cut across the bone, they are known as flanken-style.

SERVES 4 TO 6

- Rub **3 pounds English-cut short ribs** with **1 tablespoon fresh thyme leaves**; the **sliced peel of 1 orange**; **6 garlic cloves, smashed**; and **2 teaspoons black pepper**. Put the meat in a resealable plastic bag and marinate overnight in the refrigerator.

- The next day, remove the ribs from the fridge about 30 minutes before cooking to allow them to come to room temperature.

- Discard the orange peel and garlic. Season the ribs well with **kosher salt** on all sides. Heat a large skillet over high heat. Add **2 tablespoons extra-virgin olive oil** and heat until hot. Sear the ribs until dark brown and crusty on all sides, using tongs to turn. Remove the meat to a heavy-bottomed braising pot with a lid (enameled cast iron is ideal).

- Pour off most of the fat from the skillet, and add **2 medium carrots, diced; 1 onion, diced; 2 ribs celery, diced; 2 bay leaves;** and **2 thyme sprigs.**

- Preheat the oven to 325°F. Reduce the heat under the skillet to medium and sauté the vegetables, stirring occasionally, until tender, 6 to 8 minutes. Add **1 (750-ml) bottle dry red wine** and **2 tablespoons balsamic vinegar,** turn the heat up, and simmer until the liquid reduces by half.

- Add **6 cups low-sodium veal or beef stock** and bring to a boil. Pour the mixture over the ribs in the braising pot. They should be nearly submerged in the liquid.

- Cover the pot, put it into the oven, and braise the short ribs for about 3 hours, until the meat is very tender. With a slotted spoon, remove the ribs to a platter, and remove the bones. Strain the cooking liquid and skim the excess fat from the top; discard the vegetables. Pour into a saucepan, bring to a boil, and boil to thicken it slightly.

- Pour the sauce over the meat and reheat if necessary. Serve with mashed potatoes and a green vegetable.

    NOTE: To store leftovers, add the meat directly to the sauce, cover, and refrigerate for up to 3 days.

251   TIP: **Warm Your Plates and Platters**

On a cold night when you're serving something hot, such as a stew, take a minute to warm the plates, bowls, or serving dishes before loading them up. Especially if your house tends to be chilly, the vessels you serve from can cool your food down more than you might think. Simply fill bowls or plates with hot tap water and let them sit for a few minutes before drying them and serving. Or place the plates in a warm oven while you finish things up in the kitchen.

VALENTINE'S DAY

A dinner out on Valentine's Day is always welcome, but being tucked away at home is a lot more romantic. And for a host and cook, dinner for two is a great opportunity; you can serve something that requires more last-minute attention than you'd expend for a bigger party. You can hang out in the kitchen together while you cook. You can splurge on something a little pricey, since you're not feeding a crowd. But don't get too formal. Maybe serve little lamb chops you pick up with your hands or fish *en papillote* (see page 223), pretty little parchment envelopes with steamed fish inside. Of course, oysters are a traditional delicacy for valentines, and chocolate is de rigueur for dessert—fancy truffles, a simple flourless chocolate cake, or a more ambitious but doable chocolate soufflé.

252 Serving Oysters at Home

Oysters should be done right or skipped altogether. Shucking them yourself is labor-intensive, but it makes a big difference. Oysters should be alive until you eat them, and if they're in their shells, they're at their freshest. Plus, you wouldn't want to lose the flavorful juices inside (called "liquor"). So, while you could have your fishmonger do the dirty work, it's worth it to follow the steps described in the next two entries and savor the fruits of your efforts.

Talk to your fishmonger about which varieties are easiest for a novice to pry open. Some oysters clamp their shells shut extremely tightly and require serious muscle to extract. This is not the romantic display you're looking for, probably. Of course, make sure the same oysters are tasty as well; as always, the key is to shop somewhere that you trust for freshness and reliable guidance.

253 How to Shuck an Oyster

Make sure to start with well-scrubbed oysters and a good shucking knife. Hold the oyster with a dish towel as cushioning, in case your knife slips. Wriggle the point of the knife into the hinge of the shell until you manage to pry the shells apart, twisting with your wrist. Be sure to hold the oyster as level as you can, so that when it does open, the liquor inside doesn't go sloshing out: it's delicious. Once you unhinge the shell, it should be easy to open it completely. Wipe your knife off with the towel and then sweep it underneath the oyster itself, to cut the connective tissue, and loosen it completely from the shell. Now it can be slurped right out without any awkward pulling.

Oysters: Serving Dish Included

Whether they're really an aphrodisiac is debatable, but eating oysters right out of their shells is undeniably sexy, and once you get the shells open, your work is pretty much done. A lemon wedge or a bit of mignonette sauce (minced shallots in sherry or red wine vinegar with a little black pepper) gives the acidic accent that flatters oysters so perfectly. In terms of presentation, oysters are as beautiful as they are tasty, so you don't need to fuss much here, either. What's most important is to keep them from tipping over on their sides and spilling their juices. Typically, the half shells are nestled into crushed ice, which keeps the oysters cool and keeps them from moving around. You could also pour kosher salt into a platter with an edge or a shallow bowl, or use seaweed. It's true that oysters should be kept cool, but it's not necessary for them to be extremely cold, so ice is optional, as long as they've been kept cool until just before serving.

255 RECIPE: *Mushroom Risotto*

Risotto is a dish better made at home than eaten in a restaurant since it fares much better from beginning to end with careful attention, lots of TLC, and *almost* constant stirring. You can certainly putter in the kitchen getting other things done between stirs.

MAKES 6 SERVINGS

- In a large saucepan, bring **9 cups chicken stock** to a boil over high heat, then lower to a simmer. Place ⅓ **cup dried porcini mushrooms** in a liquid measuring cup and pour 1 cup of the hot stock over them. Set aside to steep.

- Heat 1 **tablespoon olive oil** in a 3-quart wide, shallow saucepan on medium high. Add **5 ounces shiitake mushrooms, sliced,** and **5 ounces cremini mushrooms, sliced.** Season with **salt and pepper** and cook, stirring, until browned. Transfer to a bowl and set aside.

HOLIDAYS AND OTHER SPECIAL DAYS

- Lift the porcini from the soaking liquid (reserve the liquid) and finely chop. Heat **2 tablespoons olive oil** in the same saucepan, add the porcini and **1 shallot, minced,** and sauté for 5 minutes. Add **2 cups Arborio rice** and stir to coat the rice with the oil. Cook the rice until it begins to turn translucent at the edges, about 4 minutes. Pour in ½ **cup dry white wine** and stir until it is absorbed by the rice.

- Carefully pour the porcini liquid into the pan of stock, being sure not to include any of the sediment in the bottom of the measuring cup. Add the hot stock to the rice one ladleful at a time, stirring continuously and allowing the stock to be absorbed each time before adding more. Keep the pan at an even, gentle bubble. The risotto is done when it has lost its bite but is still firm, not gummy, and has developed a rich, creamy coating, about 20 minutes.

- Turn off the heat and stir in ¼ **cup freshly grated Parmigiano-Reggiano, 2 tablespoons butter,** and **salt and pepper to taste.** Stir in half of the mushrooms and reheat the other half to use as a garnish. Serve immediately, topped with the remaining mushrooms.

TIP: How to Soak Dried Mushrooms

Dried porcinis pack intense flavor, but they have to be reconstituted in hot water or stock. That liquid is, in turn, infused with lots of earthy flavor. But there can also be a bit of grit left behind. Soak the mushrooms in a pitcher or a measuring cup—anything with a spout, and preferably clear glass or plastic— so you can easily pour the liquid out while keeping an eye on any sediment at the bottom and leave it behind.

TIP: Get the Truffle Aura on the Cheap

We'd all love to be shaving big flakes of pricey white truffles over our risotto, but reality doesn't always line things up this way. Using dried porcinis as a base for risotto (or soup, or sauce) adds a dose of earthy flavor. Then layer a mixture of fresh mushrooms, such as shiitakes, porcinis, and creminis (which are less expensive and can help stretch out the pricier mushrooms) to get complex flavor into the dish. To really blow away your guest, finish it off with a sprinkle of truffle salt, truffle oil, or truffle butter. (If you can't find these at your local gourmet market, take to the Internet; see Resources, page 274.) A little of any of these will go a long way in creating that decadent aroma and taste. Make sure to look for products made with real truffles, and technically you're not even cheating.

HOLIDAYS AND OTHER SPECIAL DAYS

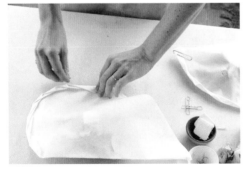

Cooking fish in an origami-like parchment envelope is a classic method that never goes out of style, and it's much simpler to do than its exciting presentation would suggest. It's also ideally suited to entertaining, since the parchment packets can be prepared a few hours—in fact, up to a day—ahead of time, and then just take a short time to cook. All the prep can be done and cleaned up long before your guest arrives. Use the recipe that follows as a starting point for your own ideas. You'll need parchment paper and scissors to make the papillotes. Then fill them with thick, firm fish fillets, or even shrimp; vegetables that will add flavor and cook quickly; and something aromatic like herbs or shallots. You can add a splash of white wine, too, but only if you are cooking them within an hour or two of making the pouches. Otherwise, the paper will get soggy. Fold the papillotes so they are tightly closed, place on a baking pan, and cook according to the recipe.

Use this recipe as a guide, but you can also add other ingredients that will flavor the fish. Try a few capers, ginger, scallions, thyme, a drop of sesame oil, some sliced oil-cured olives, or even a few chopped tomatoes.

MAKES 4 SERVINGS

- Preheat the oven to 400°F. Measure four 24-inch-long sheets of parchment. Fold each sheet in half and, starting from the folded side, cut a large half-heart shape.

- To make the packets, have ready: **4 thick skinless fish fillets, about 6 ounces each, such as striped bass, halibut, or snapper; 1 cup sliced shiitake mushrooms; 2 cups thinly sliced fennel; plus some of the fronds; and 1 large shallot, thinly sliced.**

- Open one heart on a work surface. Place one quarter of the sliced fennel a few inches from the center crease of the heart. Scatter one quarter of the shallots over it. Place a fish fillet on top, parallel to the crease, and season with **salt and pepper.** Scatter one quarter of the mushrooms and some fennel fronds over top, and, if desired, top with **a pat of butter** (you'll need a total of 4 teaspoons) or **a drizzle of olive oil** in the center.

- Fold the paper over to enclose the fish and vegetables, and begin folding the edges over: Make short folds, beginning at the deep center of the heart and working your way to the point of the heart. Each fold should overlap the previous fold; the folds will get gradually longer as you work your way around. After you fold the last pleat under, use a metal paper clip to secure it; you can also place a paper clip on the first fold to ensure a tight seal.

- Refrigerate the packets, and repeat with the remaining ingredients.

- Place the packets on baking sheets and bake for 15 to 18 minutes, or until the packages are puffy.

260 How to Serve a Soufflé

The simple answer is quickly. Make sure your guest is waiting for the soufflé rather than the other way around. A soufflé can wait a few minutes in a turned-off oven with the door ajar, but no longer. Using oven mitts (and being careful not to knock into the top), transfer the soufflé onto a tray, plate, or platter that you can use to carry it to the table. Quickly dust it with confectioners' sugar, if you want (and if it's sweet), and serve immediately. Pass sauces, if any, on the side.

261 RECIPE: *Make-Ahead Chocolate Soufflés*

Making soufflés is no more complicated than mixing up any cake batter, and they can be made a day or two ahead and popped into the oven a half hour before serving. These roux-based soufflés won't fall as fast as pastry-cream-based soufflés would, and even if fallen, they're good, very similar to a flourless chocolate cake (make a few extra and enjoy the next day). Fill individual baking dishes three-quarters full, no matter what their size.

MAKES 8 SERVINGS

- Preheat the oven to 375°F. **Butter** eight 6-ounce ovenproof ramekins and coat the bottom and insides with **sugar;** tap out excess sugar.

- Melt **8 ounces bittersweet chocolate, chopped,** in a double boiler over simmering water. Transfer to a large bowl.

- In a small saucepan, melt **1 tablespoon unsalted butter.** Add **1 tablespoon all-purpose flour** and cook, stirring constantly, for 1 to 2 minutes, until thickened. Gradually add **½ cup milk,** whisking briskly, and cook, whisking until thickened. Remove the saucepan from the stove and whisk in **3 large egg yolks** (do not discard the whites) and **1 teaspoon vanilla extract.** Pour the milk mixture over the chocolate and whisk until blended. Set aside.

- Using a hand mixer or a standing mixer, beat **5 large egg whites** together with **a pinch of cream of tartar** until they form soft peaks. Gradually add **⅓ cup sugar** and beat on high speed until the egg whites are stiff and shiny but not dry.

- Use a rubber spatula to fold the egg whites into the chocolate mixture in batches. Divide the mixture evenly among the ramekins, filling them about three-quarters full. (At this point, the soufflés can be refrigerated, covered, for 1 or 2 days until you are ready to bake them.) Run your thumb around the edge of the dishes right before baking so that nothing will hinder an even rise, and to get that nice top-hat look to your finished soufflés.

- Put the soufflés on a rimmed baking sheet and bake for 15 to 17 minutes, until the tops are cracked and the soufflés have risen but the centers are still molten. Serve immediately.

Birthday fetes can run the gamut from a simple dinner or brunch with a few friends to a surprise blowout for one hundred people to commemorate a big birthday. One thing is a constant: there will be cake. Even if you are celebrating in a restaurant, a cake usually can be brought in from the outside, and a homemade one is a great way to show you care.

262   The Tools You Need to Ice a Cake

While it's unlikely that you'll be decorating a cake in front of anyone or at the last minute, it is still good to know how to do this quickly and easily and without making too much of a mess.

Here are the essential tools.

- Turntable. This could be an inexpensive plastic one designed for the purpose of icing cakes, or a more elaborate metal model. You can also purchase a basic plastic lazy Susan in any supermarket for a few dollars. Whichever you choose, a turntable is what makes decorating a cake easy. It enables you to keep your hand in the same place while spinning the cake. It also allows you to trim the layers expertly.

- Icing spatula. Yes, you could use a butter knife in a pinch, but an offset spatula is much more efficient since the angled blade allows you to smooth the surface of the cake while keeping your fingers out of the way.

- Serrated knife. It's always good to use a bread knife—and the longer the better. It's handy for trimming and evening out cake layers.

263 *Flourish and Flair:* The Secret to Making a Perfect Cake

If you're icing a basic birthday-type cake, you will usually have two layers, and possibly three, to work with. If they're domed when they come out of the oven, trim them so they're flat. This step is essential to making a professional-looking cake. To trim, place a layer on the turntable, and hold a serrated bread knife level with the edge of the cake at the outer edge. Cut into the cake, holding the knife steady in one position while gently turning the turntable, working your way to the center. Check the evenness by looking at the cake at eye level while spinning the turntable. If it's not totally level, trim further. If it's only slightly uneven, you can even it out with icing. Just put more icing on the side that needs to be leveled out.

264 Five Steps to Icing a Cake

Once you have the tools on hand and the cakes trimmed, here's the step-by-step process for making a beautifully iced cake.

1. Place the first layer, trimmed side down, on your turntable, so you have a perfectly flat bottom facing up. Plop about a cup of icing in the center of the cake and, using a small offset spatula, spread it out almost to the edge (the icing will be pushed to the edge when you place the second layer on top).

2. Add the second layer on top, turning it upside down, so that the bottom is facing up. This will give you a relatively crumb-free top, which makes icing easier. If making a three-layer cake, ice the second layer, and then place the third layer on top (as in step 1).

3. Apply a crumb coat to the cake. This may seem like an extra step, but it will save you time later on. Spread the entire cake with a very

thin layer of icing all over, and chill it until firm, at least 15 to 30 minutes. This thin layer will trap any loose crumbs, keeping them from getting into the final, decorative layer of icing. Chilling the cake will also give the filling time to set up so the layers don't go sliding while you ice it.

4. Now that you have a smooth, firm base to work with, have fun swirling the icing onto the cake. Plop most of the icing onto the top of the cake and start working toward the edges and down the sides with your spatula, nudging it down gently and gradually as you spin the turntable slowly.

5. Let the cake sit at room temperature or refrigerate it (depending on your icing recipe) until ready to serve. Even if it doesn't require chilling, it's still best to let a cake sit for a while before serving to set up a bit as the cake absorbs some of the moisture in the icing.

How to Write on a Birthday Cake

Supermarkets sell icing gel pens that make this task easy, but if you want to do cake writing like a pro, make a small parchment cone, or use a pastry bag fitted with a small, plain round tip. You can use thin royal icing, melted dark chocolate, or melted white chocolate. These all flow through the tip very nicely, which is essential for smooth writing. The most important thing to remember is that you are not trying to form letters by pressing the tip of the cone or pastry bag right onto the surface of the cake; rather, you are trying to create an unbroken string that is suspended between the tip and the surface of the cake. Don't be afraid to go big on the first letters, adding loops and embellishments. In fact, it's easier to go large, to keep the line moving, rather than try to be small and precise. Just make sure to map out your letters with a few toothpick marks before you start so you don't run out of room on the cake when there's no turning back. Practice first on paper until you have the hang of it.

OUTDOOR PARTIES

The way we cook, drink, eat, set the table—if you are even eating at a table—loosens up and becomes a lot more fun when you're eating outdoors. Simplicity and informality rule. When the weather is lovely, just spending an afternoon or evening outdoors with friends is entertainment enough. The space is decorated by Mother Nature, the produce is plentiful, there are few concerns about how many people you can accommodate, and cleanup is easy. Any kind of party can work outdoors, but the naturals are children's birthday parties, pool parties, barbecues, and cocktail parties, which can be held before the sun goes down and the bugs come out. Dinners after dark work best on a screened-in porch, unless you're lucky enough to live in a spot that isn't too buggy.

266 Checklist for Picnics Away from Home

If you're planning an outdoor excursion that involves cooking and eating somewhere other than your yard, you will need to do some advance planning to make sure you take everything you'll need.

- ❑ **Plates, cups, napkins, and utensils.** Disposables are always an option. But depending on what kind of food and drink you are serving, you can also ask guests to bring their own "real" place setting from home.

- ❑ **Ice packs, coolers, and ice.** Take one cooler for drinks, filled with ice, and another for the food, filled with ice packs. Choose flat-top coolers so they can double as tabletops.

- ❑ **Matches or a lighter.**

- ❑ **Corkscrew and bottle opener.** It's not a bad idea to attach the opener to someone's jeans, as an opener can easily get lost, especially at the beach.

- ❑ **Sheets or tablecloths** for sitting on and for covering tables.

- ❑ **Trash bags for cleanup.** It's a good idea to take more than you think you'll need. You can stuff dirty sheets and towels in one to keep things contained on the way home. You may also want to take clear bags for disposing of recyclable cans and bottles.

- ❑ **Flashlights** to use when cleaning up after dark.

- ❑ **Wet wipes.** You'll have napkins, but these can be a saving grace for sticky fingers or unexpected messes.

- ❑ **Plastic containers or resealable plastic bags** for packing up leftovers.

How to Pick the Best Picnic Plates

When you're entertaining a crowd outside, you might not want to use your regular place settings. Here are some of the pros and cons of the old standbys as well as some of the latest options that are more kind to the environment.

- Compostable plates, made from plant-based materials such as sugarcane, wheat, corn, and potato, are pretty neat. The guilt factor is low (they biodegrade in about thirty days), and they're sturdy and microwaveable. They tend to be very plain-looking. Depending on your taste, these could be appealingly minimal, or just not fun enough. (See Resources, page 274.)

- Bamboo is quite sturdy and is biodegradable (the process takes about six months). These plates aren't reusable, but environmentalists like bamboo because it grows very quickly, making it a highly renewable material. Hostesses like it because it's chic and modern looking. The downside is that this stuff is not cheap.

- Melamine dishes are ideal for the hostess who makes regular use of her backyard or porch for dining. The hard plastic is as sturdy as ceramic or glass but nearly impossible to break, so there's nothing to worry about, even if someone drops a plate on the ground. The dishes are reusable, which means you have to wash them after your party, but they're available in many cute designs, and it's a small, onetime investment.

- Plastic plates run the gamut from flimsy to very sturdy, and the prices correspond. These are the least eco-friendly of your disposable options, and because of that, they're not as trendy as other materials and the designs aren't the most up-to-date, either. You can find simple ones, but it's difficult to find plastic plates that are elegant looking.

- Paper is not a great option for heavy, wet foods, for obvious reasons, but it can be the easiest go-to for simple uses, such as serving cake and cookies at a gathering in the park or a birthday party held at the beach. There is a waste factor, but paper is recyclable and inexpensive.

Grilling Equipment Checklist

Every grill master has his or her favorite tools, and only experience will tell you which gadgets you will personally rely on most; you might really need only a few things. Rather than buy a set, which will probably include several superfluous pieces and may well lack a utensil you do need, build up your arsenal as you go along. Here's a quick guide to some basics.

❏ A **wire brush** to clean the grill when it's hot. The bristles on these will burn and blacken, so rather than spend a lot, assume you'll have to replace the brush with some frequency if you grill often, and buy a couple of well-priced brushes at once.

❏ A **cedar plank** for cooking, especially for fish. The cedar is untreated but soaked in water, so it doesn't go up in flames. The wood imparts a hint of smoke to the food, and you don't have to worry about delicate fish sticking to the grill.

❏ **Heavy-duty gloves** are a must for handling any pots placed on the grill and for any flipping, basting, and removing that brings your hands near the heat.

❏ A set of **tongs** that are designated for the grill; they'll go through some wear and tear in the heat. Look for long ones with a silicone or wood handle, rather than uncoated metal, which will quickly become too hot to handle without gloves.

❏ An **instant-read thermometer** is a great help for grilling meat—especially pork and chicken. It will allow you to remove the meat knowing it's safely cooked through without overcooking it. Thermometers are made specifically for grilling; they have long probes that can be inserted in the meat while it's on the grill without forcing your hand too close to the fire.

❏ A **clip-on light** for grilling into the evening. (A flashlight will do in a pinch.)

- [ ] A **spray bottle** filled with water to control flare-ups.

- [ ] A **fire extinguisher, baking soda,** or a **hose** to squash a grease fire if it breaks out, though this rarely happens.

- [ ] A couple of **large trays** or **baking sheets** to place food on as it comes off the grill, unless it's going straight onto each guest's plate. Be prepared with a holding place, especially when dealing with chicken, which should never be placed back on the tray where it sat raw.

- [ ] An **iron shovel** or **extra pair of tongs** just for stirring the coals.

- [ ] Think ahead and be sure to have **olive oil, salt and pepper,** and any other crucial seasonings on hand once the cooking begins. Avoid running back to the kitchen during the grilling.

- [ ] **Grill baskets** for fish or small vegetables that might fall through the grill or stick.

- [ ] A **damp dish towel,** or **hand wipes,** so you can clean up your hands without going back inside or to the hose.

269   Charcoal vs. Charcoal

When possible, reach for hardwood lump charcoal rather than charcoal briquettes. Though briquettes will give you an even fire that will last a bit longer, they will never get quite as hot as a hardwood lump charcoal fire will. Other advantages of hardwood lump are that it costs less and never imparts a chemical taste to the food, only a hint of smoke flavor. Also, with hardwood, the coals do not need to be gray and ashy to cook with (meaning you can add more as you cook, to maintain or increase the heat), as do briquettes.

270   *In Praise of* The Charcoal Chimney

Using a charcoal chimney is a great way to start a raging hot fire without using any lighter fluid (i.e., chemicals). It uses oxygen, just like the chimney in your fireplace, and is similarly as simple. To set up a chimney, crumple up several individual sheets of newspaper—not packing them in so tight as to block air from moving through— and put them in the bottom section of the cylinder. Place the chimney in your grill, with the grate removed. Fill the chimney with charcoal and light the paper on fire, tilting it slightly to let the air travel through (with heavy-duty mitts on your hands, of course). The flames should light all the charcoal in about 15 minutes. Dump the hot charcoal out onto the floor of your grill (again, with mitts to protect your hands; the steel cylinder will now be extremely hot), and add more coals, mixing them together. When the new coals are gray and hot, spread them out, replace the grate, let it heat up for a few minutes, and you are ready to grill.

271 TIP: **Add Hardwood to a Charcoal Fire**

Hardwood burns hot, and it does not need to be ashed over to cook with, so if your charcoal briquette fire begins to fade just when you need it to be hot, throw in a few pieces of hardwood lump charcoal, and you will extend its life. Added bonus: you'll have enough heat left over at the end for toasting marshmallows.

272 Weather Permitting: Planning for Plan B

If you are throwing a party outdoors, be prepared to either bring the party indoors or reschedule if the weather doesn't cooperate. If the whole point of having this party is to be outside, say, for a summer barbecue, provide a rain date right from the start. That way, guests can pencil in the second date as well. Just make sure to keep people informed if forecasts are iffy as the day approaches. This can relieve a lot of stress for everyone, and you'll be in good form since Plan B has been in place the whole time. If expense is not a problem, think about investing in a tent, so weather won't be a worry. And if you're prepared to move your party indoors, make sure your indoor space is large (and clean) enough to accommodate your crowd, and that you've thought about alternatives to your outdoor setup: how to arrange the bar, the food, and the seating indoors. As rattling and disappointing as this change of plan may seem, remember it's really the people that make the party, and everyone will have a good time regardless of the weather.

273 How to Pack Light for a Party Away from Home

Pick dishes that are already composed, that won't suffer during travel time, and that don't requre separate dressings or ingredients. For example, go for coleslaw rather than a green salad. Lighten the load by packing only necessary amounts of condiments, such as mustard and ketchup, in handy squeeze bottles. Meat for a barbecue can be marinated or seasoned with a dry rub in advance, so it only gets tastier while it's in the cooler and you don't have to lug spices or sauces separately (although salt is indispensable).

274   The Picnic Schlep

The great thing about a picnic or a barbecue in the park or at the beach is that you don't have to clean your house—before or after. On the flip side, there's the challenge of remembering all the things you need (see the checklist on page 232) and getting it all there. For a crowd, you need wheels—or several very helpful friends. If the party is set in a spot that you can drive to, use the trunk of your car as a veritable pantry. If not, using a wheelbarrow or even a rolling suitcase beats lugging bags across a park. Pack everything, except delicate items, on wheels, and then hit the road.

275   Dealing with Bugs at an Outdoor Party

Citronella candles and torches are very effective in repelling bugs, plus they provide some light, look festive and traditional, and are natural. Spread them out, creating a sort of barrier around your backyard or picnic blanket, but not too close to your party or the food. If your backyard is prone to bugginess, provide some insect repellent for guests who want it. Fortunately, the options have expanded beyond those stinky aerosol cans. Look for natural brands of bug repellent, and chose one with a mild scent. Overwhelming aromas can get in the way of the flavors of your food.

276 RECIPE: *Salmon Cooked on a Cedar Plank*

Using an untreated cedar plank (available at most cookware stores or near the butcher's counter in your grocery store) is an elegant and easy way to cook fish on a grill without any worry of having the fish stick to the grate. The wood must be soaked for at least an hour before it hits the grill. The plank will get hot enough to smoke a little, but not to catch fire, and will impart a wonderful smoky flavor to the fish. This dish can be made with any size piece of fish; a whole side of salmon, about 2½ pounds, will serve 6 easily.

SERVES 6

• Soak an untreated cedar plank in water for at least an hour, or up to 4 hours.

• Prepare a hot fire in a grill. Rub **a skin-on 2½-pound side of salmon** with **olive oil** on both sides, and sprinkle it with **salt and pepper.**

• When the coals are hot but no longer flaming, bank them on one side of the grill so you have a hot side and a cooler side. Place the plank on the hot side and wait until it begins to smoke, about 1 minute. Turn it over and allow the other side to do the same. Lay the salmon skin side down on the plank, cover the grill, and cook for 20 to 30 minutes, checking a few times to make sure the fire is hot and the plank is smoking but has not caught fire. Have a spray bottle of water ready in case it does, and move the plank to a cooler part of the grill if necessary.

OUTDOOR PARTIES

When the fat begins to gather in white bubbles on top of the fish and the thickest part has become slightly firmer, the salmon is done.

- Place the cedar plank on a platter and carry to the table. Garnish the fish however you please (for example, with **lemon wedges, capers,** and **dill or parsley sprigs**), or pass a mustard sauce around.

How to Grill Whole Fish

Grilling a whole fish may seem intimidating, but it's easier to manage one large fish than to orchestrate the cooking time for several fragile fillets. Ask your fishmonger to clean the fish and leave everything intact. (Yes, including the head. Even if your crowd is not the type to relish the supple cheeks of the fish, keeping the head on during the cooking will make for a juicier end result. You can easily remove it afterward if you want.) Generally, round fish such as striped bass and red snapper are the best for grilling.

When you're ready to cook, stuff the cavity with slices of lemon and whatever herbs you choose, plus olive oil and salt. Make a few deep diagonal slashes in the thicker part of the fish to enable even cooking, then rub a generous amount of oil on the skin. Because the flesh is enclosed in the skin, the flesh steams, keeping it nicely moist, and the flavors of whatever you decide to place inside permeate the meat.

Depending on the size of the fish, flip it after 10 or 15 minutes, and check that the flesh in the thickest part is opaque and flaky before taking it off the grill. The only challenge is making sure the delicate flesh stays intact. A grill basket specifically designed for a whole fish is

a great gadget to use, and it means you don't have to worry about the fish sticking to the grill. When it's time to turn the fish over, you will turn the basket itself. If you're cooking directly on the grill, just be sure it's clean and well oiled in advance, and oil the fish as well. Cooking fish with its skin on will reduce the potential for stickiness; you can remove the skin afterward if you wish. Let the fish rest for 10 minutes or so before serving.

278   TIP: **Use Lemons to Create a Nonstick Grill**

Slice a lemon into thin rounds and place them on the grill to make a nonstick landing pad for the fish, and to impart a little extra flavor to the skin at the same time. When the fish—or even chicken—is finished cooking, the lemons may be stuck to the grill, but you can let them burn off and then just scrape the grates clean later. If you have large leaves handy that you know are safe to cook with, such as grape or banana leaves, these can work in the same way.

Flourish and Flair: Fillet a Whole Fish
at the Table

When you've cooked a whole fish, it's customary to serve it at the table, since seeing the whole crispy fish is part of the fun, and there will likely be someone at your table who will want to pick all the tasty bits that cling to the bones after they've eaten their portion. Filleting is simpler than it looks, as the bones tell you where to go. If you don't want to eat the skin, simply peel it back from the belly side up. Then use a large spoon or a spatula and gently divide the top fillet (facing up) into two, lengthwise, along the spine. Gently divide a portion of fish, and slide the flesh outward away from the backbone, picking it up with the spoon or spatula to try to keep it as intact as possible. Continue sliding the fish off of the bones in both directions until there's nothing left but the skeleton. Pick up the skeleton and discard; it will come right out in one piece. Set aside or discard any stuffing. Then divide the bottom half of the fish, now boneless, into portions, and serve, leaving the skin behind or serving it, as you wish.

280   How to Grill Fish Fillets

For cooking fillets, patience is a virtue. Resist the urge to fuss with the fish until the first side has had a chance to cook. Extra poking and prodding will quickly cause the flesh to tear. When the surface is nicely seared and brown, it will be easier to lift. Use a thin, flexible spatula, and if you detect any sticking, try to release the fish by scraping the spatula in short jabs under the fish with the spatula angled against the grates of the grill, metal on metal, to avoid tearing the fish. Follow these pointers to avoid sticking.

- Make sure the grill is clean. After it has heated up, use a wire grill brush to remove any past cooking residue, and do it again a few minutes later if need be.

- Make sure the fish is completely dry, and oil it well before grilling.

- Oil the clean grill with a paper towel dipped in oil; you can hold it with a pair of tongs.

- Make sure the grill is nice and hot so you can get a quick sear.

- Position fillets across the grill bars, so that the fish will end up marked with short horizontal lines.

281 How to Cook the Perfect Steak

Steak goes so well with all the summer foods we love, especially corn, tomatoes, and salad. Since it can be pricey, err on the side of undercooking. A steak can always be put back on the grill for a couple of minutes if need be, but there is no way to undo overcooking. If you aim for the center to be medium rare or rare, depending on the rarest preference in your group, there will likely be more well-done pieces toward the edges, and if you are slicing the steak for serving, which I recommend, there will be something for everyone. Follow these tips for steak success.

- Buy dry-aged prime steaks for the best flavor and the most tender meat. Porterhouse, T-bone, rib-eye, and strip steaks are the best choices for a classic steak meal. Order ahead to request steaks that are 1½ inches thick. Thicker steaks will be more forgiving and less likely to overcook. For a more economical meal, choose flank steak or skirt steak, which come only in their natural thickness of about an inch or less. These need to be cooked quickly, and they benefit from some time marinating in an acid-based marinade.

- Bring steaks to room temperature for 30 to 40 minutes before grilling.

- About 15 minutes before cooking, pat steaks dry with paper towels, and rub lightly with olive oil. Season generously with coarse salt and freshly cracked black pepper.

- Grill steaks over a very hot charcoal fire (make sure to leave a cooler spot on the grill to move the steak to in case of flare-ups or if the steak is getting too dark too fast).

- Turn the steaks over only once, but place them at a 45-degree angle to the grates of the grill, and give them a quarter turn halfway through each side's cooking time. This is not only to give them professional-looking crosshatch grill marks but also to ensure even cooking.

- Use the following cooking times as guidelines for cooking a 1½-inch-thick steak; add or subtract about 1 minute per side for every ¼ inch more or less thickness.

Rare: First side, 6 minutes; second side, 4 minutes
Medium rare: First side, 7 minutes; second side, 5 minutes
Medium: First side, 7 minutes; second side, 6 minutes
For skirt or flank steak, 4 to 5 minutes per side and 5 to 10 minutes of resting should do the trick.

- To test doneness, avoid cutting into the steak. Even an instant-read thermometer will cause the juices to pour out, and it will be difficult to know if you are measuring the very center of the meat. Give the steak the "press test" instead. Press down on the steak with your index finger. A rare steak will feel very soft, not much different than when it was raw. Medium-rare steak will be firmer, but still yielding. Medium will be barely yielding, and medium well and beyond will feel firm to very firm.

- Let the steak rest on a plate or a wooden carving board for 5 to 10 minutes after removing it from the grill. Slice across the grain, and serve immediately.

282 What Can I Make in a Foil Pouch?

To cook vegetables in a pouch while you grill meat or fish is to take full advantage of the grill's versatility, steaming some things, and charring and smoking others. Plus you won't have to coordinate cooking inside on the stove and outside on the grill. You can cook almost anything on a grill in a foil packet, as long as it will benefit from being enclosed. Shellfish is ideal, especially bivalves like clams and mussels, because

they need steam to pop open. Beets, corn on the cob, potatoes, and hardy vegetables like green beans and broccoli also come out beautifully using this method, and the opportunity for flavoring is limitless: whole garlic cloves, a few sprigs of the herb of your choice, whole spices, citrus slices, and more.

283 Steam-Grilling vs. Grill-Roasting

To use a foil pouch to steam food, such as clams or mussels, toss the food you're cooking with a little fat (butter or olive oil, most often), plus some kind of liquid that will make steam (wine, lemon juice, broth, tomatoes, even an ice cube), and any herbs or seasoning you wish to include, and then make a pouch with heavy-duty aluminum foil. Depending on what you're cooking, you may want to put it in a very hot spot for quicker cooking, or it may be best to let it cook more slowly at the edge of the grill, away from direct heat. In the case of clams and mussels, they need only cook until the shells pop open, and the time will vary depending on the heat. Broccoli or string beans need more time and a lower temperature to cook. It's hard to go wrong with this method. The only warning here is that acid, when left in contact with the foil, can develop a bitter flavor. Go ahead and use lemon juice, wine, or tomatoes, but they shouldn't spend any more time than necessary in the foil. Remove the food immediately to a serving dish and enjoy.

If you are after more of a roasted flavor, then grill-roasting is the method for you. Potatoes, corn on the cob, zucchini, peppers, eggplant, beets, cauliflower, onions, and just about any other vegetable can be roasted in foil pouches directly on the grill. With heavy-duty foil, you can create a tiny oven and even get some color on those veggies if you lay them down in a single layer and cook over the hottest part of the fire, at least for the first ten minutes or so. The pouches can be carefully flipped to cook both sides. Then they can be moved aside to continue cooking while you grill the rest of your meal. As with steam-grilling, whatever herbs or seasoning you put in the pouch will flavor the food brilliantly.

284 RECIPE: *Clams Grilled in a Foil Pouch*

Throw a pouch filled with clams on the grill when the fire's hot, and enjoy them while you cook the rest of the meal. Timing can vary a bit, depending on the size and stubbornness of the clams and the heat of the fire. You can tell if the shells have opened by feeling the top of the package with tongs or a spatula. If you open the package and see that some clams have not opened, reseal and return to the fire for a few minutes. If there are a few duds that refuse to open after 15 minutes or so, discard them.

- Stack two 2½-foot-long pieces of heavy-duty aluminum foil. In the center, heap **18 littleneck clams, scrubbed; 2 diced seeded plum tomatoes; 1 shallot, thinly sliced;** and **the leaves from a few sprigs of flat-leaf parsley** and **oregano sprigs, coarsely chopped.** If desired, add **a pinch of red pepper flakes.** Top with **1 tablespoon unsalted butter (optional).** Fold up the sides of the foil to form a pouch.

- Pour **¼ cup dry white wine** over the clam mixture, and roll the top edges over several times to seal tightly, leaving plenty of room for the clams to steam.

- Place the pouch on the hot grill and cook for 12 to 15 minutes, until the shells have opened. Serve immediately with grilled crusty bread.

The idea is to get the potatoes to brown but not burn, so pay attention to your fire, shake the packet frequently to distribute the potatoes, and turn the whole packet carefully from time to time. You will hear the potatoes sizzling if they are cooking at the right temperature.

SERVES 4 TO 6

- Scrub **1 pound small potatoes** and cut in half. Toss the potatoes with **2 garlic cloves, 1 tablespoon chopped fresh rosemary, a drizzle of olive oil,** and **salt and pepper to taste.**

- Stack two 2½-foot-long pieces of heavy-duty aluminum foil. Put the potatoes on one side, fold the other side over to cover, and fold the edges over to seal tightly.

- Put the potatoes on the hot grill and cook for 20 to 30 minutes, until golden, shaking the pouch and turning the packet occasionally.

In Praise of Grill Baskets

Traditional grill baskets sandwich burgers, fish steaks or fillets, steaks, and other foods in a flat hinged cage that opens like a book. This type of basket gives you the great advantage of being able to flip everything in one fell swoop, a big help when you're multitasking at the grill, and completely eliminates the risk of sticking. A more modern innovation is the open grill basket, sometimes called a grill wok. You can use these to cook even small foods that would normally fall between the grates of the grill, such as mushrooms, sliced veggies, small shrimp, or asparagus. You can toss a bunch of different veggies together, as you would for a stir-fry, and cook them together so the flavors marry. A little olive oil and salt and pepper are all you need to cook with a grill wok.

287   RECIPE: *Grill Basket "Stir-Fry" Vegetables*

This is a great technique if you want to serve a mixture of vegetables, like a stir-fry, with your grilled meat or fish. Start the vegetables 10 to 15 minutes before you grill your main course, so that they can get a head start. Move them to a cooler part of the grill to keep warm once they're done. Grill baskets of all shapes and sizes are available in grocery stores or cooking shops.

SERVES 6

- In a large bowl, combine **2 zucchini, halved lengthwise and sliced into ¼- to ½-inch-thick half-moons**; **1 fennel bulb, trimmed and cut into thin ½-inch wedges**; **8 ounces cremini mushrooms, cut in half, or quartered if large**; and **1 pound asparagus, trimmed and cut into 2-inch pieces.** Drizzle over

OUTDOOR PARTIES

enough **extra-virgin olive oil** to coat the vegetables, tossing.
Sprinkle with **salt and pepper** and any **chopped herbs** you choose.

- Place the veggies in a grill basket and cook on the hot grill for
  15 to 20 minutes, tossing and flipping the basket occasionally,
  until they're tender and slightly charred at the edges.

288 How to Use Your Grill Like an Oven

If you think about it, once the top is on, the only difference between
your grill and your oven is the smoke. Unlike when using an oven,
though, controlling the temperature on the grill involves some
guesswork. But that smoky flavor is worth the experimentation.
Roasting a chicken, a small turkey, or a pork roast in a covered kettle
grill is a sure way to please a crowd, and it's easy. The key to using your
grill this way is to create indirect heat, so the meat cooks slowly, turning
golden brown. Once you've lit your coals with a charcoal chimney (see
page 236), either place them in special baskets designed for this purpose
or just push them to either side of the grill, leaving an open spot in the
middle where the food won't come into direct contact with the hot coals.
(You might also want to put a drip pan into the bottom of the grill, but

this is optional.) For more smoke flavor, sprinkle the hot coals with wood chips that have been soaked in water for about 30 minutes. You will get a lovely color this way, as you would in the oven, and the meat will be juicy and flavorful. You can also baste the meat as you would in the oven. As with a regular oven, be mindful not to keep the cover off for longer than necessary, because you will be losing heat in the meantime. An instant-read thermometer comes in handy with this method, but you can also check the doneness of a chicken by shaking hands with it: the leg joint should feel loose when it is done. Cooking chicken this way will take about one and a quarter hours, in general; a bone-in pork roast will take roughly the same.

289 RECIPE: *Herbed Pork Roast*

A bone-in pork roast is a great meat to cook by the indirect heat method on a charcoal grill. It really benefits from some subtle smoke flavor, and the bones help keep it moist.

- Rub a **bone-in, center-cut pork roast (5½ to 6 pounds)** lightly with **olive oil** and season generously with **salt and freshly ground black pepper.** Sprinkle all over with **2 tablespoons dried herbes de Provence** and **2 tablespoons roughly chopped fresh rosemary.** Sliver **2 garlic cloves** and insert them into the meat by cutting a small pocket with the tip of a paring knife. This can be done several hours ahead of time.

- Prepare a grill for indirect cooking as described opposite. When the grill is ready, place the meat in the center, with the bone side down.

- Cover the grill and cook for about 1 hour and 15 minutes. Check the temperature using an instant-read thermometer. The meat is done when the thermometer reads 145°F. Cover the grill and continue cooking until it is done. Remove to a carving board and let rest for 10 minutes before slicing into chops.

Making grilled pizza is a bit of a participatory event, and is best done when guests are outside, milling near the grill. Guests can get involved in customizing their pizzas or requesting combinations. Use whatever toppings you like in addition to the tomatoes.

- Build a fire in a grill and let it burn until the coals are glowing and beginning to cool down. Bank the coals on one side of the grill to create a hot side and a cooler side.

- Divide a **1-pound piece of thawed frozen pizza dough** into 2 pieces. Roll each piece out on a floured surface. Place one piece of dough on the hot side of the grill for 1 to

2 minutes, just to toast it slightly. Flip the dough and move it to the cooler side of the grill.

- Place the other piece of dough on the hot spot, and grill for 1 to 2 minutes. Use tongs to pull both pieces to the cooler side of the grill. Flip the dough over and dress it with **sliced tomatoes, fresh mozzarella, a drizzle of olive oil,** and **a sprinkle of salt.**

- Cover the grill and cook the pizza until the cheese melts, about 5 minutes. Top with **torn basil leaves.** Repeat with the second piece of dough.

291   TIP: How to Handle a Sticky Dough

If you are trying to knead the dough and find your hands suddenly goopy, don't add lots more flour. It's a common impulse, but flour will toughen the dough, making it even more difficult to manipulate, and worse, it will make your bread dense and dry. Instead, a little water or oil on the palms can set you free. The dough should become smooth as you work up the gluten by kneading.

Cooking outside while your friends hang out and watch is fun; have all the ingredients prepared ahead of time, so you won't be running into the kitchen. And be sure to have a clean plate handy so you can set aside the meat after you brown it. Feel free to change up the ingredients, adding different seafood, such as calamari or scallops, and whatever vegetables appeal to you and are available fresh.

SERVES 8 TO 10

- Pat dry **3 bone-in chicken breasts, cut into 3 pieces each,** and **6 chicken drumsticks.** Season generously with **kosher salt and pepper** and 2 teaspoons Spanish smoked paprika (pimentón). Refrigerate until ready to cook.

- Bring **8 cups chicken stock** to a boil on the stove. Crumble in **2 teaspoons saffron threads,** reduce the heat, and keep at a gentle simmer (covered, so as not to let it boil away).

- Light a fire in a grill or a fire pit using charcoal or wood. Heat a 17-inch paella pan (or a large deep pan) on the grill and add ¼ cup **olive oil.** Add the chicken and cook until well browned on both

sides, about 15 minutes; set aside. Cook 1 **pound Spanish chorizo, sliced ½-inch thick,** until brown; set aside. Add **16 peeled jumbo shrimp** and (optional) **3 lobster tails, in the shell and cut into pieces,** and cook until pink, about 2 minutes; set aside.

- Add 1 **large onion, chopped; 4 garlic cloves, minced; the whites of 1 bunch of scallions, sliced** (save the green tops for garnish); **½ cup chopped fresh flat-leaf parsley;** and 1 **teaspoon chopped fresh oregano leaves** and cook until the onion is translucent, about 5 minutes (you may need to add a bit more olive oil now).

- Add **4 cups short-grain paella rice** and cook, stirring frequently, for 10 minutes. Add **one 16-ounce can diced tomatoes, one 8-ounce jar piquillo peppers, 1 bay leaf,** and **½ cup white wine** and cook until the wine is absorbed. Add 6 cups of the hot broth and cook for 10 minutes.

- Bury the chicken in the rice and scatter the chorizo over the rice. Arrange **18 clams, scrubbed,** and **18 mussels, scrubbed,** in the rice, seam side up. Cover the pan with heavy-duty foil, a lid, or a grill cover and cook for 10 minutes.

- Add the shrimp, lobster (if using), 1 **cup fresh or frozen peas,** and 1 **pound asparagus cut into 2-inch lengths (tough ends snapped off).** Cover and cook for 10 to 15 minutes, or until the clams and mussels have opened and most of the liquid has been absorbed and the rice is tender. If the paella is dry before the rice, clams, and mussels are done, add some or all of the remaining 2 cups stock. Discard the bay leaf. Sprinkle with **chopped fresh flat-leaf parsley** and **the reserved scallion greens, chopped,** and serve.

Fruit, especially stone fruit such as peaches and nectarines, or pineapples, cooks beautifully on the grill. The heat softens them a bit, brings out their juices, and caramelizes the cut sides. It's an easy way to take advantage of the season and make a special dessert on the spot. Cut the fruit into quarters—or in the case of pineapple, chunks—and toss them

with a mixture of brown sugar, melted butter, and a dash of vanilla extract. Use heavy-duty foil to create a grill-top pan, folding the edges to make a lip so you don't lose any of the delectable juices and to keep the fruit out of contact with the grill itself, on which you just cooked your meal. Place the fruit cut side down in a single layer on the foil. When the fruit has begun to brown and give off juice, turn the pieces over and cook the other side for just a few minutes. The fruit won't get charred, but it will brown, and the sugars (including the added brown sugar) will create their own glaze. Transfer the fruit to a platter and serve alone or with ice cream.

This salad is great at room temperature, so it could become your famous potluck contribution, and it's also perfect for buffets and picnics. The salad is hearty but refreshing, thanks to some crunchy veggies and bright orange juice in the dressing. One of the best things about it is that you can prepare it almost completely in advance.

SERVES 10 TO 12

- Bring **4 cups water** to a boil in a large saucepan. Add **½ teaspoon salt** and **one 6-ounce package plain wild rice (1 cup)**, reduce the heat, cover, and cook until about one-third of the grains have split but the rice is still slightly chewy, about 40 minutes. Drain well and transfer to a bowl to cool.

- Meanwhile, combine **2 cups jasmine rice, 3 cups cold water,** and **½ teaspoon salt** in a large saucepan and bring to a boil over high heat, then reduce to a simmer and cook, covered, until all of the liquid has been absorbed and the rice is tender, about

20 minutes. Turn off the heat and let sit, covered, for 5 minutes. Transfer the rice to a bowl to cool slightly, and fluff with a fork.

- Make the dressing: Whisk together **the juice of 1 orange; 1 shallot, minced; ½ teaspoon salt; pepper to taste;** and **2 tablespoons balsamic or red wine vinegar (or a mixture of the two).** Slowly whisk in **½ cup olive oil.**

- While the rice cooks, preheat the oven to 375°F. Spread **1 cup pecan halves** on a large rimmed baking sheet and toast in the oven, shaking the pan every few minutes so the nuts toast evenly and don't burn, about 8 minutes. Transfer the pecans to a bowl. When they're cool enough to handle, break them lengthwise in half and set aside.

- Combine the jasmine and wild rice in a large bowl. Pour the dressing over and toss. Add **1 cucumber, peeled and cut into ¼-inch cubes; 1 red bell pepper, cored, seeded, and cut into ¼-inch cubes; ½ cup dried currants or cranberries; ½ cup chopped fresh flat-leaf parsley;** and **2 tablespoons rinsed capers** and toss together well. You can make this up to 1 day ahead of time, but don't add the cucumbers until just before serving.

- Sprinkle in the nuts just before serving, so they stay crunchy.

295   RECIPE: *Minestrone Salad*

This pasta salad is a clever take on a well-loved soup. Because it's served at room temperature, it makes a great side dish at a picnic or barbecue. It's colorful and extremely flavorful, with pesto, beans, and vegetables.

SERVES 8

- Place **12 ounces fingerling or baby red potatoes** in a medium saucepan and cover with cold water. Bring to a boil and cook until

the potatoes are tender when pierced with a fork, about 10 minutes. Spread them out on a baking sheet to cool, then slice the potatoes into ½-inch coins.

- Bring a large pot of water to a boil and add 1 teaspoon salt. Prepare a bowl of ice water. Add **8 ounces green beans, cut in half,** and **1 pound asparagus, trimmed and cut into 1-inch pieces** so they're about the size of the pasta you're using, and blanch the vegetables just until they're bright green, 1 to 2 minutes. Scoop the vegetables out of the hot water with a spider or a strainer, rinse them with cold water, and submerge them in the ice water until completely cool, then drain, pat dry, and set aside.

- Add **1 pound gemelli or tubetti (or any short pasta you choose)** to the boiling water and cook until al dente. Drain the pasta and put it in a large bowl to cool a bit.

- Toss in the potatoes, asparagus, green beans, **½ cup pesto, one 15½-ounce can cannellini beans (drained and rinsed), one 6-ounce jar roasted peppers, sliced into strips,** and **salt and pepper to taste.** If preparing ahead of time, combine all of the ingredients 1 to 2 hours before serving.

This version of the Italian bread salad isn't exactly traditional: the bocconcini (tiny mozzarella balls) and capers are not standard ingredients, but they add lots in the way of texture and flavor. You'll find that the recipe welcomes improvisation. Sliced fennel, roasted bell peppers, anchovies, and any other Italian ingredients that appeal to you could be added. What makes it panzanella is the bread, tomatoes, and plenty of basil. The salad was invented as a way to use up old bread, and you should keep it in mind when you find yourself in that predicament, not wanting to waste it. But here fresh bread is grilled, which adds flavor and color and firms the bread up so it doesn't get soggy when tossed with the dressing.

SERVES 8

- In a large bowl, combine **6 medium beefsteak tomatoes, cut into 1-inch cubes; 1 seedless cucumber, quartered lengthwise and cut into chunks; ¼ cup capers, drained and rinsed; ½ red onion, thinly sliced; 3 tablespoons red wine vinegar; ½ cup extra-virgin olive oil; 10 basil leaves, torn;** and **salt and pepper to taste.** Toss well and set aside to marinate for at least an hour.

- Cut **1 loaf Italian bread (about 1 pound)** into 1-inch slices. Grill or broil the slices of bread on both sides until lightly toasted. Rub each slice with a **garlic clove sliced in half.** Tear the bread into bite-size pieces, and set aside.

- When you're ready to serve, toss the bread with the tomato mixture. Toss in **2 cups bocconcini** and garnish with more **basil leaves.**

SERVES 8 TO 10

1. Sangria

As summer concoctions go, sangria is always a hit. In your own sangria experiments, vary the fruit, use white wine (ideal for summer) instead of red, or add a little honey or perhaps a cinnamon stick.

- Pour **a bottle of dry red wine** into a pitcher. Add 1 **tablespoon sugar, ¼ cup brandy, ¼ cup orange liqueur, and ¼ cup freshly squeezed orange juice or any juice,** and mix. Slice **peaches, oranges, apples, berries, or other fruit** and toss with **a dash of freshly squeezed lemon juice.** Add to the pitcher. Pour the sangria into ice-filled glasses and top with sparkling water, if desired. Guests can hold back the fruit while pouring and then spoon out just the right amount into their glasses.

2. Planter's Punch

Planter's punch, created to celebrate the opening of the Myers's Rum distillery in Jamaica, is a perfect blend of fruit juice and fun. Mix an equal amount of orange juice and pineapple juice and then pour it into an ice-cube tray the day before you intend to serve. Use these ice cubes in the punch bowl or in glasses. Skip the rum in this drink for a family-friendly version.

- Combine 2 **cups orange juice,** 2 **cups pineapple juice,** 1 **cup dark rum,** 1 **cup light rum, the juice of** 1 **lemon, ¼ cup grenadine, and** 3 **dashes Angostura bitters** in a large punch bowl. Pour into ice-filled glasses and serve.

OUTDOOR PARTIES

298　When to Break Out the Blender

Blender drinks are most appreciated in summer when the icy drinks refresh and the loud whir of the blender takes place inside while guests are out. Make sure you have plenty of ice on hand as well as a good bar blender (see Resources, page 274) that can handle the tough job of pulverizing ice.

299　Use Frozen Fruit in Your Drinks

Frozen fruit is a time-saving and economical shortcut, and often tastes better than fresh because the fruit is harvested and packed at the height of its flavor. For a batch of Bellinis, frozen yellow peaches (even though white peaches are traditional) won't turn brown on you the way fresh ones do; and frozen fruit used in any blender drink will lend more flavor and let you use less ice, given that you are using the fruit in its frozen state.

300　RECIPE: *Peach Daiquiri*

Named for a waterside town in Cuba, the daiquiri was, ironically, the preferred drink of late U.S. president John F. Kennedy. Frozen daiquiris are festive and for some reason taste best when served next to a body of water. Flavor the daiquiri with any fruit you like (strawberry or banana are both very popular) and its corresponding fruit-flavored liqueur. Superfine sugar can be added as necessary depending on the sweetness of the fruit.

SERVES 1

- Combine 1½ ounces light rum, ¾ peach schnapps, the juice of 1 lime, and 2 ripe peaches, peeled, pitted, and diced in a blender and blend well. Add 3 ice cubes and blend again. Serve in a tall glass with a straw.

301 RECIPE: *Frozen Margarita*

Crowd-pleasing, especially when they don't come out of one of those spinning slurpee machines.

SERVES 1

- Combine **2 ounces tequila, 2 tablespoons freshly squeezed lime juice, 1 ounce Cointreau, and 1 cup ice cubes** in a blender and blend for 10 seconds. Pour into a chilled glass, rimmed in coarse salt or not as your guests prefer.

302 RECIPE: *Pimm's Cup*

A fizzy, refreshing drink that thrives in the sunshine, composed of one part Pimm's—a mild (and underappreciated) gin-based digestif— to roughly three parts fizz, dolled up with cucumbers, mint, and strawberries. Refrigerate the ingredients before mixing so the drink is bracingly cold. Multiply by the number of guests to make a pitcher.

SERVES 1

- Combine **2 ounces Pimm's Cup No. 1, 2 ounces gin,** and **¾ cup ginger ale** in a cocktail shaker, and shake well.
- Serve over ice in a highball glass. Garnish with **a mint sprig, a lemon slice, a cucumber slice,** and **strawberries.**

THE PARTY'S OVER

The reason we go to all this trouble to host a party is because we love it! The good times and good feelings that come from throwing a successful bash linger long after it's over, and this is why we return to hosting again and again. It actually enhances the quality of our lives to be able to share our time, feeding and nurturing our nearest and dearest and those to whom we'd like to be nearer and dearer. It can be a bit of a letdown when a party ends, but there are a few things to note to help bring things to a close and to make future endeavors smoother and easier. Practice makes, well . . . who needs to be perfect? Practice means more parties!

303 *In Praise of* Abundance

It's always better to overestimate the amount of food you need than to not have enough, and there's always a way to give new life to the extras. Sometimes, the second incarnation is even more satisfying than round one.

304 Six Easy Uses for Leftovers

1. Salads. Roasted or grilled meat works well tossed in a salad, whether it be a traditional chicken salad or something more inventive. A simple grilled steak, for example, could become the star of a Thai salad with the help of a little fish sauce and lime juice. This is a great way to stretch meat when there isn't enough for a whole meal.

2. Frittatas, quiches, and omelets. Leftover sautéed greens, roasted potatoes, cheese that was grated for the table, sausages that went uneaten, and even spaghetti can be cooked with eggs for brunch or lunch. Don't combine flavors that are truly incompatible, but generally it's hard to go wrong—especially with a little cheese on top.

3. Stock. Don't chuck that chicken carcass! Or those steak bones, for that matter. Homemade stock is so much better than anything you'll find at the store, and it's a great way to make the most out of random leftovers. That half onion that will likely be forgotten in your fridge, the bit of fennel that never made it into last night's salad, and extra herbs, especially rosemary and thyme, all make great contributions to a good stock.

4. Soups. Once you've made that stock (or bought some, if you must), you can make a great soup using leftover beans, vegetables of all kinds, braised meat, rice, pasta, and even day-old bread. Just make sure not to let cooked foods get too soft; wait until the last minute to add to a soup things like rice and pasta that have already been cooked.

5. Pasta sauce. There's one veal shank or short rib left and you'll have to share with your husband? Make a sauce instead. Meat that's been braised makes for delectable pasta sauce, and in no time. For a simple pasta sauce, sauté a chopped onion, a few diced carrots, a stick of celery, diced, and herbs in a sauté pan until golden brown. Add a small can of chopped tomatoes and the leftover meat, shredded. Cook just until it comes together, thickens, and tastes good, 10 or 15 minutes. Season with salt and pepper. This ragù—beef-, pork-, veal-, or lamb-based—usually goes best with a short, fat pasta, such as rigatoni, or a wide, flat noodle, such as pappardelle.

6. Sandwiches. Leftover brisket with a little horseradish mayonnaise and caramelized onions? Yes, please. Roasted meats are obvious sandwich choices, but you can go beyond sliced turkey, even if you just have the leftovers from a cheese plate. Load up a ciabatta with some ricotta, anchovies, and basil, or a baguette with sliced apples and runny Époisses.

305   What Can I Freeze for Another Day?

Some foods freeze beautifully, while others suffer, particularly in terms of consistency. Pasta will just never be the same if frozen, for example, but tomato sauce will emerge in perfect condition. As a general rule, wetter things do best in the freezer: soups and stews, sauces, and braised meat. Roasted, grilled, or pan-fried meat, certain vegetables (starchy ones), beans, and unsliced bread can be frozen with good results, too. Be prepared, though, for some change in texture. You may, upon thawing, need to alter the food to get the best use out of it. For example, roasted butternut squash can take on a mealy quality in the freezer, in which case pureeing it for a soup might be ideal. If you often cook in large quantities and like to keep your freezer stocked, it is worth investing in a vacuum-sealer.

306 What's the Best Way to Freeze Meat?

Freezing damages meat (especially raw meat), because crystals form inside and puncture the muscle cells, causing moisture to escape upon cooking or reheating. This can leave you with dry, tough meat. The quicker the meat freezes, the less damaging the process is, so turn your freezer up to the coldest temperature, and freeze the meat unwrapped. Once it has frozen, wrap it tightly in plastic and return the freezer to its normal setting.

307 What Am I Going to Do with All This Bread?

If, after your party, you are left with more bread than you can eat before it gets stale, there are still many opportunities to put it to use. If it has already been sliced, it will dry out quickly, in which case you could use a food processor to make bread crumbs to keep in the pantry. Or make a bread pudding, French toast, bread soup, or, if tomatoes are in season, Panzanella (bread salad; page 260). You can use the bread to make stuffing, or drizzle some olive oil and herbs onto the slices and pop them in the oven for croutons. If the bread is not sliced, it will do all right in the freezer if it's well wrapped, but try to use it within a month or so. Make sure to let it thaw in the same wrapping it was frozen in, which will mitigate the tendency for moisture loss.

308   TIP: **How to Keep Cheese Fresh**

If you're lucky, you'll be left with a nice hunk of cheese or two after your cocktail party. It can keep for quite a while, depending on the type. Even a hard cheese like Parmigiano-Reggiano can dry out when it's exposed to the air, so it's important to wrap cheese tightly in plastic wrap and put it in an airtight plastic bag in the fridge. If you do not finish the cheese in one sitting, be sure to use a new piece of plastic wrap every time you return it to the refrigerator. It may seem excessive, but it will make a huge difference: all cheese contains fat, and the plastic wrap will become slightly oily—and no longer airtight—once it has been in contact with the cheese.

DEALING WITH THE OTHER REMAINS

309   Just Hit "Return"

You may have a few bigger tasks to deal with when the fun is over. If you ordered any rentals for the party, you will need to coordinate the pickup, if you didn't do so when you placed the order. Generally speaking, you are expected to return items packed the same way you got them, meaning chairs folded and put back in the bags they came in, tables folded and stacked, glasses returned to their racks (but not washed), and dishes scraped and stacked (but not washed) and put back in crates. Dirty linens can be placed in the provided bags or even in trash bags.

If you have arranged it in advance with your liquor store or wine shop, you should be able to return any unopened wine or alcohol as long as it has not been iced, which would cause damage to the label. This is a great option to make sure you have enough libations to last the length of your event, without spending more than you have to.

THE PARTY'S OVER

Getting the House in Order

After the initial cleanup of dishes and glasses, there may be quite a bit more to do to get things back to normal. I tend not to rush this too much, and get it done by puttering over the next day or two. It may seem overwhelming to face all the tasks at once, so do it in stages. Wash and stack the platters and glasses, then when you can face it, put them away. Move the furniture back where it belongs. Vacuum. Do something small every time you walk past the kitchen, and before long, it will look like no one ever visited.

311 How to Keep Silver Clean

Sterling silverware can be washed just like your everyday stuff—almost. It can go in the dishwasher, but it should not touch other metals, such as stainless steel. What's most important is timing. Moisture tarnishes silver, so it's important to wash it right after the meal and dry it immediately. If you wash it by hand, don't let it air-dry on a rack; get a helper and dry each piece right away with a soft dish towel or a piece of felt, to avoid scratching.

312 Storing Grandma's Silver

Since moisture is silver's enemy, you can avoid having to polish tarnished silver by storing it properly (i.e., keeping it dry). You can buy special felt sleeves for silverware, or roll each piece in felt or acid-free tissue paper before putting it away in a drawer or box where it will stay dry and not be jostled around. Rubber and sulfur also damage and stain silver, so be careful to keep it out of contact with rubber bands, and don't use it as a serving utensil for eggy sauces.

It may seem old-fashioned to make recipe notes after throwing a party, but this doesn't have to be as fussy as it sounds. Things that didn't go exactly according to plan in the kitchen and the little changes that happened in the heat of the moment may be valuable to remember for next time. Perhaps you tweaked a recipe out of necessity (there was no mint at the market, so you substituted basil, for example) and the results were great. Or maybe you followed a recipe to a T but the finished product was not quite right (the sauce was watery and needed to be cooked down). Making a note in a journal or notebook kept specifically for this purpose means you're likely to come across it when the event is long forgotten.

If you're not the type to keep a journal, you might try a file in your computer or simply make notes in a recipe book. Jot down a note and slip it into the cookbook, or use a Post-it to make sure that next time you come across that recipe, you'll remember how to adjust it.

If you tend to veer dramatically from recipes, or cook completely from your own ideas and instincts, but then have trouble re-creating your most successful creations, it may be time to start keeping a notebook or computer file devoted to documenting them. Also keep notes on any menus, seating plans, guest lists, rental invoices, et cetera, especially if you are repeating a party annually. This reminder will help you immensely to work out the kinks each time you have a party, saving time and money and ensuring a successful event.

What is the point of having awesome cooking skills, a beautiful home, and lovely tableware if you're not going to share them? Throwing a great party creates lasting memories for all those involved. It does take some work and planning, but turning the work into creative play is the best way to enjoy the process and pass on that feeling of generosity to your guests. Think of yourself as a film director for the evening, and create something unique by bringing together different elements that create a special kind of harmony, never to be duplicated, even by you.

But let's admit it: sometimes we just don't want to host a party at home, or it isn't appropriate or possible for one reason or another. Maybe your home isn't big enough; maybe you're tired of cooking and cleaning. If you want to entertain but do not want to open up your home, there are options. You can be a gracious hostess and throw a party in a favorite bar or restaurant. If you are the organizer of such an event, there are a few things to keep in mind to ensure a smooth and successful bash.

Organizing a dinner out at a restaurant means no cooking or cleaning, but you also have less control over how the evening goes. Picking the right place, therefore, is crucial. Start researching as early as possible, so you can read lots of reviews, get advice from friends, and visit a few places before reserving. Location, price point, noise level, comfort, and cuisine are obvious considerations that will narrow your options, but the ambiance may require more hands-on investigating. If you're throwing a party for your grandparents' anniversary, that hip new spot that doesn't take reservations and plays loud music is probably not going to be a crowd-pleaser. It's always best to pick a place you're familiar with, but a drink at the bar and a chat with a manager should give you a good sense of things, in addition to reports from critics and friends you trust.

Hosting a dinner out at a restaurant makes life easier in many ways, but the question of what happens when the bill arrives can be a sticky one. If you're gathering good friends for a birthday or some other occasion in honor of a mutual friend, you don't necessarily have to pay for everyone, but you do have to make it clear what is expected. You know your crowd, so pick a place that is comfortably within their means if you intend for everyone to split the cost of the meal (an ethnic restaurant with big tables and family-style dishes can work well). When you send out the e-mail or make the phone call inviting everyone, make the financial situation clear by saying something like, "Let's take Karen out for her birthday." Your contribution here is the organizing, which will be appreciated as long as there is no surprise cost, and naturally, the honoree shouldn't be allowed to contribute to her own dinner.

Just as it would be in your role as host at home, your job is to make your guests comfortable and to keep the evening running smoothly. Make sure everyone is well informed in advance of the event, and communicate frequently with the staff to keep things moving at the right pace.

A good party is much more than the sum of its parts. The gathering takes on a life of its own, and it almost always works out, even when it doesn't. Bad weather, a burned roast, a spill on a tablecloth, an unsolicitous guest—none of this will be remembered, except maybe with humor. Problems have a way of working themselves out and turning out to be not nearly as important as we thought they might be.

What is important is to remember that the crucial thing about any gathering is the people and the interaction and the conversation that happen around the table (or the picnic blanket, for that matter). So, the bottom line is, even if you don't have awesome cooking skills, a beautiful home, and lovely tableware, you can still throw an outstanding party if you remember that the essence of it is the feeling of connectedness that everyone comes away with, and the feeling of pure satisfaction that you, the hostess, feel from being the one who created it all.

RESOURCES

SPECIALIZED INGREDIENTS

Bedford Cheese Shop
141 North Fourth Street
Brooklyn, NY 11211
(718) 599-7588
www.bedfordcheeseshop.com
For specialty cheeses. Mail order in New York City only.

Dean and Deluca
(800) 221-7714
www.deandeluca.com
For truffle products and other gourmet foods.

Despaña
408 Broome Street
New York, NY 10013
(212) 219-5050
www.despananyc.com
For Spanish cheeses, meats, and olives.

Dufour Pastry Kitchens
251 Locust Avenue
Bronx, NY 10454
(800) 439-1282
www.dufourpastrykitchens.com
For puff pastry dough.

East Village Cheese
40 Third Avenue
New York, NY 10003
(212) 477-2601
For specialty cheeses.

Far West Fungi
1 Ferry Building, Shop 34
San Francisco, CA 94111
(415) 989-9090
www.farwestfungi.com
For truffle products.

Ideal Cheese
942 First Avenue
New York, NY 10022
(212) 688-7579
(800) 382-0109
www.idealcheese.com
For specialty cheeses.

Lamazou
370 Third Avenue
New York, NY 10016
(212) 532-2009
www.lamazoucheese.com
For specialty cheeses and meats.

Murray's Cheese Shop
254 Bleecker Street
New York, NY 10014
(212) 243-3289
www.murrayscheese.com
For specialty cheeses.

Niman Ranch
1600 Harbor Bay Parkway,
Suite 250
Alameda, CA 94502
www.nimanranch.com
For bone-in whole hams.

Russ and Daughters
179 East Houston Street
New York, NY 10002
(212) 475-4880
(800) RUSS-289
www.russanddaughters.com
For smoked salmon and "appetizing."

Zingerman's
620 Phoenix Drive
Ann Arbor, MI 49108
(888) 636-8162
www.zingermans.com
For specialty ingredients.

KITCHEN TOOLS AND EQUIPMENT

Bowery Restaurant Supply Company
2 Delancey Street
New York, NY 10002
(212) 254-9720
www.bowerykitchens.com
For kitchen gadgets and chef tools.

Broadway Panhandler
65 East Eighth Street
New York, NY 10003
(212) 966-3434
(866) 266-5927
www.broadwaypanhandler.com
For kitchen must-haves: cast-iron skillet, enameled Dutch oven, immersion blender, bar equipment, kitchen tongs, fish spatula, instant-read thermometer, offset spatula, Microplane grater, Japanese mandoline, and more.

Didrik's
190 Concord Avenue
Cambridge, MA 02138
(617) 354-5700
www.didriks.com
For Libeco aprons, table linens, glassware, and flatware.

Home Depot
(800) HOME-DEPOT
www.homedepot.com
For the Home Hero fire extinguisher.

Macy's
(800) 289-6229
www.macys.com
For chafing dishes, warming trays, and other serveware.

Sur La Table
(800) 243-0852
www.surlatable.com
For kitchen must-haves: cast-iron skillet, enameled Dutch oven, immersion blender, kitchen tongs, fish spatula, instant-read thermometer, offset spatula,

Microplane grater, Japanese mandoline, and more.

Williams-Sonoma
(877) 812-6235
www.williams-sonoma.com
For kitchen must-haves: cast-iron skillet, enameled Dutch oven, immersion blender, kitchen tongs, fish spatula, instant-read thermometer, offset spatula, Microplane grater, Japanese mandoline, and more.

SERVING AND PARTY SUPPLIES

ABC Carpet & Home
888 & 881 Broadway
New York, NY 10003
(212) 473-3000
www.abchome.com
For platters, serving bowls, and woodenware.

Amazon.com
www.amazon.com
For bar blenders and Mydrap dinner napkins.

Bed Bath & Beyond
(800) GO BEYOND
www.bedbathandbeyond.com
For ice-cube trays.

CB2
(800) 606-6252
www.cb2.com
For plates and dinnerware.

General Home Store
100 Park Place
East Hampton, NY
11937-2467
(631) 267-6108

www.generalhomestore.com
For paper napkins and other tabletop goods.

Global Table
107-109 Sullivan Street
New York, NY 10012
(212) 431-5839
www.globaltable.com
For platters and serving bowls, and melamine plates.

La Plates
www.laplates.com
For customized melamine plates.

Restaurantware.com
(800) 851-9273
www.restaurantware.com
For bamboo plates.

Save-On-Crafts
(831) 768-8428
www.save-on-crafts.com
For mint julep cups, silver plated or plastic.

The Spoon Sisters
(800) 716-4199
www.spoonsisters.com
For ice-cube trays.

Levenger
(800) 667-8034
www.levenger.com
For clipboards and organizers.

Totally Bamboo
1810 Diamond Street
San Marcos, CA 92078
(760) 471-6600
www.totallybamboo.com
For bamboo plates.

West Elm
(888) 922-4119
www.westelm.com
For platters and serving bowls.

World Centric
www.worldcentric.org
For compostable paper plates.

STATIONERY

Emilie Friday
www.emiliefriday.com
For invitations.

Evite.com
www.new.evite.com
For e-vites.

Invitation Consultants
www.invitationconsultants.com
(888) 381-4400
For menu cards.

Invitation Land
www.invitationland.com
For invitations.

**Martha Stewart Place
Card Template**
www.marthastewartweddings
.com/article/
click-print-place-cards

Minted
(888) 828-6468
www.minted.com
For menu cards.

Paper Direct
(800) 272-7377
www.paperdirect.com
For place cards.

Pingg
36 East 20th Street, Third
Floor
New York, NY 10003
www.pingg.com
For invitations.

Polka Dot Design
(877) 816-0884
www.polkadotdesign.com
For invitations and party supplies.

Punch Bowl
www.punchbowl.com
For e-vites.

Purple Trail
www.purpletrail.com
For e-vites.

Send-O-Matic
www.sendomatic.com
For e-vites.

CLEANING SUPPLIES

Amazon.com
www.amazon.com
For 3M Scotch Fur Fighter.

Bed Bath & Beyond
(800) GO BEYOND
www.bedbathandbeyond.com
For Oxy carpet cleaner.

Wine Away
(888) 946-3292
www.wineaway.com
For red-wine stain remover.

INDEX

Affogato, 173
Ambrosia Trifle, 173
apples, 76, 77
apricots
Apricots with Mascarpone, 174
Baked Chicken with Apricots
and Olives, 107–108
aprons, 20
asparagus, 161
avocados
Avocado, Grapefruit,
and Lobster Salad,
208–209
Guacamole, 57
shopping for, 57

bacon, oven baked, 184
bagel and lox feast, 185–186
bagna cauda, 130
Baked Chicken with Apricots
and Olives, 107–108
Baked French Toast, 190
Baked Orecchiette with Sausage and Broccoli Rabe,
100–101
Bananas, Sautéed, with
Caramel Sauce, 174
bars, see also beverages
amounts of alcohol needed, 90
on a budget, 89
ice, 85
liquor list, 84
mixers, 88
placement, 31
returning leftovers, 269
temporary, 87
tools, 86–87
bartenders, 85
bathroom checklist, 48–49
Béchamel Sauce, 105
beef
Braised Short Ribs, 215–217
doneness chart, 149
filet mignon, 145

Lasagna with Ricotta and
Mushrooms, 103–106
Roasted Filet of Beef, 146–147
steaks, cooking perfect,
243–244
Thai Beef Salad, 192
beer, choosing, 88–89
Belgian endive, braised, 159
Bellini, 188
berries
Berry Tarts, 177
Mixed Berry Crisp, 117–118
Strawberry-Rhubarb Lattice
Pie, 113–114
beverages, 261–263
aperitifs, 135
beer, 88–89
Bellini, 188
Bloody Mary, 186–187
champagne, 212–214
champagne cocktail, 92
cosmopolitan, 91
Frozen Margarita, 263
lemons and limes, 92, 93
Manhattan, 93
margarita, 91
martini, 91
mint julep, 93
mixers, 88
Negroni, 92
Paloma, 92
Peach Daiquiri, 262
Pimm's Cup, 261, 263
Planter's Punch, 261
Ramos Fizz, 187
Sangria, 261
wine, 88–89, 168, 169,
212–214
birthday parties, 226–229
blanching vegetables, 160–162
blenders, immersion, 26
Bloody Mary, 186–187
Boston shakers, 86
Braised Short Ribs, 215–217
braising vegetables, 158–160

bread
Baked French Toast, 190
Panzanella (bread salad), 260
Savory Bread Pudding,
188–189
serving, 167–168
using leftover, 268
brining, 201–202
broccoli florets, blanched, 161
broccoli rabe
Baked Orecchiette with Sausage and Broccoli Rabe,
100–101
blanched, 161
brown sugar, 118
brunches and lunches, 180–193
bacon, oven baked, 184
bagel spread, 185–186
Baked French Toast, 190
dessert course, 185
drinks, 186–187
entrée salads, 191–192
Cobb Salad, 191
Italian Chicken Salad, 191
Mexican Shrimp Salad, 192
Salade Niçoise, 192
Thai Beef Salad, 192
Layered Frittata, 183–184
menus, 180–182
Savory Bread Pudding,
188–189
bruschetta and crostini stations,
63
Brussels sprouts, 156
buffets, 94–125
arranging the table, 120–121
menus, 96–97
platters, 112, 124–125
recipes (desserts), 113–119
Malted Brownies, 119
Mixed Berry Crisp, 117–118
Strawberry-Rhubarb Lattice
Pie, 113–114
recipes (entrées), 97–101,
103–112

buffets *(cont.)*
  Baked Chicken with Apricots and Olives, 107–108
  Baked Orecchiette with Sausage and Broccoli Rabe, 100–101
  Carnitas with Tomatillo Salsa, 98–99
  Glazed Ham, 108–112
  Lasagna with Ricotta and Mushrooms, 103–106
  Meat Loaf, 106
  refrigerator space, 102
  seating plan, 121
  tips, 122–123
butter dishes, 35

cabbage, 160
cakes
  icing and decorating, 226–229
  Meringue-Sorbet Layer Cake, 175–176
cake stands, 121
Campari, 135
candles, 39, 41–42
Carnitas, 98–99
carrots
  glazed, 151
  roasted, 156
carving
  boneless roasts, 148
  ham, 110–111
  turkey, 200–201
caterers, 17–20
cauliflower, 156
caviar, 211–212
celeriac, 156
centerpiece dos and don'ts, 45
chafing dishes, 25
champagne, 212–214
champagne cocktail, 92
charcuterie, 78–79
chargers, 34
cheese, 70–78
  after-dinner cheese course, 171–172
  amounts to buy, 74
  Cheese Straws, 75
  finding and choosing, 70–71, 171–172
  fruit accompaniments for, 76–77
  Gorgonzola Dip, 70
  Gougères, 55–56
  leftovers, 269
  Mac 'n' Cheese, 99–100
  serving whole, 69
  types, 72–73
cheese knives, 77–78
chicken
  Baked Chicken with Apricots and Olives, 107–108
  doneness chart, 149
  Italian Chicken Salad, 191
  rescuing dry white meat, 200
  Tarragon Roasted Chicken, 138–139
Child, Julia, 1
children, 12, 14–15
chocolate
  Chocolate Soufflés, 224–225
  chocolate stations, 64
  Gelato with Chocolate Ganache, 173
  Malted Brownies, 119
Clams Grilled in a Foil Pouch, 246–247
cleaning, 46–49
  bathroom checklist, 48–49
  during the party, 49
  pet hair, 47
  post-party cleanup, 270
  pre-party decluttering, 46
  spills, 47
clearing the table, 170
coatracks, 49
Cobb Salad, 191
cocktail garnishes
cocktail parties, 50–93
  amounts of food to prepare, 62
  bar basics, 84–90
  cocktail recipes, 91–93 (*see also* beverages)
  hors d'oeuvres (*see* hors d'oeuvres)
  menus, 52–55, 58
  task list and timeline, 59–61
  using food stations, 62–64
cocktail trays, 87
coffee mugs, 35
corkscrews, 86, 169
cosmopolitan, 91
crudités, 68
Cynar, 135

decorating, 38–46
  candles, 39, 41–42
  centerpiece dos and don'ts, 45
  cuisines and, 38–39
  flowers, 42–45
  foliage and greenery, 45–46
  lighting, 39–40
  simplicity, importance of, 39
dinner parties, 126–177
  after-dinner migration, 169–170
  aperitifs, 135
  budgeting, 130–132
  cheese course, 171–172
  clearing the table, dos and don'ts, 170
  desserts, 172–177
    Affogato, 173
    Ambrosia Trifle, 173
    Fresh Apricots with Mascarpone, 174
    Gelato with Chocolate Ganache, 173
    Glazed Figs, 173
    Greek Yogurt Parfait, 172
    Ice Cream Sandwiches, 174
    Individual Berry Tarts, 177
    Meringue-Sorbet Layer Cake, 175–176
    Nutella Sandwiches, 174
    Peach Melba, 172
    Sautéed Bananas with Caramel Sauce, 174
  entrée recipes, 138–147
    Hoisin-Glazed Salmon with Soba Noodles, 142–143
    Lamb Tagine, 140–141
    Pork tenderloin with Pomegranate Sauce, 143–145
    Roasted Filet of Beef, 146–147
    Tarragon Roasted Chicken, 138–139
  garnishing dos and don'ts, 166
  menu cards, 134
  menus, 128–130, 136

dinner parties *(cont.)*
place cards, 134
plating vs. family-style,
164–165
salads, first course, 136–137
seating arrangements, 133–134
serving pieces, 164
side dishes, 150–163
Glazed Carrots, 151
pasta as, 150
potato dishes, 152–154
Sautéed Mushrooms, 151
vegetable dishes, 155–163
task list and schedule,
132–133, 147–148
water, serving, 167
dips and sauces
Béchamel Sauce, 105
Gorgonzola Dip, 70
gravies, 203–204
Guacamole, 57
store-bought, 56
Tomatillo Salsa, 97
drinks, *see* beverages
drinks trays, 87
Dutch ovens, 26

eggplant, 155
eggs
Baked French Toast, 190
Layered Frittata, 183–184
Savory Bread Pudding,
188–189
e-mail invitations, 9–10
en papillote, 163, 222–224
eucalyptus, 46

family-style vs. plating, 164–165
fennel, braised, 159
figs, 77, 173
filet mignon, 145
fish, *see also* salmon
en Papillote, 222–224
filleting, 242
grilling whole, 240–242
flower-preservative recipe, 43
flowers, 42–45
foil-pouch cooking, 244–248
foliage and greenery, 45–46

food stations, 31–32, 62–64
French Toast, Baked, 190
Frittata, Layered, 183–184
Frozen Margarita, 263
fruit
accompaniments for cheese,
76–77
dried, 77
grilled, 256
furniture
arrangements, 30–31
renting, 19

garnishing
cocktails, 90, 92
dos and don'ts, 166
Gelato with Chocolate Ganache,
173
gin, 84
glasses, 19, 24, 35
Glazed Ham, 108–112
Gorgonzola Dip, 70
Gougères, 55–56
grapefruit, sectioning, 208
Grape Schiacciata, 81–82
graters, Microplane, 27
gratin dishes, 26
gravies, 203–204
Gravlax, Home-Cured, 209–211
Greek Yogurt Parfait, 172
green beans, 162
grill baskets, 240–241, 249–250
Guacamole, 57
guest lists, 6
guests, *see also* invitations
after-dinner migration,
169–170
delegating jobs to, 15
flowers from, 43
mingling, 13
seating arrangements, 133–134
traffic jams (bottlenecks),
30–32
uninvited, 12–15

ham, 108–112
haricots verts, 162
Hawthorne strainers, 86
help

caterers, 17–20
family, 16
guests, 15
hired, 16–17
Hoisin-Glazed Salmon with
Soba Noodles, 142–143
Home-Cured Gravlax, 209–211
hors d'oeuvres, *see also* cheese,
charcuterie, and salumi
crudités, 68
dips, 56–57
Gougères, 55–56
Grape Schiacciata, 81–82
Guacamole, 57
menus, 52–55
Parmesan Palmiers, 83–84
piping bag techniques, 68
Pissaladière, 80–81
ten quick ideas, 66–67
White Bean and Tomato
Toasts, 64–65
hosting, art and etiquette of
afterward, 264
drinking and, 23
four golden rules, 4
managing guests, 12–15
parties in a bar or restaurant,
272–273
record keeping, 272
role of a host, 273
skills to impress guests, 32
toasts, 214–215

ice, 85
ice cream
Affogato, 173
Gelato with Chocolate Ga-
nache, 173
Ice Cream Sandwiches, 174
pre-scooped, 175
immersion blenders, 26
instant-read thermometers, 27
invitations, 7–12
dealing with regrets, 11
e-mailing, 9–10
and kids, 12
last-minute or replacement,
10–11
mailing, 9
phone, 10

invitations *(cont.)*
   RSVPs, 10
   timing, 8
Italian Chicken Salad, 191

jiggers, 86
juicers, 86

**kitchen equipment, must-
   haves,** 26–27

lamb
   doneness chart, 149
   Lamb Tagine, 140–141
**Lasagna with Ricotta and
   Mushrooms,** 103–106
leeks, 160
leftovers, 266–269
lemons
   cutting, 93
   lemon slices for nonstick grill-
     ing, 241
   twist of, 92
Lillet, 135
limes, 93
lists, 6–7, 21–23, 147–148
lobster, 208–209
lox, 185–186
lunches, *see* brunches and lunches

Mac 'n' Cheese, 99–100
Malted Brownies, 119
mandolines, 27
Manhattan, 93
margarita, 91, 263
martini, 91
Mashed Potatoes, 152
Meat Loaf, 106
meats, *see also specific meats*
   charcuterie, 78–79
   doneness chart, 149
   freezing, 268
   Meat Loaf, 106
   resting, 145
   salumi, 78–79
menu cards, 134
menu planning

brunches and lunches, 180–182
buffets, 96–97
cocktail parties, 52–55, 58
dinner parties, 128–130
do what you love, 5
New Year's Eve parties, 207
outdoor parties, 237–238
ten important questions, 5
Thanksgiving, 193–194
timing and, 21–23
Meringue-Sorbet Layer Cake,
   175–176
Mexican Shrimp Salad, 192
Microplane graters, 27
Minestrone Salad, 258–259
mint juleps, 93
mise en place, 132
Mixed Berry Crisp, 117–118
mixers, 88
mostarda (mustard fruit), 76–77
mushrooms
   Mushroom Risotto, 219–221
   Sautéed Mushrooms, 157
music, 40–41
mustard fruit (mostarda), 76–77

napkins
   cloth, 24
   cocktail, 87
   paper, 25
   placement, 34
Negroni, 92
New Orleans Fizz, 187
New Year's Eve parties,
   207–217
   Avocado, Grapefruit,
     and Lobster Salad,
     208–209
   Braised Short Ribs, 215–217
   caviar, 211–212
   champagne basics, 212–214
   Home-Cured Gravlax, 209–211
   menus, 207
   toasts, 214–215
No-Fail Piecrust, 114–117
Nutella Sandwiches, 174

outdoor parties, 230–263
   bugs and, 238

checklist for picnics away from
   home, 232
drinks, 261–263
   Frozen Margarita, 263
   Peach Daiquiri, 262
   Pimm's Cup, 263
grilling
   charcoal, 236, 237
   charcoal chimneys, 236
   Clams Grilled in a Foil
     Pouch, 246–247
   covered-grill roasting,
     250–251
   equipment checklist,
     234–235
   fish, whole, 240–242
   fish fillets, 242–243
   foil-pouch cooking,
     244–248
   Fruit on the Grill, 256
   Grill Basket "Stir-Fry"
     Vegetables, 249–250
   Grilled Pizza, 252–253
   Grill-Roasted Potatoes, 248
   Herbed Pork Roast, 251
   lemon slices as landing pads,
     241
   menu planning, 237–238
   Paella Valenciana on the
     Grill, 254–255
   Salmon Cooked on a Cedar
     Plank, 239–240
picnic plates, choosing, 233
salads, 257–260
   Minestrone Salad, 258–259
   Panzanella, 260
   Wild Rice Salad, 257–258
transporting food and equip-
   ment, 238
weather and, 237
oysters, 218–219

Paella Valenciana on the Grill,
   254–255
Paloma, 92
Pan-Asian food stations, 64
panini stations, 63–64
Panzanella, 260
Parmesan Palmiers, 83–84
parsnips, 156

parties in a bar or restaurant,
272–273
pasta
Baked Orecchiette with Sausage and Broccoli Rabe,
100–101
Lasagna with Ricotta and
Mushrooms, 103–106
Mac 'n' Cheese, 99–100
Minestrone Salad, 258–259
sauce from leftovers, 267
as side dish, 150
pastry bags (piping bags), 68
peaches
Bellini, 188
Peach Daiquiri, 262
Peach Melba, 172
pepper, 38
Pernod, 135
pets, 47
picnics, *see* outdoor parties
pie, strawberry-rhubarb,
113–114
piecrust, no-fail, 114–117
Pimm's Cup, 263
piping bags (pastry bags), 68
Pissaladière, 80–81
Pizza, Grilled, 252–253
place cards, 134
place mats, 32
Planter's Punch, 261
plating food vs. family style,
164–165
platters and serving pieces,
25, 112, 124–125, 164,
206, 217
playlists, 40–41
pork
Baked Orecchiette with Sausage and Broccoli Rabe,
100–101
Carnitas, 98–99
doneness chart, 149
Herbed Pork Roast, 251
Pork Tenderloin with
Pomegranate Sauce,
143–145
potatoes
boiled, with parsley, 154
gratin of, 153
grill-roasted, 248

mashed, 152
roasted fingerling, 153–154
puff pastry, 75, 80–81, 83–84

quesadilla stations, 64
quince paste, 76

Ramos Fizz, 187
rentals, 19, 269
risotto, mushroom, 219–221
roasted vegetables, 153–154,
155–156
RSVPs, 10
rum, 84
runners (table linens), 33

Salade Niçoise, 192
salads
Avocado, Grapefruit,
and Lobster Salad,
208–209
Cobb Salad, 191
dinner party, first course,
136–137
dressing and tossing, 193
Italian Chicken Salad, 191
Mexican Shrimp Salad, 192
Minestrone Salad, 258–259
Panzanella, 260
Salade Niçoise, 192
Thai Beef Salad, 192
Wild Rice Salad, 257–258
salmon
bagel and lox feast, 185–186
Hoisin-Glazed Salmon with
Soba Noodles, 142–143
Home-Cured Gravlax, 209–211
Salmon Cooked on a Cedar
Plank, 239–240
salmon platters, 112
salt and saltshakers, 37–38
salumi, 78–79
Sangria, 261
sauces and dips
Béchamel Sauce, 105
Gorgonzola Dip, 70
Tomatillo Salsa, 97
sautéing vegetables, 157–158

"save the date" notices, 7–8
Savoy cabbage, 160
seating arrangements, 133–134
serving pieces and platters,
25, 112, 124–125, 164,
206, 217
shopping lists, 6
Short Ribs, Braised, 215–217
shot glasses, 86
shrimp, Mexican Shrimp Salad,
192
silverware, 34, 35, 206, 270
simple syrup, 187
simplicity, importance of, 4,
22, 39
skillets, cast-iron, 26
slider or burger stations, 63
snack tables and food stations,
31–32
snow peas, 157
sorbet, Meringue-Sorbet Layer
Cake, 175–176
soufflés, 224–225
spatulas, 27
spiders (Chinese strainers), 163
spills, 47
squash, 158
stain removal, 47
steaks, 243–244
sterling silver, 206, 270
stock, 109, 266
Strawberry-Rhubarb Lattice
Pie, 113–114
stuffing, 204–205
sushi stations, 63
Swiss chard, 158

table linens, 24, 32–33
table-setting rules, 34–37
task lists and timelines, 6–7,
21–23, 147–148
teacups, 35–36
tequila, 84
Thai Beef Salad, 192
Thanksgiving, 193–206
menus, 193–194
turkey, 195–203
thermometers, instant-read, 27
timelines, *see* task lists and
timelines

toasts, 214–215
to-do lists, *see* task lists and
    timelines
Tomatillo Salsa, 97
tongs, 27
traffic jams (bottlenecks), 30–32
truffles, 221
turkey, 195–203
    basic preparations, 195
    brining, 201–202
    carving, 200–201
    cooking times, 149, 199
    one vs. two, 203
    pan gravy, 203–204
    rescuing dry white meat, 200
    roasting or grilling parts,
        195–196
    roasting whole, 197–198
    stuffing, 204–205
    trussing, 198
turnips, 156
twist of lemon, 92

unsticking food from pans, 150

Valentine's Day, 217–225
    Chocolate Soufflés, 224–225
    Mushroom Risotto, 219–221
    oysters, 218–219
vases, 44
vegetables, *see also* potatoes;
    salads
    blanching, 160–162
    braising, 158–160
    crudités, 68
    en papillote, 163
    frozen, 162
    Glazed Carrots, 151
    Grill Basket "Stir-Fry"
        Vegetables, 249–250
    roasting, 153–154, 155–156
    Sautéed Mushrooms, 151
    sautéing, 157–158
vodka, 84

warming trays, 25
warm plates and platters, 217
water, serving, 167
wheatgrass, 46
whiskey, 84
White Bean and Tomato Toasts,
    64–65
Wild Rice Salad, 257–258
wine
    champagne basics, 212–214
    choosing, 88–89
    opening, 169
    pairing, 168
    saving a corked wine, 89
wine and cheese stations, 63
wineglasses, 24, 35, 36, 37–38

yellow squash, 158

zucchini, 158